Sven Ingmar Thies (ed.)

Teaching
Graphic Design

Approaches, Insights, the Role of Listening and
24 Interviews with Inspirational Educators

Birkhäuser
Basel

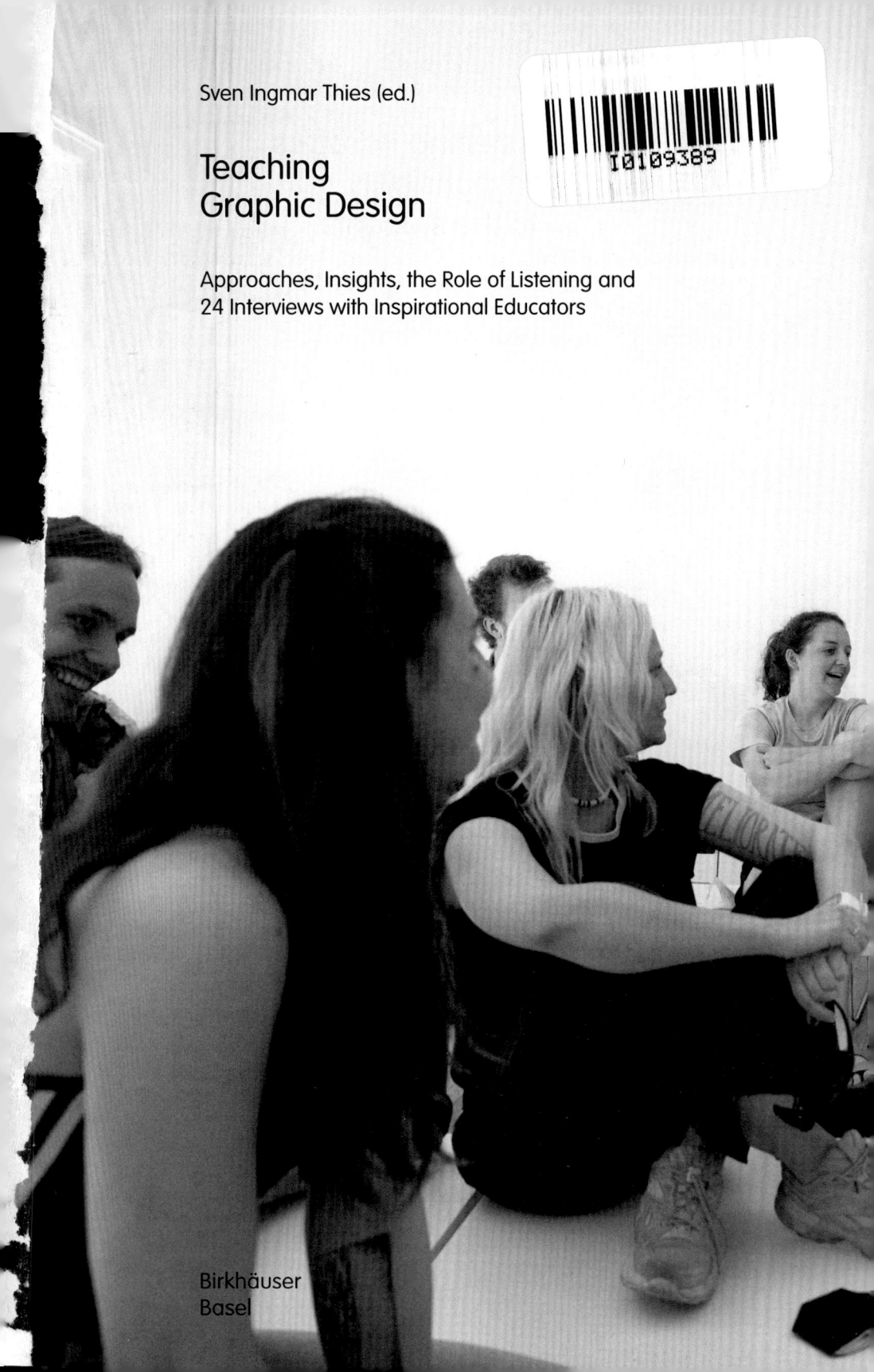

'Listening transfers
responsibility
to the students.'

Sven Ingmar Thies teaches
Graphic Design
Page 17

'We have to deal with
uncertainties and
keep an open mind.'

Katrin Androschin teaches
Strategic Design
Page 87

'I believe that
remote teaching
is a granted
enrichment.'

Masayo Ave teaches
Sensory Experience Design
Page 94

'Language is the most accessible tool we can use to reflect.'

Paulus M. Dreibholz teaches Typography

Page 101

'My goal was to educate my students to prevent products from being made.'

Fritz Frenkler teaches
Industrial Design
Page 110

'Cultivate your curiosity and creative hunger and learn to learn.'

Nikolaus Hafermaas teaches
Transmedia Design
Page 117

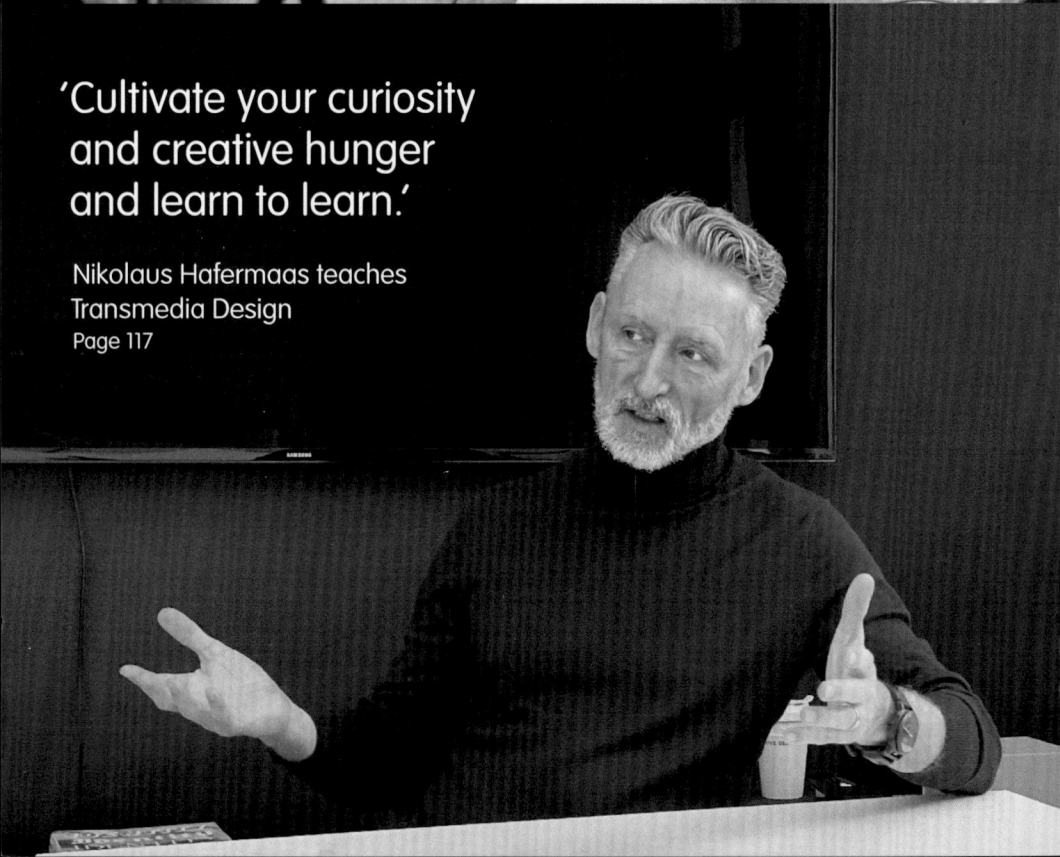

'... to prevent people from trying to perceive everything on a purely intellectual level.'

Brigitte Hartwig teaches
Communication Design
Page 127

'You can neither impart nor teach design.'

Jianping He teaches Poster Art
and Visual Language
Page 133

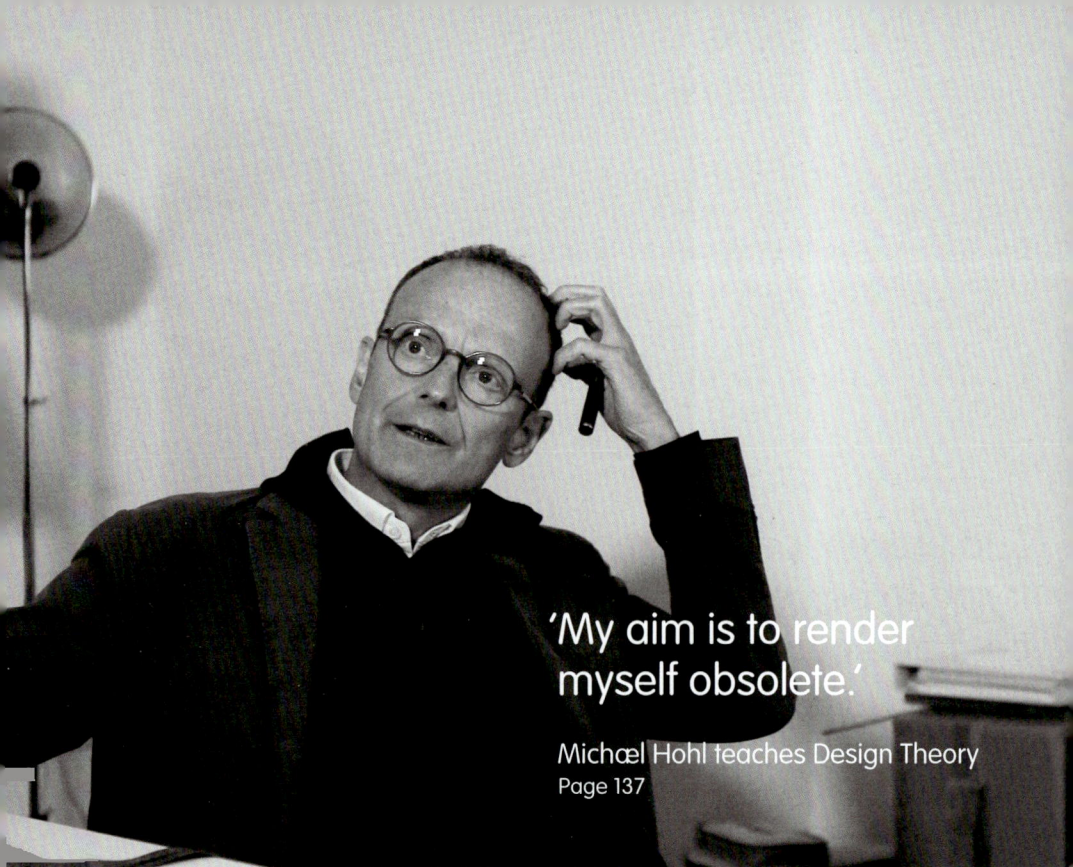

'My aim is to render myself obsolete.'

Michæl Hohl teaches Design Theory
Page 137

'I create an experiential space.'

Gesche Joost teaches
Design Methods
Page 143

'It's okay to fail.'

Katsuya Kato teaches
Design Basics and Media
Page 152

'I write down what I find fascinating and what I have learnt myself.'

Ruth Mateus-Berr teaches Didactics
Page 158

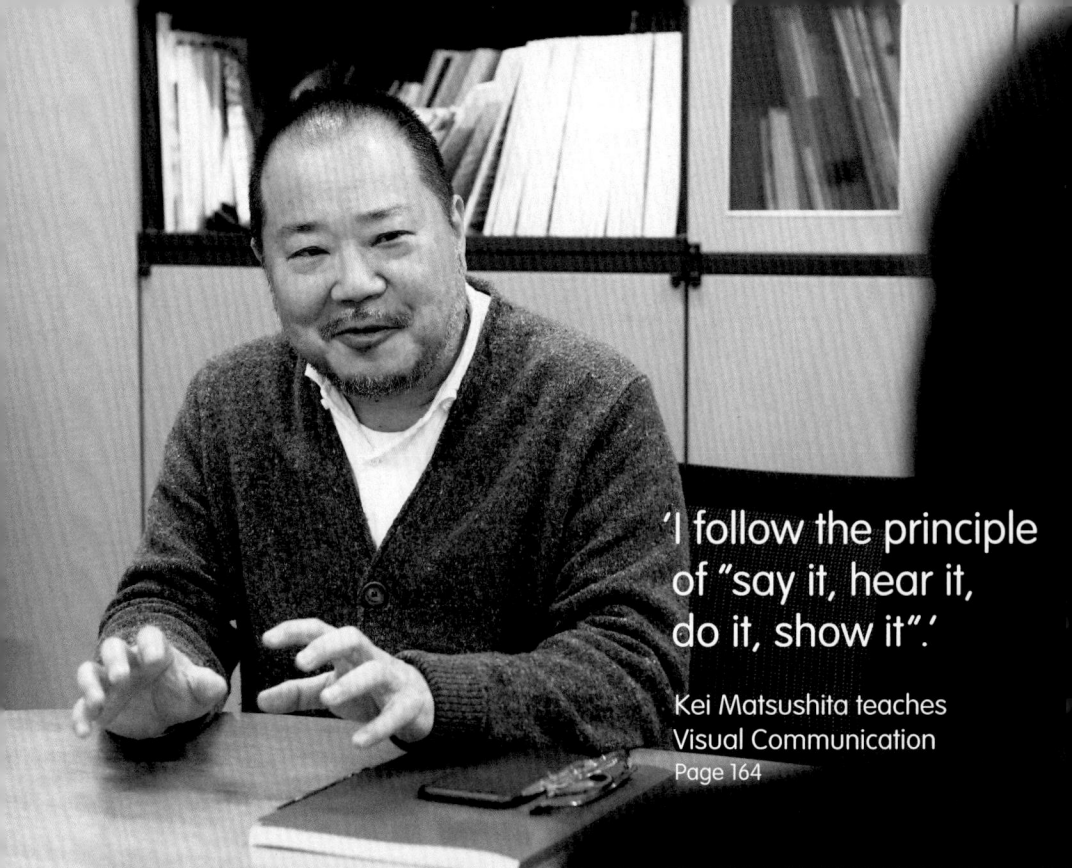

'I follow the principle of "say it, hear it, do it, show it".'

Kei Matsushita teaches
Visual Communication
Page 164

'It's crucial that we begin to rethink with these new generations.'

Johanna Pirker teaches
Game Design, Game
Development and Social
Media Technologies
Page 171

'They realise they
need to function
first as a human.'

Rathna Ramanathan teaches Typography
and Graphic Communication Design
Page 181

'Ask more questions, use the body and motion.'

LeeAnn Renninger, expert in Adult Learning
Page 191

'A university is basically a place where the future is of overriding importance.'

Ichiro Saga teaches Typography and Design History
Page 198

'They should learn how to touch someone's heart with design.'

Stefan Sagmeister teaches Graphic Design
Page 204

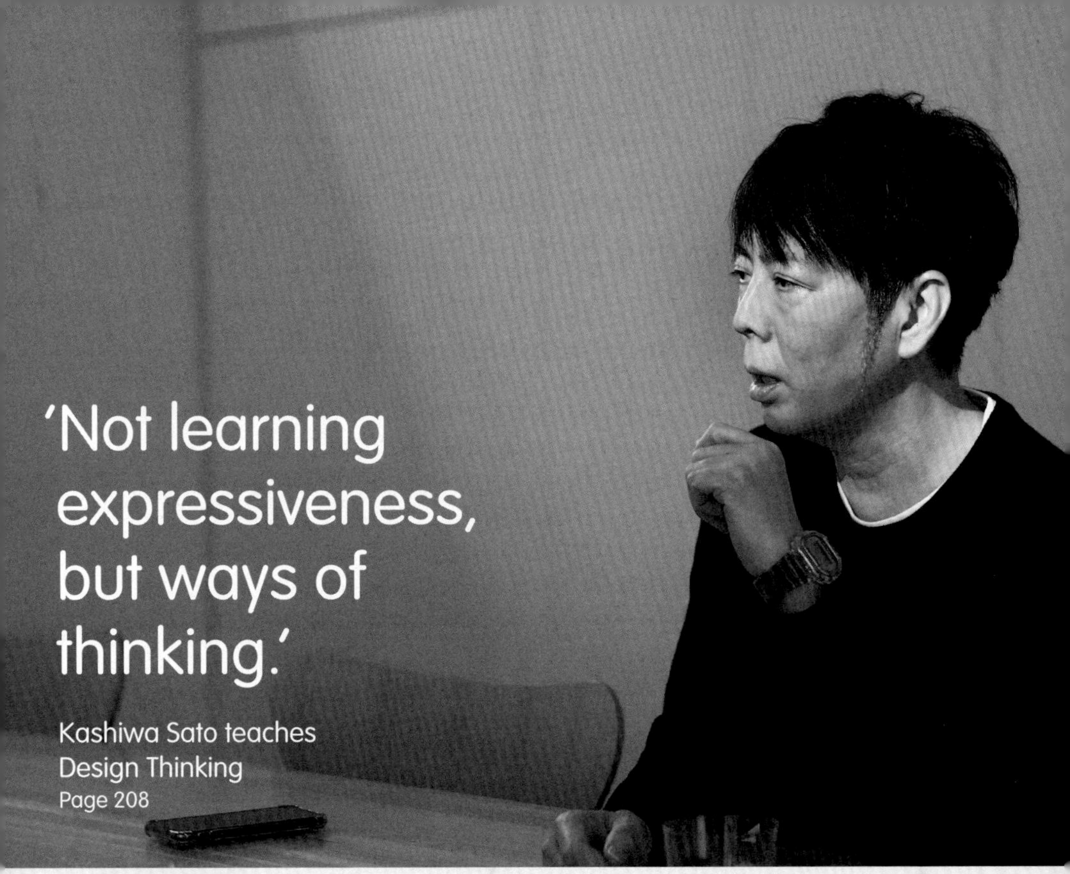

'Not learning
expressiveness,
but ways of
thinking.'

Kashiwa Sato teaches
Design Thinking
Page 208

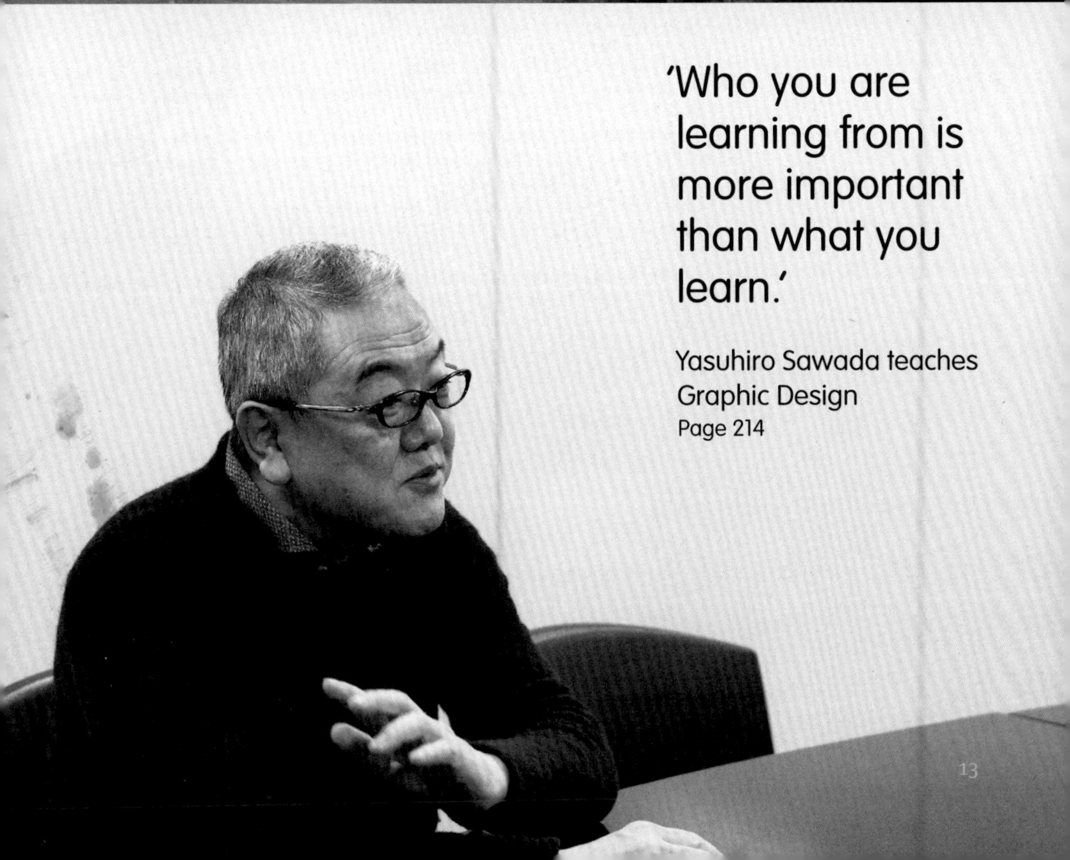

'Who you are
learning from is
more important
than what you
learn.'

Yasuhiro Sawada teaches
Graphic Design
Page 214

'We always manage to quickly build an honest feedback culture.'

Mathilde Scholz teaches Integrated Design
Page 220

'First of all you motivate by preventing demotivation.'

Matthias Spætgens
teaches Conception
Page 227

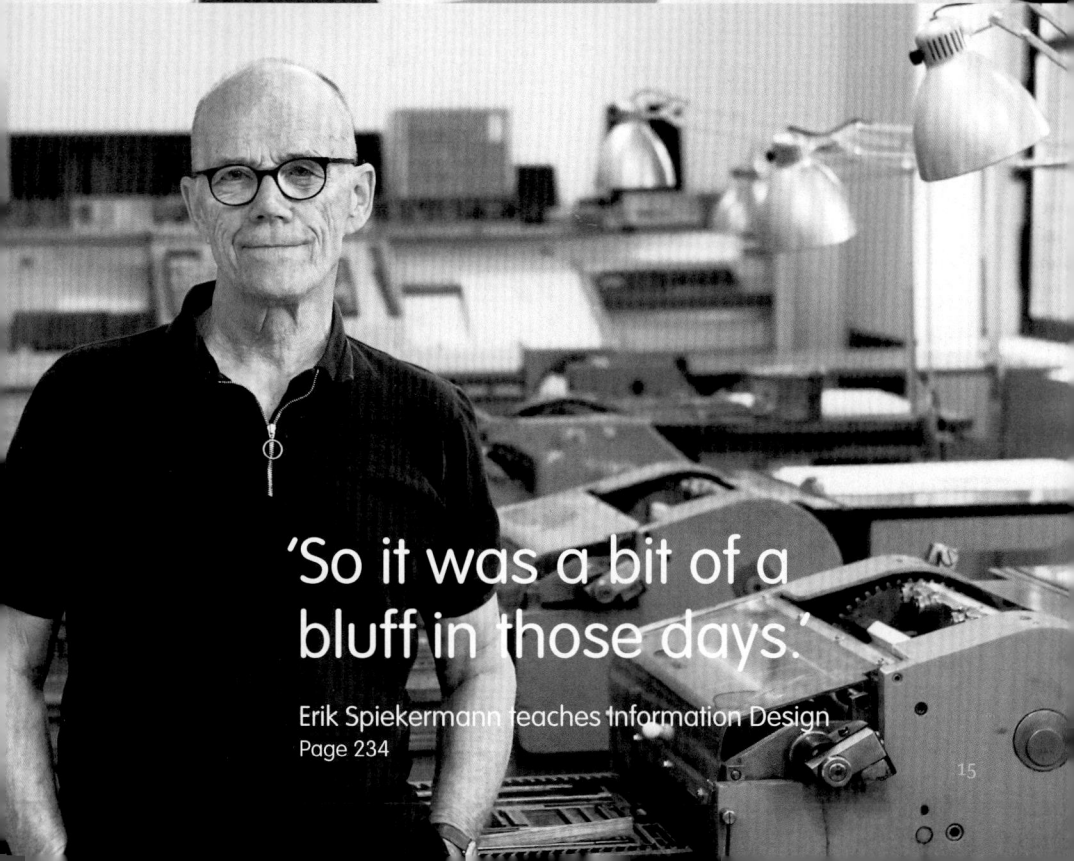

'So it was a bit of a bluff in those days.'

Erik Spiekermann teaches Information Design
Page 234

'Students are allowed to adopt and develop any ideas from their fellow students.'

Takeshi Sunaga teaches
Interaction Design
Page 244

'I think it's high time to reflect on human beings again.'

Toshio Yamagata teaches
Graphic Design and
Design Management
Page 250

INTRODUCTION

INTRODUCTION

What does this book intend to offer?
This book provides the opportunity to get to know various approaches and opinions on design education and to examine one's own position from a new perspective. It hopes to inspire awareness for options and actions in class in order to enable students to gain maximum experience and insight. Ideally, it will persuade educators to try out something new and contribute to making learning even more enjoyable for teachers and learners alike.

The book pursues the following four goals:
- to create an overview of potential teaching parameters
- to listen more consciously in class
- to receive feedback for one's own teaching
- to foster more spatial variety.

The chapters focus on the following questions:
- What is it we are teaching? – *Introductory thoughts*
- How do we enable learning? – *In-depth considerations*
- How do others teach? – *24 interviews*
- What are their project briefings like? – *12 examples*

Why write a book on teaching design?
I think the main reason is because we all ask ourselves similar questions. What was it like, for example, when you first walked into the class you were going to teach? What did you expect of yourself, and what did the students expect of you? Looking back on several years of teaching experience, would you now walk into the same room with the same attitude? Has your teaching style changed? Is the institution you teach at changing its requirements? Have new challenges arisen from design practice or from society?

Just like everyone else, I started on the other side of the classroom as a pupil on my first day at primary school. Back then, seated in the second row, I was curious and excited, but felt insecure at the same time. On my first day at university, I experienced the same three emotions again, this time sitting in the second-to-last row. And then suddenly it was me standing on the other side of the classroom as the teacher of a university class. Again, on my way into class, feelings of instinctive curiosity, pleasurable excitement and – at least initially – slightly inhibiting insecurity accompanied me. At the same time, those three companions of mine served as an incentive to do my job well.

Many weeks before I walked into the university building as a teacher for the first time, I had already asked myself how I would teach. *What I would teach*, the subject and the goal, seemed clear, as I had been able to choose those myself. But *how I would teach* was not at all clear. I only knew that I wanted to share the passion I felt for designing with my students and to find a way in which both they and I could learn something new. Was there a *perfect* way to do that? Which methods would be successful? What do others do? And what do people from other cultures do?

These questions still linger on after ten years of teaching, which is why I decided to write about my professional experience and ask questions in a wider context.

To that end, I interviewed 24 specialists from China, Germany, Great Britain, Japan, Austria and the USA, many of whom have accumulated teaching experience beyond the borders of their countries. And I spoke to many students. I conducted my first interview in December 2019 and my last one in January 2023. During that time, the Corona pandemic not only affected teaching methods, but left its mark on this publication project as well.

This book is conceptualised and written from the perspective of a practising designer and committed educator; I teach graphic design with a holistic approach in the Class of Ideas at the University of Applied Arts Vienna. Design is becoming increasingly important as a means to deal with social, economic, ecological and political issues and find solutions for them. It is against this backdrop that I describe my work as a teacher and conduct interviews with various other teachers. Essentially, we all recount our personal experience.

Who is this book aimed at?
Above all, teachers. At the same time, however, it is inextricably committed to students and to people who strive to enhance their personal development.

In that sense, then, the content of this book focuses on the *how* in teaching without excluding the *what* and the *why*, because ultimately all three of them are dependent on and influence each other. The subject of scrutiny is not the structure of a curriculum or individual courses, but the collaboration between teachers and students. After all, we do learn from one another.

Seen from that perspective, listening is instrumental to collaboration in class. It is one of several ways to actively accompany students and support them in their endeavour to drive their personal development. Moreover, the potential of listening is transferable to professional practice: for example, when you, as the agent, listen to a client's briefing or a designer listens to a colleague in day-to-day agency life.

The specialist focus here is on graphic design. Since the *how* in teaching can be regarded as interdisciplinary, however, people from the fields of design strategy, industrial design, game design, design theory, design research, sensory design, didactics and cognitive psychology were interviewed as well. That included a wide array of experts ranging from a Dean of Academic Strategy and heads of institutes to class-leading professors and a lecturer responsible for university courses. All of them have one thing in common: the desire to allow their students to experiment, gain experience and develop their own potential.

Does this book intend to pigeonhole or to classify?
No, on the contrary. Its intention is to enable comparison and deepen insights. It wishes to describe the passion for teaching and learning.

It aims to provide inspiration for learning.
I truly hope it does.

GRAPHIC DESIGN

GRAPHIC DESIGN

Let's start with the world we move in: graphic design.

In search of a definition

Do you work as a graphic designer? Do you teach communication design? Are you a professor teaching a class for graphic and information design? Or are you starting to study visual communication next semester?

Of course, the list of questions could go on and on – as could the names for the discipline. Some extend the sphere of activity in order to realign the name with the action involved. Others denote a specialisation and become new disciplines.

From a historical point of view, graphic design originally referred to designing two-dimensional printed material. Over time, however, a greater range of media needed designing. With package design, a third dimension surfaced. At some point, it became evident that services also required design. And now, everything connected to the virtual world is opening up further dimensions.

Due to this continuous expansion, the wish to rename graphic design has come up again and again, which seems understandable at first. After all, a new term seeks to capture and reflect the latest developments. At the same time, however, it seems a bit like inventing new professional titles so that every single employee has an individual position to show on their business card. In the end, though, that only points to prevailing hierarchies. Does it reflect modern practice? Why insist on new nomenclature when technological change gives rise to new media and forms of communication, but the substance remains the same? Graphic design has embraced such changes up to now and responded to current societal, social, political, economic and ecological requirements.

Moreover, a new name would face the almost irresolvable contradiction between a definition that needs to be precise and differentiate clearly, and the dynamic development of content and meanings, which creates ambiguity. In his reference to culture theorist Raymond Williams's book *Keywords*,[1] Professor for Design History Jeremy Aynsley[2] points out that, just like many other terms, graphic design has its own history, and its use and meaning are subject to change over time.

So graphic design does not need a new name. However, it must retain its readiness to change constantly and to interact with other disciplines.

Etymologically, the term 'graphic design' has two roots: 'graphic' stems from the Greek word 'graphikḗ' (téchnē), which means the art of painting and drawing, while 'design' comes from the Latin word 'designare', meaning to intend or designate. Painting and drawing allow something new to take shape, even if it sometimes means reproducing what is seen. On further reflection, graphic design could actually stand for the ability to express something new.

In order to express something new, one must have the will to change. This enables a critical approach to given facts or to an assigned task – so that one can ultimately understand it. Then the ideation process can begin. Only afterwards does the final result obtain its form – a design – through realisation.

Essentially, then, graphic design aims to change, understand, ideate and realise. These four activities can be regarded as fundamental to graphic design.

Graphic design aims to change

The driving force behind every designer is to change or to improve a situation, a phenomenon that is aptly described by social scientist and Nobel laureate Herbert A. Simon in his book *The Sciences of the Artificial*: 'Everyone designs who devises courses of action aimed at changing existing situations into preferred ones.'[3] He then goes on to explain that, regarding the intellectual activity involved, there is no difference between someone producing material artefacts, someone prescribing remedies for a sick patient, or someone devising a new sales plan for a company or a social welfare policy for a state.

The difference between these exemplary actions practised by people from other professions and those of a designer is that design, like graphic design, relies on individual attitudes and methods to enable change. Hence, 'the combination of imagination (visioning) and the ability to present things (visualisation) is considered the core of all practices in design.'[4] This definition of core competences is from the book titled *Designing Design Education*, which is the result of an international research project on the future of design studies. Social scientist Ekkehart Baumgartner comes to a similar conclusion in his essay 'The Thinking Hand' in the same book. Designers are perceived in their workings because 'the designer can design both in a creative and in a thinking vein informed by knowing reality', which makes designers unique compared to other professions.[5] Bryan Lawson, who studied architecture and psychology and taught architecture, compares the approach of scientists to that of architects thus: while scientists focus on discovering rules, architects are obsessed with achieving the desired result and trying it out.[6]

Graphic design aims to understand

Before any change is possible, graphic designers must understand the purpose of the task in question. And in order to understand something, it is not only necessary to penetrate the relevant subject matter, but to question it as well. 'Critical thinking' is not only critical towards a given task, but also in relation to one's own environment, attitudes and actions. Graphic designers challenge other people, their ideas and goals. That is why they need to understand all kinds of tasks and have a genuine empathy for their fellow humans.

Graphic design aims to ideate
In graphic design, goals are often described as 'solutions to problems', but I prefer to use the term 'idea'. An idea may well solve a problem, but puts a stronger emphasis on conceiving something new. Graphic design aims to enhance the existing or even to create something previously unimaginable. This creative process is comparable to that of other design disciplines. Graphic designers analyse (think), produce ideas (conceive) and revise (rethink) in order to assess whether their outcome or fledgling idea might already have its justification. That process is reiterated as often as needed to reach the defined goal and allow the final result to take shape.

Graphic design aims to realise ideas
Graphic design aims to implement what was developed as an idea. During implementation, the reiterative process of continuous reconsideration and revision comes into play again until the idea assumes its final form. Giving form to an idea requires expert knowledge and a commitment to excellence. Graphic design aims to launch the idea with the greater intention of making it perceptible, impactful and, ideally, generate change. Accordingly, graphic design employs means of communication that appeal to as many senses as possible, as in the case of holistic design. To find the right way to achieve this, graphic designers use open-ended methods that frequently require visualisation tools.

Communicating
In all four basic activities of graphic design, designers require the ability to communicate comprehensibly and clearly. This has twofold significance: communication is designed for those who perceive the final result. At the same time, communication is also an essential part of the design process: communicating with all those involved in the process on their way to the final result. This approach is gaining ground in interdisciplinary and inter-cultural teams. Finally, two additional competences, genuine curiosity and intensity, are required – here the latter stands for in-depth involvement with all other participants as well as with the task itself.

Taking responsibility
Depending on the problem, the objective is to contribute to the cultural, social, political, economic and ecological development of our society. This is where graphic designers step in and assume responsibility.

Graphic design is always at the service of humankind.

Design practice

Design practice has a twofold meaning: it describes what designers do, or practise on a daily basis, while also alluding to design as a practice in the course of which something is created. In this sense, graphic design is also a process that generates knowledge and produces results based on findings acquired in the process. In this way, ideas are realised.

Design practice as a creative process
Applied practice also aims to change, understand, discover ideas and realise them. Designer and educator Victor Papanek, who is notably associated with socially and ecologically sustainable design, says, 'Design is the conscious and intuitive effort to impose meaningful order.'[7] This applies to both the creative process and the act of giving final form to the idea. Here, 'giving form' encompasses everything that is intangible or immaterial, thus also virtual things or services.

Design practice as a profession
Daily practice can perhaps be best clarified with an example:

The alarm goes off at 7 am in my hotel room. Outside it is pitch black and raining. The workshop begins punctually at half past eight. It is part of a brand development process consisting of two parts, starting with a summary of the jointly formulated brand purpose. This is done by two brand consultants from the partner enterprise that invited me to participate. I am to play my role in the second part. We call it design intervention. It involves collaboratively developing a feeling for the meaning of holistic design, which can range from a website and the design of seminar rooms to the behaviour of all staff members in order to establish a consistent experience. So today's session is not about developing a design, but rather agreeing on the course of action and decision criteria. The client is a leadership and management academy. Upon our arrival, we – that is, three external participants including myself – are joined by four client representatives: two CEOs, the head of marketing and a tutor.

After about two hours, a break with fruit and refreshments offers an interesting opportunity to talk about private matters, tea and enthusiasm for brands. Open questions and answers help create a pleasant atmosphere.

After that the design intervention begins. Meanwhile, the rain is drumming on the floor-length windows of the conference room. We begin with a walk around the building. Do the orientation system's pictograms guide us clearly? What is the atmosphere like when you enter the large classroom?

Do we all perceive the same noises and smells? What at first seems a bit strange to the four people from the academy then leads to an increased sense of awareness. Design is much more than an external appearance. Design is always *experienced*.

Everyone gathers again in the conference room to consider the appearance of other educational institutions. Later on, assessment criteria and a procedure for the design process are established in a playful approach. Lively discussions that also invite contradiction alternate with clarifying sketches and numerous memos on a large wall. Listening to each other carefully, we are able to find the best-suited terms. This participative approach to encountering internal and external participants on an equal footing is maintained in the later design process. For there is no need to persuade anyone of anything that has been achieved in a collaborative effort.

At the end of the day, something has been *created*: a shared understanding – for the task, for the common course of action and for one another.

This example shows that, depending on the project dimensions, graphic design is mostly part of a greater process requiring a variety of expert opinions from different people alongside continuous harmonisation. At the very least, the project team will consist of a client and a graphic designer. While the final result itself is always about communicating content to a wider audience, personal communication and interaction pave the way towards achieving it. However, that process cannot be planned or guided throughout – on the contrary: a situational approach is prerequisite to engaging all of those involved and enabling them to become a team. Since decisions have consequences for others, designers must have a sense of responsibility.

The same applies to teaching.

Design education

The objective of design education is to prepare students for their future job as designers. However, since practice is subject to constant change, design education must remain open-minded towards all future questions and leave no room for any kind of forces that might restrict independent critical reflection and academic work. In that context, studying graphic design is a way to enhance oneself in the discipline. Embedded in a wider educational context, its supreme goal should be to foster one's individual personal development.

On the other hand, the nature of education is influenced by the society, culture and community of which it is a part. Former rector of the University of Applied Arts Vienna, Gerald Bast, views education against the backdrop of digital transformation, which is seen as a cause of additional insecurity and uncertainty in our society. Education should therefore respond to complexity and mutual dependencies in society, politics, economy and environment. For him, the fact that artificial intelligence, digitisation and robotics are increasingly shaping our world requires people to face the challenge and develop hitherto inconceivable connections using creative cognitive processes. Intellectual, intuitive, social and emotional processes are therefore crucial in order to bring something about. In that respect, Bast believes that 'a new "holistic thinking"' would be necessary.[8]

Change affects many aspects of our lives, including our attitudes and needs. However, graphic designer and co-founder of brand consultancy Wolff Olins, Michael Wolff, is convinced that some things do not change: 'And yet all people's need to be well-treated, loved and respected is still the same as it has always been. With all this change, design is still intended to serve, satisfy, improve life and delight people.'[9]

Bast and Wolff emphasise the importance of interpersonal skills. These very skills are an essential ingredient of education as a social process, which has a huge influence on society while also being an intrinsic part of it. Education thus has both small and large-scale effects.

A brief glance at the big picture reveals that not everyone has access to education. India-born Dean of Academic Strategy at Central Saint Martins in London, Rathna Ramanathan, comes from a region where many people cannot afford books. On a critical note she asks, 'How can we claim that we make knowledge accessible if we can't even make knowledge affordable?' Ramanathan has worked out a hypothetical solution by viewing the problem from a different perspective. She calls for a radical change of mindset: Couldn't there be different copyrights depending on the type of publication? Printed books would cost something in that case. But the same digital texts would be available online for free.[10]

Key competences

Changing one's own perspective leads to insights and allows new ideas to emerge. And ideally it leads to a change of what has already been recognised as worth changing. The World Economic Forum has listed the ability to solve complex problems, think critically and be creative among the top ten professional skills of 2025.[11] These are competences that are still being learned, tried out and applied in graphic design study courses, including the ability to use solution-oriented methods whatever the thematic content. Hence, design education also enables people to learn how to learn. And in the process, our discipline changes us as a person, but we change the discipline as well.

These theoretical considerations lead to the question of how to teach graphic design in practice.

TEACHING

TEACHING

The focus of this book is on teaching in the tertiary education sector. In Austria, this sector encompasses federal and private universities, higher educational institutions and universities of applied sciences. Much of the experience and procedures from those institutions is transferable to colleges for higher vocational education, as I can confirm from my own teaching experience at an Austrian higher technical college.

The equivalent of 'teaching' in German is twofold: *unterrichten* (to teach; literally, to inform) and *lehren* (literally, to lecture). While the former is commonly practised in the primary and secondary educational sector, the latter is applied almost exclusively in tertiary educational institutions. However, when educators from the tertiary sector speak about their job, they will often use both terms interchangeably.

When I began teaching, I felt that both *unterrichten* and *lehren* always implied the 'authority' of giving someone instructions. Meanwhile, I use both words without hesitation because in common parlance they also communicate the relevance of teaching through experience and reflection. The English word, by contrast, never embodied anything authoritative for me. It stems from the Old English word '*tæcan*', to show, explain and demonstrate.

What does it mean to teach?

How can students learn sustainably through experience? This question is key to the meaning of teaching, for it is all about learning. Changing the term and perspective from teaching to learning is essential here because it shifts the focus to those concerned, namely the learners. However, this by no means excludes teachers; on the contrary, it explicitly includes them. For we all learn new things together in the classroom context. At the same time, this shift of perspective also requires us to put ourselves in the learners' situation and to reflect on teaching from their point of view.

The following chapters, which deal with different aspects of teaching, are headed by questions that all teachers will probably ask themselves at some point in their careers.

Who am I?

Why did you begin to teach? Did you know what it meant to teach? Was it the desire to pass on knowledge? Did you want to become a researcher?

Whatever their individual motives may be, teachers are there to accompany learners. I do that consciously because my maxim is to learn along with my students. On my first day as a university teacher, though, this idea had not yet occurred to me. My hope was rather to spread my enthusiasm for graphic design and to raise awareness for the diverse and exciting sphere of activity opened up by design. And I was intrigued by the idea of finding out whether I could convey my ideals to students. That also meant encouraging contradiction from the very start, which I had got to know and learnt to appreciate during my own studies at university. I wanted to discover other perceptions in discussions in order to revise my own if necessary, but it also pleased me every time I was able to convince students of my viewpoints.

Meanwhile, I have consciously practised collaborative learning in class and have changed from a conveyor into a companion who asks a lot and listens attentively.

In that respect, my motivation is threefold: first, it is fulfilling to learn new things together with others; second, it is a rewarding experience to alternate between professional practice and research-oriented teaching, thereby defining one's expression and choice of words more precisely; third, this coincides with a serious commitment to the discipline, in this case graphic design, whose further development is also determined by, and in collaboration with, students.

The task of accompanying students demands intensity, or as graphic designer Ken Garland put it, 'Teaching was entirely devoted to students'[12], which is why his office could not reach him when he was teaching.

Expectations of oneself
Defining one's own expectations will always be an individual matter. The following questions can help to structure one's own goals and expectations:
1. What do I do when I teach?
2. How do I teach?
3. Why do I do that?

The *how* and *why* are more important here than the *what*.

As educational theorist David Cohen posits, it is essential to ask *why* because 'teachers work at a profession of human improvement. Like psychotherapists, social workers, pastors, and organization developers, they work directly on other humans in efforts to better their minds, lives, work and organizations.'[13]

In their book *Teaching as a Subversive Activity*[14], Neil Postman and Charles Weingartner advocate for learners be given more control over what they learn and how they learn it. In order to find out what is worth learning, they suggest the following thought experiment: Imagine all written works such as textbooks and curricula no longer existed and you were required to create a new curriculum solely by formulating questions. Looking at eight questions given by the above authors, you can find out whether or not the questions in your new curriculum have a favourable influence on learning.

Those eight questions could also be translated as the *how* of teaching. To that end, write a list, for example, describing how you teach, which mode of teaching you use and how you handle students and challenges. Everything you write down must be formulated as a question. In order to ascertain the impact of your teaching, analyse your questions based on those compiled by Postman and Weingartner:

- *Will your questions increase the learner's will as well as his capacity to learn?*
- *Will they help to give him a sense of joy in learning?*
- *Will they help to provide the learner with confidence in his ability to learn?*
- *In order to get answers, will the learner be required to make inquiries? (Ask further questions, clarify terms, make observations, classify data, etc.?)*
- *Does each question allow for alternative answers (which implies alternative modes of inquiry)?*
- *Will the process of answering the questions tend to stress the uniqueness of the learner?*
- *Would the questions produce different answers if asked at different stages of the learner's development?*
- *Will the answers help the learner to sense and understand the universals in the human condition and so enhance his ability to draw closer to other people?*

If your answer to all these questions is yes, you are pursuing the ideal of putting learners and their independent development centre stage.

Expectations placed on the teacher

First, let me reassure you that there is no such thing as *the* perfect teacher. However, it might be disconcerting to discover that learners are able to judge how teachers teach in less than ten seconds. A study using silent video recordings lasting only a few seconds revealed that high school students were able to assess a teacher without ever having met that person before. Their assessments corresponded to those of the teacher's real students.[15] Still, that does not worry me; it rather suggests that it is best, and even necessary, to be authentic.

By and large, learners regard fairness, personal respect and magnanimity as important.[16] For me, that also means admitting to mistakes or to not knowing something every now and then.

Similarly, learners appreciate being supported in their independence and autonomy as well as getting sensible and precise feedback that motivates them and puts learning in a positive light.[17] This was confirmed to me by all of the students I spoke to, without exception.

Who are the people who have those expectations of teachers?

Who am I teaching?

Teachers mostly teach people who want to learn, but just sometimes want to have fun as well. For example, at a class party:

The party takes place one night after the authorities have lifted the strict Corona lockdown regulations. Now, anyone can visit restaurants, bars and clubs without a face mask. Outside it feels chilly, but it is nice and warm in the club where the celebrations are in full swing.

The students have also invited other students from a neighbouring class and have booked a separate room. A flight of steps leads down to the location: a reddish glow on the walls, a few lights moving to the rhythm of the music, and brightly lit bottles standing in a fridge with a glass door, self-service and prepaid from the class's savings account. The music is not too loud, so you can talk to people standing nearby. Everyone is chattering away. About their day and about the Corona pandemic, of course. Most of it has nothing to do with design. Some of them are dancing. Later on, almost everyone joins in.

The founding director of the Vitra Design Museum, Alexander von Vegesack, stages weekly costume parties as part of international workshops at the Domaine de Boisbuchet in France. He thinks that dressing up and celebrating without any purpose or constraints can help people discover new projects and make new experiences, which the mind can activate later on.[18] In that sense, a class party does not serve any purpose. And the partygoers will gather together in the classroom at some point. So who are those people?

Developing
imaginativeness

All learners are individuals who are different from one another in many ways, for example with respect to their social background, age, basic education, personality and learning experience as well as their motives, goals and convictions.

Educational background and general education
Students' educational backgrounds can vary greatly. The university class I teach, for example, covers a broad range of applicants including school leavers from higher educational institutions and universities of applied sciences as well as university graduates and people who wish to acquire further qualifications after years of professional practice.

School leavers from higher educational institutions often come from school systems based on hierarchical assessment. While correct solutions are rewarded, mistakes will earn bad grades. The interviews in this book confirm that. Some of my interview partners in Japan told me, for example, that the objective of the first few sessions is to introduce students to an open-minded way of working and thinking.

Having a good general education and the will to keep on expanding it is fundamental to studying graphic design because it helps one to understand contexts and contextualise graphic design. Only then will students be able to think and act with the necessary sense of social responsibility.

Personality and talent
Collaborative learning success depends on how groups are composed in terms of the students' personalities.

Personality psychology differentiates five personality traits: How does a person respond to human interaction, and how open is that person toward seeking new experiences? Does a person act in a conscientious, targeted and accurate manner, and how agreeable are they in terms of being helpful and empathetic? Finally, how does a person cope with negative emotions?[19]

Curiosity and intensity are especially important personal traits for design students. Does that person want to discover new things and are they willing to embrace and experiment with unconventional ideas and perspectives in the process? Will that person go into depth on specific topics and are they able to recognise a relevant idea amongst many others?

'Artistic talent' only comes second to that. And although that does not necessarily imply requiring a strong sense for aesthetics, it will certainly ask whether a person is able to draw. Not with the goal of finding a budding young Albrecht Dürer, of course, but of being able to translate one's thoughts to a drawing so as to enhance one's communicative ability. 'Talent' as a development factor to acquire expertise is even characterised as problematic by educators John Hattie and Gregory Yates because assumed talent will rarely predict long-term development. Talent could also lead to a person automatically performing actions and skills without giving them any thought, which is quite the opposite of conscious exercise.[20]

However seriously you may take teaching, though, it always helps to have a great sense of humour to ease and cheer up day-to-day collaboration in class. Course director for fashion and journalism at London College of Art Andrew Tucker, for example, looks for creativity, ambition and a sense of humour in applicants.[21]

Entrance examination

The first step in forming a successful learning group begins with the entrance examination.

The smaller the class, the more subtle the choice and combination of individual characters will be. Around 120 people per year apply for admission to the class I teach and from those an average of 25 are invited to partake in a four-day entrance examination. The test ranges from texting a headline to conceptualising a communication campaign with a free choice of media. In addition, applicants are asked about their educational background and interests and take part in individual interviews and group sessions.

The ability to communicate with others and to collaborate in a team is essential at university and in later professional life as well. So it would make sense for entrance examinations to include a task that requires working in a team. This would necessitate more time and targeted observation, but it would also shed more light on how applicants behave in groups.

At the end of the selection process, eight to ten applicants are admitted per year.

Number of students from different years

Teaching quality is determined by the availability of time and, equally important, by the ratio of teaching staff to learners. In my case, an average of 15 to 25 students from different years study together within one course. This has the advantage of strengthening the class community and the mutual learning effect.

Guest students

One to two guest students are admitted per semester. They enrich life in class by providing other perspectives and approaches, sometimes through a different culture and other languages: not only foreign languages, but other ways of explaining design as well.

What range of skills do a diverse mix of students like this need to learn?

What do I aim to convey?

The goal of teaching should be to foster the following skills in students, based on the four fundamental activities of graphic design:
- graphic design aims to change – *thinking critically*;
- graphic design aims to understand – *getting to the heart of the topic*;
- graphic design aims to ideate – *being creative*;
- graphic design aims to realise ideas – *producing outstanding results*.

All four skills are interlinked and dependent on one another. *Thinking* stands for questioning a task and all of the steps in the design process. *Getting to the heart of the topic* means to profoundly understand the topics and given tasks. *Being creative* aims to discover the idea, while *producing results* not only involves trying things out in the design process, but also realising the final result.

How can teachers contribute to helping students improve those skills?

Teachers offer students topics and tasks that enable self-reflection and self-development, or they search for them together with their students. In this way, an open form of collaboration emerges between teachers and students. To allow for constructive and productive learning on both sides, teachers and students should be on equal footing.

During my university studies, most of my professors told me what was right and how one should go about doing things. Many went to pains to explain why; others merely established facts. Having trust in a teacher means believing that person and endorsing and then adopting the same or similar opinions. If, however, students have no trust in a teacher, they will challenge – either directly or even just in thought – what that person has to say. This leads to the development of a personal opinion, which is a vital factor in the process of independently finding answers. When these established perceptions and opinions merge to form a conviction that acts as a guiding principle for one's actions, we call that an attitude. Having an attitude provides students with an 'inner compass' both at university and in their later professional lives, in the course of which that attitude will often be readjusted.

Adopting an *attitude*.

People define their attitudes and vice versa. This applies to the creative as well as to the social, societal, political and ecological context. In all of these cases, graphic design can and should exert influence. Essentially, influence also means having consequences for oneself and having an impact on one's environment as well. This leads to responsibility.

Taking on *responsibility*.

Attitude and responsibility result from having the will not only to question given things, but also to challenge oneself, one's approaches and perceptions, all of this on the premise of bringing about improvement. At the same time, the will fuels self-motivation: one's determination to be persevering and conscientious at all design stages. Or to sometimes cross the line that one has drawn for oneself, which may include working all night in order to achieve a project goal, accepting other people's opinions, although one may not agree with them, or taking on discussions.

Displaying *openness*.

Openness thrives on one fundamental prerequisite: curiosity, which is essential for the unbiased discovery of new things. Translated to the creative process, curiosity allows a person to approach topics and ideas playfully, and in the best of cases, it spawns fascination. As a student of graphic design, I was fascinated by the variety of things I could form out of three equal lines arranged on a predetermined surface. And it thrilled me to see how differently one could interpret those compositions. Today, I am equally fascinated by the fact that every student generation discovers ever new compositions. And even more so when I notice how confidently some students leave the trodden path to let those three lines go beyond the defined format.

Cultivating *curiosity*.

Curiosity leads from the familiar into uncharted territory and opens up novel contexts. In doing so, curiosity causes questions to be asked, followed by answers one listens to and which again initiate new questions. With respect to design, curiosity drives content-related creative decisions. Because only those who are truly aware of the purpose of an enterprise will be able to design an appropriate corporate design. And only those who know users' needs will be in a position to develop a suitable app. In view of this, curiosity should embrace all of our senses. For example, a university is not only made up of teachers and learners, but also of its website, building forms, door handles, the sound of an elevator or the taste of lunch at the students' dining hall.

Forming *sensitisation*.

Being sensitive also means paying attention to one's own and other people's thoughts. As a consequence, perceptions must then be accordingly put into words and recounted to others. In that way, one can perceive and then positively influence a disproportion between the demand and action of an enterprise in the course of a design process. Or the smell of a material could lead to choosing alternative materials that are environmentally friendlier at the same time. However, in order to stimulate such changes, it is vital to communicate with other people,

Building *communication skills*.

Communication connects designers primarily with the people who commission them. In this case, it is equally important to ask questions, to listen and to express oneself clearly. Later on, communication connects the design result with the people actually using the design. A website that addresses consumers, for instance, requires different functionalities and visual characteristics than an intranet site for company employees. It is key to understand all of those people, and vice versa. It is just as decisive to communicate clearly and comprehensibly when collaborating with others on a project.

Searching for *collaborations*.

Complex projects require the ability to collaborate for example with game developers. In that sense, collaborations open up opportunities to benefit from other people's specialist knowledge, to tread new paths in the ideation process or to account for other people's opinions in the implementation phase. To do all of this, one must be able to empathise with others.

Developing *empathy*.

Having empathy for others is essential. This applies particularly to intercultural and interdisciplinary projects such as developing print media or an interface providing mnemonic training to people with dementia. Or finding imagery that appeals to young people. The best way may be to speak to those concerned or even to integrate them into the design process. Whatever the case, the more one empathises, the more knowledge will be accumulated. Hence, designers who are creating something for a winegrower will know what effect dosage has on sparkling wines. Just as designers collaborating with a cabinetmaker will know that fumed wood has nothing to do with smoke.

Expanding *knowledge*.

Detailed knowledge one has already acquired is often transferable to other projects. Sometimes it is the method of how aquiring knowledge or knowing how to treat other people. Every conversation held, every question asked and every observation made will open up new horizons. General knowledge, languages, travel, anything heard or devised; all of that knowledge serves as a pool in the ideation process.

Initiating *ideas*.

The very first idea in the ideation process should initiate a never-ending train of thoughts that knows no bounds. However, that requires constant practice in order to exclude everything that is negative while moving in the border zone between what one can know and what one cannot know. Later on, the selected design idea initiates users such as listeners of a radio spot or podcast or even rock music fans, who are then enabled to participate interactively in the production of a new song. In order to provide that functionality, an appropriate design needs to be implemented.

Perfecting *implementation*.

Once the idea, concept and basic design are established, the implementation phase can begin. During this phase all of the details are determined, which of course need to be technically feasible. 'Perfecting' therefore relates to the implementation process on the one hand, meaning: how do I achieve a very good result in a reasonable amount of time? How do I optimise processes and how do I ensure a smooth interplay between all participants and tasks in larger projects? On the other hand, 'perfecting' also relates to the final result, and in that regard, there is not only a single excellent result. On the contrary, outstanding graphic design can range anywhere between being appropriate or inappropriate. One has to maintain a critical eye all along the way to perfection. This critical stance will not only apply to one's own work but also to that of participants.

Establishing *critical thinking*.

Constant observation, differentiation, testing, judging and the resultant will to improve circumstances accompany creative people in every phase of a project. That requires a positive attitude towards questioning oneself and one's environment in a consistent manner.

From doing to being

Students improve their skills through continual practice and reflection, which, in the ideal case, will become second nature to them.

Which topics are best suited for students to develop and practise their personal attitudes and skills?

Which topics do I choose?

Global and regional contexts and new technologies inevitably give rise to a host of different challenges. It is vital to be able to respond to those changes. However, it is not only necessary to find the appropriate responses, but also the responding processes. And these need to be tried and tested, then adapted to current topics. In this way, students learn to adopt different approaches, identify challenges, develop essential activities and implement change. For that reason, the topic is of secondary importance.

Those who prefer topic-based teaching or think that every age has 'its own topics' which call for individual approaches could well be tempted to contradict this statement. Nevertheless, the topic is still less important. This is because it is always possible to learn design processes from the design of a milk carton or an app or when developing a business idea for an empty shop.

Requirements may change, but processes and interpersonal communication remain basically the same. The topic only becomes significant in connection with motivating students, so it ought to be relevant for them. In this sense, then, the question 'Which topics do I choose?' instead shifts to 'How do I choose a topic?'

We can differentiate between the following approaches:
- the teacher proposes a topic or a choice of topics
- teacher and students decide jointly
- several teachers decide and plan jointly
- other people decide

The teacher proposes a topic or a choice of topics
Teachers who put a particular topic on the agenda intend to focus on project processes or design knowledge, for example. Or they might have a personal interest in analysing a topic within a larger group. In both cases, students then tend to learn what teachers regard as important. In order to counteract that effect, the teacher could propose a topic such as 'environmental protection' as a broad thematic area within which students discover *their individual topic*. Again, the medium used for the project result can either be determined or freely chosen. The advantage of given topics or media is that the resulting works are comparable.

Another method would be to propose two to three topics, discuss them with the students and then decide on one of them, thus already incorporating that step into the design process.

In this regard, topic sources can differ hugely. Other related disciplines such as sociology, ecology or specialist fields like biodiversity and mobility management could spawn additional ideas as they offer a whole range of interesting tasks and basic topics that are adaptable and realisable from the perspective of graphic design. This can sometimes also lead to interesting collaborations.

Teacher and students decide jointly
Of all procedures, the joint decision variant puts the strongest focus on selecting a topic as part of the learning process. What is taught is not what the teacher knows, but what the learners want to know. Together with the students, their interests are discussed with an open outcome: what makes them tick? What would they want to change? Their topics do not have to be of global concern, but could address issues around shared student housing or family. The process of addressing and presenting their interests will ultimately help the students to give the topic serious consideration and to clarify their thoughts and choice of words.

As regards topic selection, it might help to let the students complete a given sentence – like Kyle Schwartz who asked her third-graders to finish the sentence 'I wish my teacher knew…' in order to get a better understanding of, and relationship with them.[22] Another approach would be to get together with the students and explore the neighbourhood, seeking out concrete places or events that they would like to change.

When all topics have been presented, it can then be decided on whether everyone is going to work on one chosen topic or develop their own topic in an individual project. To what extent a teacher codetermines or supports the decision-making process has to be decided on an individual basis.

Several teachers decide and plan jointly

This procedure provides the opportunity to view a topic from different perspectives. Here students can also learn that teachers sometimes have varying opinions and different approaches. If this includes people from other disciplines, there will be an even greater variety of opinions and expertise.

The topic could be elaborated simultaneously or consecutively, for example, in a marketing course, a typography course or in a course on digital media. Optionally, guest lecturers from other disciplines could contribute fundamental content to the topic which would then serve as a basis for teaching in class.

Other people decide

Principally, an assignment submitted by external persons can determine the nature of a topic. However, what is meant here is to involve externals in the process of topic selection by letting them define a topic that is relevant for them. This could be a village community whose problems and wishes are discussed, or an individual person requesting help, or an institution one approaches in order to listen to issues that are important to it. A digital variant would be to use platforms or social media channels to ask people to name topics.

This procedure makes addressing, questioning and listening a key part of the project process. And maybe the result is not to have provided a solution delivered by designers, but to have accompanied people or a community who did the designing themselves.

Combinations

A project that was implemented by Matthias Spaetgens's Class of Ideas to mark its tenth anniversary combines a number of different approaches.

The umbrella topic 'changing ideas' evolved in the teaching team. This project title has a dual meaning: humankind changes something through ideas, but at the same time, ideas change humankind as well. Topic and title were preceded by lengthy discussions: Is the umbrella topic too open-ended? What makes it cohesive? Does it express what students and teachers do in class? Finally, it was decided that the content framework should remain in place in order to offer the students greater freedom in their choice of topics. The objective of the project was to exhibit the results at designforum Wien as part of a retrospection of, insight into, and outlook on the class.

Several teachers joined the students in search of their own topics. The focus was on social transformation. The task was for the idea to stimulate thinking, action and change, a challenge that some students found extremely daunting at first. 'As students, who are we to believe we could bring about social change?' and 'Why do we always have to start with something that big?' are just two amongst many reactions. Other students found their topic very quickly. Many discussions later, everybody was aware that it was not about changing the world at large, but that small changes can have positive effects too. A broad variety of ideas was developed. The self-selected topics ranged from a future vision of the poster as a medium that could fly using drone technology to illustrated and animated info graphics on Austrian democracy and women's political participation, and a smartphone app offering further information on 'stumbling stones' placed into the pavement to commemorate victims of the Nazi regime. Both the visual identity and exhibition concept were developed in my course. The exhibition's publicity campaign was conceptualised by another teacher.

Once the topic has been chosen, it is then a matter of deciding which teaching format would best suit the topic as well as the students.

Which teaching format do I use?

Teaching formats are also known as teaching-learning formats, meaning that they focus on learners. The question is: which teaching format transforms individual experiences into a wealth of experience for students?

The format is determined by the type of learning method and applied technique as well as by activities during and outside the course. Typical formats include lectures, seminars, exercises, tutorials and work placements. The most sustainable format besides these classical formats, in my opinion, is project work.

Project-based learning

I consider project-based learning worthwhile because it combines theory with practical work across different courses and disciplines and takes the various approaches and opinions of all participants into account. Not only students, but also teachers, external people or organisations can participate. This procedure is closest to professional practice and motivates students to work independently. The practical relevance of such projects is a good argument for holding them as block courses.

I use several teaching-learning formats within one project in order to offer more variety and to quickly move on to practical work. Most classroom time is clearly spent on project work. From time to time, it is useful to expand on specialist knowledge together with students or experts, for example through guest lectures, short presentations or excursions such as a visit to a printing shop.

Real or fictitious projects

Projects can involve working on assignments from external clients or formulating them oneself. If this basic difference is discussed with students, it will encourage them to take a closer look at the various roles that designers could play.

Real projects

Universities are often thought of as places that have nothing to do with 'real life'. Graphic designer Adrian Shaughnessy does not agree with that. For him, professional life represents the 'non-real world', which includes disadvantages such as irrational clients and unrealistic deadlines.[23] In my view, there is no need to divide the world into two places, as both of them are part of one and the same 'real world'. We have to find our bearings in both places, and in each of them it is up to us to act and react. Isn't it actually a designer's job to try and positively influence the 'one real world' which is likewise 'out there', beyond the walls of academia? Shouldn't students already learn to collaborate with all those involved in a project, say, with clients and external specialists, during their time at university? That would enable students to deal with possible client objections and discussions in real projects – during a briefing, intermediate coordination or their final presentation.

An art programme that is disconnected from the real world, but which is supposed to prepare students for 'real life', is a paradox that could be considered an advantage. Philosopher and media theorist Boris Groys describes it as an education without rules – just as in 'real life, where we are subject to an endless variety of improvisations, suggestions, contusions and catastrophes ... Ultimately, teaching art means teaching life.'[24] The same goes for studying graphic design, too.

Examples of real projects could include developing a film production company's corporate design, a wine label or the communication concept for a congress held by the media and communication sector.

One advantage of real projects is that students are familiarised with content-related and interpersonal requirements directly through praxis. If those assignments are financially compensated, the students will also become acquainted with the economic dimensions of a project.

Fictitious projects

One great advantage of fictitious projects is the freedom of choice of topics, procedure and choice of results, as exemplified by the following project.

The semester project's objective is to develop the visual identity of a fictitious photo museum. First, the museum's location is determined, which would probably not be possible in reality: it is decided to locate the photo museum at Haas Haus in the middle of a busy pedestrian zone in Vienna's urban centre. The curator of a Vienna museum for contemporary art and photography and the former director of a contemporary art centre are invited to the kick-off event. They start with the subject of photography and elaborate on the significance of preserving and exhibiting cultural objects. According to the cultural professionals, a museum such as this would be a long overdue addition to other institutions. Since the students have many questions to ask, a lively discussion emerges.

In addition to its visual identity, the students also develop ideas for the museum's marketing strategy and first drafts of an orientation system within the building. The broad range of media accordingly reflects the requirements of holistic design. During the semester, the group visits a photo exhibition together. Both guests are again invited to the final presentation, during which they give thorough feedback on the students' works.

Like the above project, fictitious projects can be realistic, but they can be futuristic, too: together with his students, Kashiwa Sato conceptualises projects such as the colonisation of Mars (interview p. 208).

Paulus M. Dreibholz, who teaches typography, has a different approach to fictitious projects. He lets students search for or write their own texts, which are then designed by their fellow students. In that way, the students turn into clients and designers and learn how to operate in both roles (interview p. 101).

Over many semesters, it has proven successful to strike a balance between real and fictitious project types.

Knowledge is based on past experience. Trial and error focuses on the future.

Working individually or in groups

Experience has also shown that it is best to keep a good balance between working individually and in groups. Both forms cover professional practices that designers require for their later careers, whether they are self-employed, freelancers, part of a studio team or working on the interface between various other specialist areas.

Working individually

Working individually helps students to go their own way and to make their own conscious decisions. Both are key to successful learning. Feedback can be obtained from others, or alternatively, acquired in a process of self-reflection as specified by the teacher.

Working in groups

My preferred group size consists of two to three people, although a greater number would allow participants to experience specific group dynamics. Groups can form randomly or be put together by teachers, but students can also make up their own groups. If similar constellations emerge during the courses, teachers should tend to intervene in order to help students learn to create a positive atmosphere regardless of the group's composition.

I consider group work per se an elongated brainstorming process in which nothing of a negative nature should be said that could impede action that is solution-oriented and forward-looking. Having said that, of course, there should be room for critical remarks or retrospection, but the teacher must always explain that any criticism should be constructive so that everyone concerned can learn something new.

Many group works are performed collaboratively, when all group members are involved in all stages and results. Teams can also work cooperatively by distributing tasks. Both forms correspond to later professional practice and are learnt even more effectively in cooperation or collaboration with people who specialise in a different area.

Peer-to-peer teaching

In this type of project, students teach their fellow students without the supervision of a teacher. The aim of this teaching method, which can take place with or without teaching staff, is to enable students who have already acquired skills on, say, a computer programme, to impart that knowledge to other students, or to share their insights on work experience and semesters abroad. In any event, projects such as these are self-organised and students should be able to contribute their own topics.

Once the topic and type of project have been established, the actual teaching, the *how* of interaction in class, can begin.

How do I teach?

As a teacher, I aim to provide students with experiences that will help them to acquire new knowledge independently. They should use this knowledge to improve themselves in a continuous rethinking process and develop their own approach to designing.

Again, the *how* of teaching does not refer to a teacher's behaviour alone, but to the way teachers engage with learners. This is crucial, as it not only places extra emphasis on the people receiving tuition, the students, but also on where the *how* happens – between people.

My role in this interaction is to support students along their way. I am not an advisor, but an asker and a listener. At the same time, I am a learner who seeks to learn more about content and designing and hopes to improve as a teacher as well. In that context, it is helpful to be aware of which courses of action you have in class and how to take them in a targeted way. This chapter intends to explain what they are and how to employ them.

Acting consciously

It is Wednesday morning, a winter's day. While many students turn up in class shortly after quarter past nine, others arrive punctually at half past nine when class begins. And one of them, it is always the same person, is late as usual.

After they have all taken their seats and had a chat about their morning moods and experiences, I ask them to stand up and follow me to a flip chart in order to start a discussion in a different constellation. A semicircle forms quite naturally and I am part of this formation. My opening question is: 'What is graphic design?'

Reactions range from a still sleepy gaze and deliberate look the other way to the beginning of a discussion between two students and the first answer. Another student responds to this immediately, saying, 'I see that differently. For me, that word is no longer up-to-date.' One student agrees with her, while another tries to define what the word originally meant to him, then goes on to explain why his perception has since changed. I remain silent, pleased that the discussion is warming up; I listen and use a flip chart to make a note of individual statements and catchwords.

Different opinions spark a lively discussion in which the initially bleary-eyed student also participates. When pauses in the conversation occur, I allow them to take effect as such. Only now and then do I break the silence by asking one of the two people who are always reluctant to join in whether they have the same view as their fellow student. And that person has an opinion and voices it, too. Another student, who always supports his statements with lots of arguments, asks, 'Wouldn't our class need to be renamed?' Meanwhile, one-to-one conversations evolve, but they always find their way back to the middle of the group. 'Shouldn't we define the word "design" first?' one student argues, which leads to the question as to whether design generally entails commitment. New insights and outcomes now fill the flip chart.

I ask them whether and how we want to organise our insights and outcomes visually, and listen again. One student remarks that it would be good to organise everything in circles because that would help to include umbrella terms as well. A second flip chart is brought in, its metallic legs squeaking while being set up. Organising the terms visually helps to categorise thoughts and to clarify ambiguities. When a new thought is voiced, I ask the students to add it to the flip chart themselves, in that way literally activating the discussion.

The final result is a diagram with an arrangement of words that most people agree on. After a short break during which all windows are opened to let the winter air in, we begin with this semester's topic 'Design & Environment'. This Wednesday, the aim is familiarising ourselves with the topic. At the end of the session, I leave the class, thinking about next Wednesday when we will be discussing the word 'environment'.

What do we teachers do in class?

We act. It is a succession of interwoven events that we deploy not only consciously and in a targeted way, but often also intuitively. Ruth Mateus-Berr compares her action with that of a dramaturge. As head of the Center for Didactics of Art and Interdisciplinary Education, she endeavours to create motivating contexts in educational settings in order to facilitate experiences (interview p. 158).

Courses of action

In order to raise awareness for courses of action that can be freely combined in the process of teaching, I break them down and ascribe different doing words to them, since these verbs express decisive action.

Students act, too. Their courses of action can be summarised in the following order of verbs:

asking — listening — speaking — rethinking — doing

If these courses of action are translated to a semester project, they could stand for the following: *asking* stands for initial familiarisation – asking questions opens up a topic and triggers interaction with it; *listening* stands for receiving information – it expresses attentiveness and enables people to learn with and from others; *speaking* stands for formulating and articulating oneself – thoughts, concerns and ideas are voiced and views develop; *rethinking* accompanies the whole process and leads to change – it stands for critically viewing and assessing; *doing* is giving form – it represents getting started, experimenting and creatively implementing all other steps.

Teachers' courses of action require an additional word:

asking — listening — speaking — rethinking — letting do

doing becomes *letting do* because it is the students' job to create something and make decisions. Teachers accompany that part of the actions, but do not do anything themselves in the sense of a course of action.

The order of the courses of action begins with asking because I often start with a key question, and questions frequently initiate discussions in class. All actions, however, are equal in value; no action need be given priority and they can be used in any order depending, of course, on the situation. Asking is followed by listening. Sometimes though, a question can also trigger immediate rethinking. Additionally, just as in design processes, it is also possible or even necessary to go back to an earlier step. Individual actions affect each other just as interpersonal communication is affected by a person's voice, facial expression, gesture, posture and movements.

Is there any action that teachers tend to employ less consciously? Is it the asking, listening, speaking, rethinking or letting a person do something? My experience from observations and conversations with teachers and students is that teachers tend to listen less often. The interviews in this book also seem to confirm that.

I am convinced that listening ought to be practised more frequently – or at least more consciously – because it motivates students more strongly to think, decide and act themselves. Listening transfers responsibility to students.

Below, I have placed listening at the centre of all actions in order to emphasise its key role:

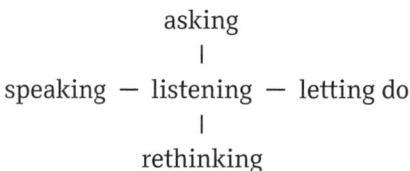

                    asking
                      |
speaking — listening — letting do
                      |
                  rethinking

A detailed description of these individual courses of action and how to employ them in practice is given in the following. They appear in the order of verbs set out above.

Asking

'I can't see inside other people's heads and so I have to ask questions to find out who they are, what they think, how they think, how they are doing today and what they expect from their lives.'[25] This is how Professor of Design Theory Michael Hohl (interview p. 137) explains the importance of communication to learning, which is a social project just like research.

Questions are the first step towards gaining insights – and learning is based on them. The same applies to graphic design. Teachers can ask questions, for example, to help students:
- clarify their statements
- formulate subsequent questions
- find other answers
- adopt other perspectives.

If a teacher listens carefully to answers, an exchange of ideas happens. Questions posed by the teacher can initiate a learner's train of thoughts – and sometimes even lead to 'aha!' moments. In order to encourage that, teachers should
- always formulate questions openly,
- offer any advice in the form of a question whenever possible, and
- begin now and then with the question as to how they can help at all.

The latter paves the way for students to express their intention clearly and to realise that formulating their own answers and subsequent questions will help them move forward and ultimately make independent decisions. If students ask themselves questions, topics will emerge that are relevant for them.

At the same time, the question as to how to give any help can prevent one from offering immediate advice. Another strategy in that sense is to begin one's own questions with *what* in place of *why*. Instead of asking students *why* they chose a certain font for an application, ask them *what* they chose it for. Therefore, an alternative to 'Why do you think this concept is suitable?' would be 'What made you think in that direction?'

Sometimes students try to provide answers they think will fulfil the teacher's assumed expectations. If so, that needs to be addressed at once, as it is not what class is about.

If a question is met with prolonged silence, it is best to 'scale it down' and reformulate it.

By asking questions, teachers can influence learning processes positively in many aspects of their teaching, as the following four examples show:

Beginning of a project

On the first day in class, questions can help teaching staff to become acquainted with their students. If the latter are able to ask their teacher questions too, this will help create an open atmosphere right from the start. Moreover, the choice of questions plays a specific role in that respect: questions reflecting a general interest are more favourable than subject-related ones.

Questions can also ease group interaction, for example, when pairs of students are required to ask each other questions in varying dialogue situations without using typical words such as 'design' or 'communication'.

At the beginning of a project, asking questions can help to establish the students' degree of knowledge and their expectations.

Alternatively, certain questions may be used to awaken interest in design history and the works of other designers. British graphic designer Richard Hollis, for example, analyses different design works together with his students as a means to help them use precise language and to subsequently speak about their own and other people's works. To do this, he often uses two questions to stimulate critical discussion: 'What was the person who made it trying to do?' and 'What am I trying to do?' In such a discussion, asking further questions can foster reflection on social, technical and aesthetic issues and thus awareness of one's own values.[26]

Briefings

Asking questions also reflects a person's curiosity, and teachers should be role models in that respect, for example, with regard to briefings:

External clients assign a wallpaper design for a new Vienna hotel offering 178 rooms. The accommodation is within walking distance of Vienna University of Economics and Business, the surrounding urban district and the Prater, Vienna's famous amusement park and gateway to a greater recreation area. The wallpaper motifs are intended to highlight the diversity and individual style of each interior. The written briefing is followed up by a summary in the classroom, which the clients, the architect and the designer who initiated the project are invited to attend. In line with the predetermined motto, there is a distinct 'passion for adventure' and 'fun of discovery' at the hotel and the assignment requires the wallpaper motifs to reflect that spirit.

At first, only a few questions crop up. I try to break the ice by asking general questions about the hospitality sector. These questions may initially have nothing to do with the actual briefing, but make an interesting contribution on how to manage a hotel and fill it with life. This helps develop an understanding for the clients and the topic, as does the question of how to find good staff. Gradually, the atmosphere becomes more relaxed and the students begin to ask assignment-related questions.

A lively discussion emerges in which everyone tries to define the 'passion for adventure' more closely and the students learn more about the history of the urban district. When the discussion comes to a halt, I reinitiate it and sometimes ask people if they could explain something more precisely.

Feedback and asking

The design process ranges from initial research and the ideation process to the elaboration and realisation of the idea. During this process, it is essential to motivate students to follow their own line of thought by putting questions to them. For instance, if students who are conceptualising or designing a logo ask, 'How could I tackle this problem?' then well-meaning teachers tend to either offer a solution or suggest three alternatives in the hope of inspiring the person seeking advice. That is one possibility. However, if a teacher asks questions in response to the student's query, they will search for their *own* answers. An opening question could be: 'What were your initial thoughts on the topic?' The reply to that question should be followed by another question: 'Do you see any alternatives to that?' Again, the question to follow this answer could be: 'Do you have any other ideas you could try out?' This question-and-answer process should only stop when students have no more answers to give.

Besides that, another aspect needs to be considered when asking questions on students' design proposals: questions are not meant to ask for any personal feelings (of the person doing the designing), but for the impact of the design (on other people). In that way, such questions offer a chance to step into someone else's shoes. That could be someone of a different age or social background who is seeing this creative work for the first time. What effect does the design have on them? Which questions are those people asking themselves?

Maintaining an objective view of your own work can be learnt by looking at it together with non-designers – or by involving the people for whom the design is intended in a participatory design process.

Study trips

Asking questions can also become a guiding principle, for example on a study trip:

36 students, four teachers and ten days. Our destination is Tokyo. The aim of the trip is to get to know the country, the people and their culture. Ahead of the trip, there are preparatory workshops with a Japanese designer, a calligrapher and with a student presenting a report of her personal experience in Japan during the 2011 Fukushima nuclear and natural disaster. Initial questions are already asked at those kick-off events in Vienna.

'Meeting Tokyo's Creatives' is a semester project that builds on questions itself. It is an interview project with many stages and challenges: researching creatives in Tokyo, getting in touch with them from abroad, developing a set of questions, meeting those people in Tokyo, dealing with language-related difficulties, interviewing and portraying the selected person. The final result is a collection of eleven booklets that present different perspectives on the working methods, attitudes and lifeworlds of each of those creatives. Their specialist areas range from architecture to illustration and photography.

How to improve one's questioning skills
Whatever the occasion, it is vital to ask the right questions and to do so without hesitating. Concerns as to whether or not the answers are useful for the project and ideation process can be analysed afterwards. Likewise, the person to whom the question is addressed is equally important: fellow students, clients, or those who are going to perceive or use the design later on?

Is it possible to improve your questioning skills? Yes, by asking questions as often as you can. How is that taught in class? By asking questions as a teacher and requesting students, if necessary, to formulate their questions differently and more precisely. Ideally, that is achieved by asking counter questions and not by correcting the original question.

Going back to the initial list of things Michael Hohl seeks to find out about people by asking questions, he also makes reference to how a person is doing. This is a key point, because learning in terms of class collaboration is not just a matter of learning together in a group, it is also an accumulation of different personalities and moods. Therefore, instead of guessing what mood a student is in, teachers should address them concretely and discuss them if need be – providing, of course, they wish to get involved with the student's emotional world. If that is the case, the teacher needs to listen as well.

Listening

If asking questions is looking into the future, listening is acting in the present.

In a general sense, listening stands for the ability to receive and interpret messages in the communication process. Listening should not be confused with hearing, which is the ability to perceive sound through the ears.

Hence, listening means focusing our attention and concentrating on what we hear, on the person speaking. Besides the content, we also perceive the speaker's intonation as well as their body language: we hear verbal messages and see nonverbal signals. At the same time, the listener needs to perceive the feelings behind the content and respond empathically to them. In that context, it can help to repeat what we have heard in our own – non-judgmental – words. Psychologists Carl Rogers and Richard Farson refer to this kind of listening as *active listening*.[27] Psychologist Michael P. Nichols puts it in a nutshell: 'The essence of good listening is empathy, which can only be achieved by suspending our preoccupation with ourselves and entering into the experience of the other person.'[28]

Listening is therefore not a tool, but an ability that is fundamentally determined by our attitude. It requires sensitivity towards students and ourselves. Mafalda Spencer, who studied under graphic designer, photographer and author Ken Garland, confirms that students are well aware of that: '…although he likes pontificating – which he can do at length – he does actually listen to students. And that's a rare thing. Plus, this amazing rapport he has with youth. Not dismissing youth; taking young people seriously, and treating students as equals.'[29] When teachers listen carefully to their students, they:
- give them their undivided attention
- make them feel appreciated
- treat them with empathy
- do not judge what has been said
- create an atmosphere which makes everybody feel confident
- give them time to think things over.

By listening to their students, teachers also activate them. They hand over responsibility to students for their thinking, acting and decision-making. Feedback sessions are one good example of mindful listening.

Feedback and listening
Feedback sessions sometimes begin with questions from teachers. If students are familiar with the procedure, it may not be necessary to ask any questions. The candid request to 'show me what you've got', for example, can trigger a conversation in which teachers listen and students codetermine what and in which order to talk about matters.

It is Wednesday again, shortly before the summer holidays. The goal of the semester project is to develop the corporate design of a new drink – white wine combined with maté and elderberry. Besides the taste, the bottle's design is crucial, and this is to be developed alongside the logo and other media. Today's feedback session is all about the drafts for the bottle's design. The students work in pairs in small groups. They arrive in that constellation at the conference room, which is adjacent to the actual classroom. There are always two groups of two students, that is, four in all. Today however, three groups enter the room last in order to ensure that no one group ends up without any feedback from their fellow students. The old parquet floor creaks as the six enter the room and take their seats at the round table.

My role is to listen and help students improve their asking and listening strategies. Who will begin is quickly established. It is the group that has already spoken up quite often. Although the procedure of showing drafts and getting feedback does not follow any given order, the students are familiar with it from previous feedback conversations. These sessions are basically about conveying and listening to observations and opinions. Now and then, I am also asked a question, for example, what I think about an idea. I then pass that question on to one of the groups.

It is easier to conduct a discussion with smaller groups in feedback sessions because there is usually somebody who will say something. If nobody says anything, though, I do not intervene. If critique is too harsh or even offensively formulated, students tend to notice that themselves. If not, it is my job to bring it to their attention. And this can also happen by asking questions in order to remain in the listener's role.

At the end of the discussion, I ask an open question, 'How can a label, considering the whole bottle as an object, be conceptualised in an unusual way? Is there a way to create ideas that go beyond the conventional adhesive label?' At the next session, I am listener again and am taken by surprise by two outstanding ideas: one label consists of two superimposed carrier media, one of which can be turned around to create an analogue text and image animation. The other bottle can be used to play music.

This example clearly shows that one course of action is rarely used on its own, which is why some points such as feedback are addressed in several courses of action. In all cases, it is about encouraging students to think for themselves without prescribing a certain direction.

Intentional silence

Interestingly, the words *listen* and *silent* consist of the same letters, which suggests that they are related to one another: silence can be intentionally employed after listening to a person in order to give them time to reflect. Hence, the listener should not immediately voice their thoughts as soon as the speaker stops talking. Research results from the USA show that silence gaps lasting for more than four seconds may cause a feeling of discomfort. According to social psychologists Koudenburg, Postmes and Gordijn, this is because we tend to associate silence with rejection.[30] Translated to tuition, however, a silence gap can last even longer if a positive discursive culture prevails. One should therefore curb the urge to interrupt the silence too quickly.

How to improve one's listening skills

The first step on the way to improving one's listening skills is the decision to focus more intently on listening. If this strategy is proactively pursued on a regular basis, it often leads to an improvement. Prompting students to get started, or even an open question as to how to take joint action, fosters one's own listening ability as well.

In discussions, one should then ensure that the conversation is linear: speaking – listening – speaking – listening. People who interrupt others should be made aware of the interference.

In the same way, it is essential to practise focusing on listening in order to avoid judging something purely by appearance. This applies both to the person being listened to and what they are saying. Something that may have initially sounded wrong in terms of content can be clarified by asking further questions.

Since situational factors have an additional influence on one's own listening capacity, one should create a situation that is found preferable: am I standing in front of the whole class? Is everyone sitting in a big group around one table? Do I prefer listening to dialogues or to smaller groups when I walk around the classroom and sit down next to students doing their work?

In order to judge one's listening skills from a critical perspective, two questions could be of further help:
- What advantage do students have when I listen to them?
- How should I listen in order to be of advantage to them?

The following two examples suggest how to focus more on listening:

Soundwalking

This term was coined by sound ecologist and composer Hildegard Westerkamp.[31] Instead of concentrating on spoken words, a soundwalk is about perceiving sounds that are often ignored in our day-to-day environment. In order to sensitise the ear in that respect, the group could walk along a predetermined route, for example, and pay attention to all kinds of sounds. This could be a walk through streets or in the woods. During this activity, participants are not supposed to talk, but just take in the sounds around them. Afterwards in a feedback session, participants discuss what their impressions were and what they triggered inside.

This exercise can also be performed using spoken content. It requires closing your eyes and listening to someone else, thus drawing more attention to nuances that are otherwise missed.

The role of listening skills in lectures or discussions
In order to be receptive to spoken content during discussions or lectures, it may help to first appreciate *why* you are listening to it – this is also something you can ask your students:
- What do I want to take away with me?
- What goal do I have in mind when listening?

Listening to oneself
Listening also prepares students for their future careers, because professional designers – according to the International Council of Design's Code of Conduct for Designers – are especially characterised by humility, which comes from the ability to listen: 'It is easy to fall in love with our ideas, but we do not design for our own pleasure. Good design comes from the ability to accept and value criticism, be open-minded, work in teams, and listen (to experts, to the client, to the end user, their peers, their collaborators and the general public).'[32] To that list of people, I would add: one should also listen to oneself. Paying attention to one's own thoughts and feelings, to questioning them and responding empathically by putting oneself in other people's positions, is a type of listening that should be permanently implemented in the creative process. Only then will the ability develop to encounter others open-mindedly, to accept criticism and learn from it. Listening to oneself also means acting intuitively at times and tolerating mistakes. This sometimes requires a basic change to one's own attitude. And in order to change one's ways at all, one should not try, as Carl Rogers puts it, to function at all times in the way one would like to function.[33]

Is listening more important than asking questions?
No, listening is not more important in that respect, but it is implemented less often and less consciously by teachers. There seem to be several reasons for this: as mentioned previously, teachers sometimes wish to support their students by giving them advice, or they get the impression that it would speed things up if they gave hints to students. Moreover, teachers may even give a piece of advice with the sole intention of achieving a perfect result, at least from their own perspective.

Of course, students can learn from recommendations, too, but I am convinced that open-ended questions can significantly help students to tread their own path to learning, practising and making decisions – because asking questions does not interrupt a student's train of thought as much as giving advice does.

Listening shapes dialogue with others as well as one's own thoughts. It has an effect on what and how something is said.

Speaking

To speak means to formulate something in words and to transport appropriate meanings along with them. Hence, language is meaningful in every conversation and lecture as well as in the communication of specialist knowledge. In professional practice, an equally precise language is required to communicate clearly with clients, collaboration partners or programmers.

Teachers should express themselves clearly. And they should demand clarity from their students, too.

In that context, the spoken word is also influenced by nonverbal communication, while interaction is determined by the voice, facial expression, gesture and posture as well as by one's movements and position in the room. If, for example, a teacher sits down next to rather quiet students, they will receive more attention. Conversely, a teacher can attract more attention by changing pitch and speech tempo.

Our body language not only has an impact on how we are perceived by others, but also on ourselves, our feelings. What effect does it have for example, when I smile? Psychologist Fritz Strack and his team looked into that question in a study with participants who were asked to watch an animated cartoon and then rate it. Participants who were instructed to hold a pencil between their teeth, making their mouth form a smile, found the cartoon funnier than those who had to hold the pencil between their lips, resulting in a frown.[34]

At the same time, however, it is essential to remain authentic. Teachers who smile or speak less often will tread other paths than their counterparts who like to kick off their projects with a lively and lengthy monologue. Whatever the case may be, everybody should be aware of their courses of action and the consequences they bring with them.

Clarity

Clarity is necessary for successful communication: what one intends to say should be uncomplicated and generally comprehensible. Foreign words should be avoided or otherwise explained. Communication is clear when everyone listening is able to repeat what they have heard correctly – albeit in their own words.

Language also promotes a contextual understanding of existing and potential conceptions. For instance, describing one's own design, literally putting it into words, makes it easier to understand.

One can foster clarity of expression by addressing individual words along with their use and meaning. Clarity is achieved by repeatedly asking students to define their statements more precisely. This occurs mostly in discussions, in group or face-to-face conversations or in presentations. In addition, non-design-related literature can enhance a person's repertoire of linguistic nuances.

Writing – readable language
Another good way of learning how to express oneself more precisely is by formulating and writing down one's thoughts. Methods such as the following are suitable in class:
- preparing creative briefs
- describing concepts and ideas
- doing intermediate and final presentations
- concluding project descriptions.

Therefore, relevant concepts should have working titles that include just a few key words, and each idea should be described in one brief sentence. This will not only help learners to express themselves more effectively, but in most cases, also to clarify the concept and idea behind it.

According to Volker Albus, who studied architecture and teaches product design, one's relationship to an object changes when it is 'put into words'. Writing about something thus becomes an act of appropriation. Albus advocates a qualified description that can be either direct or associative and addresses the existing lack of specific design vocabulary.[35] The same applies to graphic design. Using largely familiar words in terms of design vocabulary means that people from other disciplines and non-designers can also make sense of specialised content.

Drawing – giving language a form
Is it sometimes easier to give thoughts a form instead of putting them into words? Well, it does at least present an additional way to address undiscussed matters with students and to enhance their linguistic skills by asking them to explain a drawing. In that sense, then, drawing is a means to translate ideas into images.

Video tutorials – recorded language
Today, teachers are increasingly using video tutorials to teach students online. They use this format, for example, to explain what branding means. The usefulness of that kind of knowledge transfer depends on its purpose. In her capacity as teacher of game design, game development and social media technologies Johanna Pirker points out that in a course, whether distance

learning or class teaching, one always has the option to activate students by interacting with them, which a video cannot provide (interview p. 171). Besides that, a video also lacks the opportunity to discuss and clearly define things with students.

Whether articulating content orally, in written form, as a drawing or in a video, though, it is essential to express oneself understandably, or even better, unambiguously.

Speaking about experiences

For teachers, *speaking* is a course of action that could also mean talking about their own experiences. How does one handle clients? Did difficult situations sometimes arise? How were they resolved? What can one do to extend personal knowledge – working in the profession or as a teacher? If one wishes to speak about topics that are relevant for students, it is best to ask about their interests beforehand.

Addressing situations and moods

There are occasions that need to be directly addressed, three of which are presented below:

Discomfort

If situations arise that are uncomfortable for one or more people, or for oneself, these need to be addressed proactively. Depending on the situation, that could happen directly or sometime later on in a smaller group or face-to-face talks. The aim should always be to foster a positive and constructive atmosphere.

Multitasking

How does one respond to a student who insists on being able to concentrate on classwork while simultaneously doing an illustration, or who appears to be otherwise distracted? This happens often while a lecture or presentation is going on or when everyone is involved in a discussion. One could ignore such behaviour in favour of devoting more attention to those who are genuinely interested, as Yasuhiro Sawada does in his graphic design classes (interview p. 214). Alternatively, one could deconstruct the multitasking myth: several studies have shown that if activities are demanding, it is only possible to cope by switching from one task to the other, which has a negative effect on knowledge acquisition as well as intellectual participation in and reflection on content in class. So we cannot perform two demanding activities at the same time.[36] [37]

Making use of group situations

Sometimes it can be helpful to make a person aware of the disturbance they are causing and to involve the group as well. One example of this is being late. If this happens frequently, one's initial reaction might well be to issue a warning or give bad marks. But one could instead ask the person how they intend to remedy matters in the future, or one could discuss the consequences of being late in the group.

Alternatively, a kind of working agreement involving jointly negotiated rules could be set up in advance between teacher and group.

Nevertheless, there are situations which call for a clear statement from the teacher in order to heighten attention and bring about a quicker change to teaching in class. Students can also perform this kind of moderation provided that there is prior agreement to take on the task as part of their personal responsibility.

Feedback and speaking

Feedback should be specifically and clearly formulated so that students can use it to improve their performance, but it should not contain any working instructions. However, clearly explained feedback can sometimes be applied to correct details where there is no question, such as wrongly using inch marks instead of inverted commas in direct speech.

As far as sustainable learning and individual learning progress is concerned, therefore, it is advisable to offer students guidance and steer them in the right direction. Seen in that light, then, failing to use the correct inverted commas can even provide a deeper insight: 'What does the incorrect use of punctuation marks suggest to people who can differentiate between them?' or 'What is the origin of inverted commas?' and even 'What do those differentiations tell us about our language?'

When giving feedback, one could be tempted to praise students. Although this will be taken as a compliment, it will not be of any genuine help to learners. Praise only shows learners what teachers have found laudable, and it can – if employed frequently – lead to habituation. Since, however, studying design is all about learning new things self-dependently, students should be able to recognise good results without praise. They need to develop their own evaluation criteria and be a yardstick of quality. This should go hand in hand with personal motivation, which students are also expected to build themselves.

Teachers encourage students to think ahead by what they say and how they say it. In that context, then, speaking is closely related to the act of rethinking things.

Rethinking

Teachers are required to rethink their actions regularly in order to improve their teaching: how do they and others judge their teaching? What needs to be changed? Suggestions in that regard can be found in the chapter 'How can I improve my teaching' (p. 74).

In this chapter, it is essentially about critical thinking and continuous rethinking – the basis of any creative process.

In order to establish both, universities need to be safe spaces where everything is allowed as long as it does not interfere with others. This applies to ideas as well as designs. Hence, enough room should be given for experimentation in a stimulating atmosphere of confidence.

Critical thinking

Critical thinking is the unbiased analysis of a circumstance or a situation, enabling one to draw the best conclusion. To do that, it is essential to formulate questions unambiguously, to observe and to also perceive things that are inconspicuous. For the purpose of evaluation, it is important to weigh information and to provide an objective assessment that in no way reflects one's own opinions. Conclusions should rest on clear, constructive and appreciative grounds.

When speaking about his students, Katsuya Kato, who teaches design basics and media, describes the essence of critical thinking as follows: 'I don't want them to assume a formal way of thinking, to have preconceptions. I want them to learn to think freely and to question everything' (interview p. 152).

In a completely different context to teaching design, while in a yoga course, graphic designer Milton Glaser realised that openness was key to thinking freely. He recalls the yoga teacher saying: 'Spiritually speaking, if you believed that you had achieved enlightenment, you have merely arrived at your limitation. I think that is also true in a practical sense. Deeply held beliefs of any kind prevent you from being open to experience, which is why I find all firmly held ideological positions questionable.'[38]

This openness and constructive questioning represents a positive critical basic attitude that begins long before the actual design process and embraces political, social, economic and ecological issues of our society, affecting students beyond academia too. At university, though, this basic attitude must be maintained not only in terms of assigned topics, assigned tasks, one's own and other people's creative work, but also with regard to tuition itself.

Teachers should demonstrate that basic attitude and seek to shape it together with their students by making critical thinking an issue, giving relevant tasks or developing them collaboratively with their students.

Continuous rethinking

While critical thinking is a basic attitude, continuous rethinking is fundamental to all creative processes because it enables insights and changes.

This principle resembles that of permanent self-correction found in the theory of cybernetics, which suggests that dynamic systems effect changes through continual feedback.[39] In an ideation process, correcting, rethinking and conceptualising often happens 'intuitively'. Chemist and philosopher Michael Polanyi uses the term 'tacit knowledge', meaning knowledge that we are not able to express in words.[40] How we can transfer this knowledge to immediate practice is described by philosopher and urban planner Donald Schön in his concept of 'reflective practice'. In learning and working processes, professionals often alternate between thinking and acting, which leads to further development and improvement.[41]

In visualisations of design process models such as the 'Double Diamond' of the Design Council[42] or 'Human-Centered Design'[43] which centres on the human being, continuous rethinking is not explicitly stated. It governs all actions and is thus link and prerequisite to the creative process. This continuous questioning aims to generate changes.

The following semester project shows the effect of critical thinking and continuous rethinking on project work:

The project's title is 'Gender Equality'. It is a cooperation project between the China Academy of Art in Hangzhou, Tama Art University in Tokyo and the Class of Ideas which I teach in Vienna. Students in all three cities are given the same tasks.

In Vienna, students arriving in the classroom on the first day are welcomed by *Somewhere over the Rainbow* booming out of the loudspeakers as if it were a clubbing event. Some of them smile while others look bewildered. One student moves to the music as he enters the long classroom.

Topic, scope of the project and procedure during the semester are quickly explained. One important thing will be to take a critical view of the chosen topic. The first question, therefore, is: what does gender equality mean to us all? A discussion unfolds that develops momentum. What can we designers do to contribute to equality? What do we want to make others aware of and reflect on? Now and then, I put questions to students who seem reluctant to join in.

After the discussion, it is time for individual research, and everyone is given freedom of choice within the topic's definition. The students select aspects of gender equality that they consider important and do in-depth research on them. During research, small groups form around tables pushed together. If those groups repeatedly consist of students who know each other well, I sometimes suggest forming new ones. Walking from table to table, a conversation with one of the groups comes back to critical thinking again. It starts with the question of whether criticism always aims to be negative and finishes with experience reports, when they start thinking critically without always being aware of it.

The project's goal is to express one's own perceptions and suggestions for improvement in words and images – and translate them compactly to a poster.

One week later, we begin with the question of what makes a good poster, while also challenging the medium itself: is it up to date? Is there a difference between the requirements of commercial posters and those intended for display in an exhibition? My questions on how posters could be used in other ways as a medium and whether it would be worth breaking out of the two-dimensionality of a flat sheet of paper spark a discussion on animated variants including posters which we call Animated Display Images (ADI).

When it comes to focusing on the topic and designing the poster, discussions are held in small groups across several sessions in which students are able to demonstrate their progress and give feedback to one another. They are busy asking, listening and speaking and are additionally encouraged to rethink content and design-related decisions or experiments. When I ask, 'Is there anything you still want to improve?' they begin to cast a critical eye on their own work. Besides these targeted feedback sessions, exchange amongst students takes place permanently during collaboration in class. Everyone learns from everyone else.

As the semester progresses, classwork focuses more strongly on the actual design. Based on printed posters, we assess their long-range and close-range effects. To that end, all of the students meet up frequently. Many of them feel that it is rewarding and a good experience to observe their own design process and to critically question it over a period of several weeks as opposed to the thrill of short-term projects that are implemented within a couple of days.

The project culminates in exhibitions taking place simultaneously in the three cities involved. Over one hundred posters by all of the students participating in the cooperation project offer insights, perspectives and outlooks on other cultures and ideas.

As a course of action, *rethinking* focuses on how teachers can help students to analyse their ideas. However, when it comes to the doing, students should work independently.

Letting do

Letting do has a twofold meaning. First, it stands for letting students do a practical exercise, for example, on a specific topic. Second, it means giving students complete freedom and having faith in what and how they will do things.

Exercises
Sometimes it can make sense to limit freedoms, for example, by determining the parameters of a creative exercise to help students focus their attention on a specific task instead of getting too involved with fonts or colours:

Identity
Our task is to design the visual identity and communications media of the University of Applied Art Vienna's annual festival. Before we begin, we want to find out what identity means and what identity the university has. The students are given a portrait photo of themselves or someone else. They are asked to cut or tear them or to alter them in any other way and to then place them on a square surface, with the aim of depicting their own or the other person's identity. Afterwards, the results are analysed in small groups where conversations are initiated by asking questions: What distinguishes the terms 'personality' and 'identity'? Is it possible to express complexity using photos and forms?

At the same time, it is an entertaining way of getting to know each other better.

Signalling effect
The semester project's objective is to create a poster for a symphony orchestra's open-air concert. Following the research and ideation phase, one of the sessions begins with a composition exercise. All students receive a black and white printout from which they are to cut out a white base area (60 × 85 mm) and a black square (35 × 35 mm), which they again cut in half to obtain two equal shapes. The task is to arrange both shapes on the base area to form a signal.

All compositions are hung up on the wall for collective scrutiny. This begins two metres away from the wall, followed by a quick retreat to the door where we view them again from a distance of five metres. Next, we open the door and stop to scrutinise everything from a distance of about twelve metres. Finally, we go even further back through another door to take everything in from a distance of nearly 25 metres. Viewing the compositions from various distances helps us to gain insights into what it takes for a signal to catch the eye. Additional categories such as 'very striking', 'exciting' or 'rather dull' initiate discussions on the meaning of these words and the reason why some compositions fall into those categories.

Trust
Giving students complete freedom in their actions is based on trust, on having confidence in them. In that regard, Johanna Pirker is convinced that teachers can consciously build confidence in their students' ability to work independently by asking them activating questions (interview p. 171).

If one has great confidence in students, then class teaching will become easier, not least because the responsibility for learning is transferred from teachers to learners. Having confidence in students allows them to tread their own paths and have personal experiences. And that is precisely how valuable learning evolves, meaning that students are able to get mutual feedback and collaborate outside of the classroom without the presence of teaching staff.

In class, teachers should be patient and leave it to individual students to determine their own pace. The same applies to approaches and solutions that may appear unusual at first. In that setting, one should adopt a supportive role as often as possible to encourage reflection, foster critique among students and attempt to create a culture of failure. For the latter, it may be useful to discuss the assumption that all ideas are based on failures, and then perhaps also to establish that failures occurring in the creative process are better described as 'failed attempts'.

Project work is ideally suited for those attempts.

Project work
Project work requires what Tadao Ando learnt through boxing, which also helps him as an architect: 'Courage and risk, moving into areas that are not so known…you have to take that extra step into the unknown.'[44]

In order to help students take that step, in most cases it is best to let go completely, because only then will they feel free to try things out. This will yield the following results without any intervention from teaching staff:
- *self-determination* in the choice of topics and team partners as well as in the project and time schedule
- *self-efficacy* by directly experiencing their own action, a sense of achievement and encouragement from others
- *self-motivation*, which also includes motivating others
- *self-criticism* that also involves fellow students.

How a free choice of topics can work is exemplified in the 'Artificial Intelligence and Design' project:

At the start of the project, the basic topic of 'AI and Design' sparks a discussion as to whether all students should receive the same task. Two arguments in favour of this are that results would be easier to compare and everyone could start designing more quickly. Arguments against it range from the position that some of them are keen on exploring their individual fields of interest to the fact that everyone is starting with different levels of prior knowledge. Finally, we all agree on defining our individual choices autonomously – an important step on the way to doing things independently. All of the students are highly motivated when they get started with researching *their* topic.

My role in this is to support them in doing so. If someone asks, 'I have three topics to choose from; which do you think I should pick?' I reply, 'Which of your topics are not only relevant to you, but also to exhibition visitors, for example?' And then I sometimes give a little extra encouragement by telling them to simply decide and trust in their own judgement. Afterwards, I ask what had been crucial to their decision. This helps students to understand their own learning.

The process of letting do is interspersed with feedback sessions in which teachers encourage the students to reflect on their work: where do you see strengths and weaknesses in your design? Which assessment and decision-making criteria evolve? Try to see things from your audience's perspective. However, do not adopt that perspective, but question the audience.

Project conclusion
The same applies to finalising projects: students should be given free rein. From that perspective, then, if we ask which project conclusion contributes most to learning and how to best get in touch with an audience, the answers are:
- presentations
- documentations
- exhibitions.

In order to reach a broader audience, it is a good idea to invite non-participant students, other classes or specialists from other disciplines to topic-based presentations.

Documentation can be made either in digital or printed form. To make it complete, it should include all outcomes and insights.

Exhibitions should motivate students to use the exhibition period for other activities such as guided tours that provide opportunities to speak to interested visitors, or student-led workshops with topical relevance. A real exhibition is clearly preferable to a virtual one as only the former enables real experiences, unless an attempt is made to redefine the virtual experience.

All courses of action mentioned above should be understood as suggestions to invite experimentation. However, it is essential to offer a wide range of variety as well.

Variety

Learning new things should be a varied experience; not only during the semester, but in every session as well.

My tuition covers a variety of short lectures, guest lectures, discussions, research and ideation sessions as well as experimental implementation that alternates with exercises and frequent feedback phases, including special focuses on certain days and within individual sessions. My weekly teaching sessions last three and a half hours. Sometimes I give tasks which are to be completed by the next session. At the end of every semester, results are shown in a presentation in the classroom or, whenever possible, to the broader public, for instance in an exhibition. An example of what we do is given below:

It is the beginning of the semester. And it is Wednesday again. Class starts at nine thirty as usual. The first five minutes are reserved for getting settled and organisational questions. Then I begin with a 20-minute lecture on different types of posters and assessment criteria followed by a 15-minute in-depth discussion with the whole class. After that, each student chooses three posters which they think are outstanding and one which they think has distinct weaknesses. They are all theatre posters in order to ensure comparability. After hanging them up on a wall, everyone gathers around to see them. This is followed by a longer discussion which flares up briefly, but calms down again after a while, partly thanks to some funny remarks someone makes. During a ten-minute break, some of us go to the class kitchen to fetch some tea or coffee. For me, it is green tea.

The next exercise focuses on the question of whether texts or images attract more attention. Students select printouts with predetermined words and photos of toy dolls, cut them into pieces and glue them onto a small rectangular piece of paper. Gradually, the students hang up the results in a different room in order to analyse their impact; the change of location generates fresh attention. After one of the students has given a short summary of all insights, everyone begins researching the semester's poster topic. At the end of the session, we talk about the semester plan again.

In the next session, all of the students present their research results and have the opportunity to ask their class colleagues questions. The rest of the session is spent on ideation and discussions with those who still have open issues. A week later, class starts in a neighbouring museum. A member of the museum staff explains the historical posters in the context of their time and analyses them with us. The next session begins again with a short exercise followed by discussions on initial ideas for posters, which is done in pre-organised smaller groups. With the end of semester approaching, the session often begins with students working on plans for the exhibition before focusing on the feedback.

The exhibition opening is a rewarding experience for everyone in view of their commitment during the semester.

A glance at the overall course of a study programme shows that, on average, students deal with poster formats once during their studies.

Time factor

Everything described so far – and everything to come – is always dependent on the amount of time available. It will not always be possible to do everything one would like to. Nevertheless, it is important to try out as much as possible.

Atmosphere in class is not only created by the actions of teachers and learners and the amount of variety offered, but it is also determined by the learning environment.

Where do I teach?

This book focuses on teaching in real spaces. There is no doubt, however, that virtual spaces affect teaching practice.

Is it possible to sustainably implement my preferred concept, which is project-based learning, in both 'worlds'? The fundamental goals I wish to achieve are transferrable to both: critical thinking, continuous rethinking, self-dependent learning and individual personal development. The same is true for the choice of topics and teaching methods as well as the conscious use of courses of action. However, there are some differences in the requirements and general framework.

Virtual space

Virtual space offers many people simultaneous access to videoconferences, not only enabling people to engage in tuition from different locations, but also to bring in experts from all over the world. In that sense, virtual space can extend almost infinitely in terms of perceived spatial dimensions. Once accessed though, it does have its limitations: one watches a screen and hears noises and voices coming out of a loudspeaker. This not only restricts one's field of vision and the sounds one hears, but practically excludes all other senses as well. Virtual Reality is quite similar: it may let us forget that we are viewing a screen, but it excludes all other senses just the same, resulting in a loss of group experiences.

If these challenges are embraced, though, working in a virtual group can be enriching and even contribute to building a sense of community. In that respect, it is a good idea for all participants to use the same background from the outset, suggests Masayo Ave, who teaches sensory experience design (interview p. 94). Letting do is an important course of action in the virtual group, too: groups form and decide on their working methods themselves. Later discussions on how that happened is of interest to groups and teaching staff alike. As providers of support, teachers should always be available for talks with groups in order, for example, to initiate a change of perspective from outside.

Just like classroom teaching, distance teaching needs to be planned carefully in order to provide sufficient variety. These plans should distinguish clearly between online time spent together and offline time when people work on their own. In some cases, students are even able to concentrate better on their work when they are offline. In any case, distance learning does not leave much room for spontaneous exchange or a glance at a fellow student's work.

To sum up, virtual space has its advantages and disadvantages, which some of the interviewees address in this book, besides making suggestions that are definitely worth trying out.

I agree with Masayo Ave that although virtual space is still largely unexplored, it can enrich class teaching at the same time.

Real space
Real space is a place where meetings take place physically, thus providing for personal exchange, empathy and improvisation. In that context, the meaning of 'space' extends beyond the built structures surrounding it which are determined by the architecture of the building:

Classrooms
What furnishings does a classroom have? And who decides? Architects, administrative departments of universities? Or teachers and students? Would it be conceivable to design and build the furnishings oneself? Do couches promote or hamper the learning atmosphere?

Whatever the approach, classrooms should be able to cater to variable teaching situations and enable focused learning. A change of spaces could have an inspiring effect and promote attentiveness. It is therefore meaningful to raise students' awareness of the impact that spaces and their usage have on the class community.

To get ready to try out new things, it can be helpful to question routine situations: must a circle of chairs always form a circle? What will students find on their chairs at the beginning of a session? Would it be better to stand perhaps? How could students alter available rooms for topic-related purposes? Is there a possibility to book different rooms at university for the next sessions?

Work and project rooms
Ideally, students are provided with a room for the project duration or even for a period of several semesters. This room should be able to become *their* space, and they should be able to leave materials there, says Brigitte Hartwig, who teaches communication design (interview p. 127).

Workshops
Hartwig also suggests that students should be allowed to use workshops around the clock, all with the goal of increasing the amount of time students spend together – because this is when much of the learning takes place with each other and from each other, in interaction.

Excursions
Do the immediate environs offer any opportunity for project-related exploration? Could classwork be moved to a green space? Or would going for a walk help groups to get to know each other better and foster an exchange of ideas?

A change of location could also mean visiting external experts in their working environments, which might include a museum, a production site or even project-related places in connection with possible clients.

Study trips
In a wider sense, a study trip is certainly one of the greatest changes of location. It does not even have to be a whole week: a two-day trip would do, explains Gesche Joost who teaches design methods. On days such as this, she merely outlines the scope, while students and colleagues decide on the programme and organise the necessary groceries for the joint cooking session as well as the evening get-together (interview p. 143).

Every real-life relocation – whether on a small or large scale – is a valuable experience for all of our senses.

The *where* also leads to a bigger question: does studying graphic design need to be restricted to a university building? In a similar context, art and media theorist Peter Weibel suggests new usages of museums as a contribution towards educating the general public. He sees museums as an experimental space in which people can exchange ideas, think together, acquire knowledge and autonomously partake, both actively and creatively, in so-called 'work stations' (former art works).[45] This could translate to questions related to teaching design: do we make use of all available rooms effectively? Does classwork really have to take place in a certain room? And could available rooms be opened up and used more flexibly? Should universities be generally accessible and provide education to all citizens?

Traditionally, most universities are still place-based institutions where teachers are required to assess their students' performance.

How do I assess?

Assessment at university level usually involves awarding grades: a numerical score that enables comparison with other students and previous grades. However, it does not reveal any details about a person's individual learning progress. It is often said that grades are not necessary. Arguments in favour of this range from self-motivated learning and personal responsibility in the frame of university studies to demotivation caused by negative grades.

I regard feedback in the form of a grade as legitimate as long as two criteria are met.

First, teachers should use the 'final feedback' to review their own actions:
- Did everyone reach the learning target?
- Were all contents understood?
- Were the teaching mode and the media I used appropriate?
- Could I have helped in a more targeted way?

Second, teachers must communicate to students that the assessment is based on justifiable criteria such as:
- profundity of research
- idea
- quality of implementation
- collaboration
- further development
- punctuality.

All the assessment criteria must be explained to students in the first teaching session. Their learning success, which also includes motivation and commitment, can then be evaluated on the basis of those criteria. The aim of providing an individual justification and communicating openly is to enable students to perceive assessments within a wider context and as constructive feedback. Whether that justification be written or oral is merely secondary and dependent on the number of students and the amount of time available. It is also of minor importance whether the assessment contains a numerical score or not. As long as the structures of the performance assessment or, for example, merit scholarships are grade-related, it will be necessary to award them.

Self-assessment

One approach to getting students involved with their own performance is to ask them to make judgements about their own work. Most of them will assess themselves realistically. Up to now, self-assessments made by students in my class have largely corresponded to those I had worked out myself. Peer assessment is a variant of self-assessment that requires students to rate other students' work. Peer assessment, however, should be anonymous and taken into account as a component of the teacher's overall assessment.

In that context, the question inevitably arises as to whether teaching staff should also be given grades and justifications as a means of improving their performance.

How can I improve my teaching?

A good start to teaching begins with one's own education and preparation. In some countries, this is promoted through a mandatory one-year university training course in didactics offering both theoretical knowledge and practical insights.

Getting better in the course of one's teaching career is what continuing education aims to do. At the same time, it is helpful to rethink one's actions and interactions with students and to obtain feedback on them. Feedback is a form of self-assessment insofar as the person requesting feedback is able to specify what kind of feedback is given, and when. This could either occur on one's own initiative or due to requirements established by the teaching team or the institution itself. In the case of mandatory assessments, time intervals can vary from university to university. Shorter intervals appear to make sense for teachers beginning their careers. However, even after many years of teaching experience, regular feedback still helps to improve one's teaching skills.

In my own class, I vary the ways in which I obtain feedback, as each type of feedback has its own key aspects and takes different amounts of time. What they all have in common, though, is that feedback is only given after events have ended. The feedback process, however, should already commence before relevant events occur.

Right from the start, it is important to convey to students that their feedback is welcome during the course of class. It can also be helpful to jot down one's own expectations in advance. These can be discussed with colleagues or checked later on.

Asking about expectations

In addition, students can be asked what they expect from class from the very start, before discussions on the actual semester topic commence. Although this may be done in writing, a conversation will certainly support the open atmosphere mentioned before. If you are teaching those students for the first time, a conversation will also help in getting to know one another better. Should you wish to transfer responsibility to a student in that context, you could ask them to conduct the conversation.

Evaluating one's own actions

Teaching often happens intuitively by simply reacting to situations. If a structured self-assessment is desired, the following three approaches, which are based on the courses of action *asking, listening, speaking, rethinking* and *letting do* may provide valuable help.

Assessing individual situations in class

The above is achieved by writing down chronologically one or more situations experienced during the session, including various details and what the atmosphere was like. Every situation is then reassessed on the basis of courses of action: would a change in action have improved class cooperation? Would it have been better to listen a little longer instead of explaining how to do something? Would it have perhaps been more useful to have told the students in a different situation how the process unfolds in order to save time? Conclusive notes on presumed improvements can help to respond more positively to similar situations in the future.

Reassessing a single teaching session

It is equally possible to reconsider the course of a single teaching session. If the structure is not predetermined, the session can be broken down into phases and blocks afterwards, in order to ascertain, for example, whether teaching in class might benefit from a targeted use of certain courses of action.

Assessing the course structure
If one of these self-assessments is undertaken regularly, comparisons can be made at the end of the semester: what caused the improvements? Were there any problems that kept on cropping up? Did the actions and tasks provide sufficient variety?

All self-assessments are open-ended. The first one may already suggest that the teacher has done everything correctly – which is rather unlikely. Or that the students might be to blame for all the mistakes – which is also unlikely. In the best of cases, these considerations will ensure that whatever one perceives as a failure, there is always room for improvement. In that way, self-criticism may well result in increased awareness of how to act in class. Hence, it is not about changing one's style, but about one's personal enhancement within self-defined limits.

Although it takes more time and effort, it can be revelatory to discuss one's notes with another person. This could be either a colleague or an external person. Involving students, on the other hand, can help to distinguish between one's own self-perception and interpersonal perception.

Receiving feedback
Feedback can be used to evaluate conditions and concepts as well as processes and the effects of individual measures in class. It can also help to create transparency, encourage dialogue, and monitor performances or document successes.

Types of feedback
There are many types of feedback, four of which I have found to be the most effective, which several of my interview partners and colleagues have also acknowledged. They have no clear-cut designation and are known by different names at different institutions and in various languages. The terms I have chosen aim to differentiate clearly between these types of feedback:
- feedback from students
- feedback from colleagues (peer observation)
- feedback through casual conversations
- feedback from external specialists (peer review).

Whatever the type of feedback, it is essential to accept criticism. The goal is to collate ideas for improvement. It is not about contradicting criticism or beginning a discussion to justify oneself for the action taken and for wanting to adhere to it. Rather, students need to feel that they can voice their opinions freely – and that these will be taken seriously.

Feedback should be given in the first person singular: 'I feel...' instead of 'you have...' Similarly, questions need to be asked in a way that will provoke answers in the first person singular.

Feedback from students

Many universities use standardised feedback forms. Some of them are questionnaires that use evaluation scales to give a quantitative overview in the form of a trend representation. In addition, others use openly formulated questions to facilitate a qualitative overview. Sometimes it is a combination of both approaches.

The following open questions have proved useful to me:
- What was good?
- What was not so good?
- How do I or we improve this?
- What have I learnt?
- What did I miss?

First, it should be determined whether the whole class, groups or individual students are to be questioned. Participants are then given an explanation of how the feedback process will proceed. Using the phrase 'It's not about my improvement as a teacher, but about optimising our collaborative learning experience' emphasises that it is a group achievement and adding 'Everything needs to be constructively formulated without using any abusive language' will mostly make it easier to get started.

One advantage of giving written feedback is that students are able to voice their opinions anonymously. Besides that, the feedback can then be retrieved at a later date.

Meanwhile however, I almost always ask these questions in connection with oral feedback. Conversations have the advantage of creating an atmosphere that is more open to critical response, of spontaneously addressing additional details or clarifying issues, in order to *jointly* ascertain how to improve the issue identified. Questions can then be asked as to whether everyone in the group feels the same in that respect, on people's behaviour during class or the feedback process. All of those questions need to be openly formulated and should not communicate any criticism of one's own. Asking 'You lost your motivation to generate ideas after only about ten minutes. What was the reason for that?' is bound to provoke other reactions than 'You stopped generating ideas after only about ten minutes. Why did you lose your motivation?'

Lively discussions may also prompt hesitant students to participate more actively in enhancing class cooperation, which often has noticeable effects from one feedback session to the next. However, it may be perceived as a disadvantage to have to jot down answers in brief oneself, and if need be, to write them out in full after class.

Another variant of the feedback talks would be to ask an external person or student to moderate the feedback process, in that way placing the critics on an equal footing with teaching staff.

Teachers should tailor the frequency, scope, questions and duration of their feedback sessions individually. Improvements resulting from just one feedback session at the end of the course will only have an effect on later courses. If those sessions are included in class on a regular basis, though, everyone will benefit from those improvements straightaway.

Alternatively, feedback phases can also form an integral part of every teaching session, as in the case of Michael Hohl (interview p. 137) and Mathilde Scholz (interview p. 220). In their *Transformative Teaching* concept, the last ten minutes of class are always reserved for feedback. For the first five minutes, everyone is invited to write down their reflections on five questions similar to those named above; the rest of the time is spent on an open exchange of feedback in a conversation. In that way, improvements are implemented on an ongoing basis from one teaching session to the next. Regularity, openness and the deconstruction of hierarchical models lead to a change of mood in students – from frustration to motivation.[46]

Feedback from colleagues (peer observation)
Also known as teaching observations or critical friends, this type of feedback is provided by colleagues sitting in on someone else's classes. Peers may either come from the same discipline, from other specialist areas or even other institutions. Also, peers from somewhat more remote disciplines can contribute valuable feedback, as they are able to add quite different perspectives to the context.

Sitting in on someone else's classes entails observing events and then giving either general or more detailed feedback on certain predetermined aspects depending on the agreed goal.

Ideally, peers will give their feedback in a conversation directly after class. This feedback requires further classification into positive points and those in need of improvement in order to build constructive cooperation between teacher and peer. Again, with regard to those points, it is essential to differentiate carefully between observation (a neutral description of the situation) and analysis (a subjective appraisal of the situation). Observation also enables teachers to analyse and understand their own actions.

If several peer observations are possible, it is crucial to record the feedback in writing in order to recognise and comprehend how and why changes and improvements have occurred.

Final exam observations
Final exams are often a forgotten part of feedback culture. A board of examiners has different dynamics to those of a class headed by one teacher; however, in my opinion, both require an equal share of regular self-critical scrutiny.

Feedback through casual conversations
Day-to-day exchange with, for example, colleagues must not be underestimated as a source of feedback. Although in most cases, the people you are conversing with will not have participated in class and sometimes no more than a few words are exchanged on your way to the classroom, that brief encounter can still offer food for thought. Even a quick question such as 'What would you do this semester: assign group work or individual work?' can ease your decision or lead to a diversified use of teaching formats in class.

I consider individual chats with students, which sometimes happen spontaneously in the kitchen, as belonging to that category of feedback. The same goes for talks with assistants, administrative colleagues, family members and friends who are not involved in the same field and who are therefore able to view the situation from an unbiased perspective.

Feedback from external specialists (peer review)
The same can be said for peer review, as it also ensures unbiased perspectives. It not only provides feedback to individual teaching staff, but, on a comprehensive level, to teachers of a whole class or an entire degree course as well. For that purpose, external specialists are invited.

At the University of Applied Arts Vienna, for example, the head of a class can request a peer review. Together with all the other teachers of that class, it is then decided on which areas feedback is required. The review applies to all main teaching sessions and is undertaken by an external agency, which then proposes peers in agreement with the head of class. This process usually lasts for a year.

Advantages of this procedure are not only the elongated period of time during which fluctuations are ruled out and adaptations can be taken into consideration, but also the external unbiased perspective. Disadvantageous, though, are the higher costs in comparison with other types of feedback presented above.

Accepting criticism
How we deal with criticism is an essential issue, which is why it cannot be stressed enough that whatever form feedback may take, it is fundamental to accept criticism. The priority must be to focus on what to improve and how to improve on a personal level.

Trying out new approaches

Accepting criticism should help teachers to gain new perspectives, try out new approaches – and dare to experiment as well.

Ensuring quality

Insights from feedback processes can also help to define quality criteria of teaching in a class, an institute or an entire university. If these are defined in agreement with all or the majority of teaching staff, they could form the basis of quality enhancement. Moreover, quality criteria should also be communicated in mandatory continuing education courses. To me, it seems important to engage intensively with all experiences and to collate them in a practical way to ensure that insights from all teaching staff are identified and accounted for. Besides that, quality criteria should not just be laid down in writing, but also put into practice. Only in that way will students benefit from them.

Consequently, quality criteria will also help teachers who are entering the classroom for the first time.

How do I apply that?

The preceding chapters suggested trying out new methods and details or questioning known methods and details. In this context, it is the actual doing and trying out that is crucial. Otherwise, the book remains just text. It is just as important to find your own way, to perceive your own and the students' reactions and to adapt your behaviour as a teaching person in a constant learning process.

The first day in class

How do I know which path to choose if I have never taken any of them before? Teachers at the beginning of their career always face the same problems. Regardless of their country of origin or cultural background, the following questions, which crop up regularly in many conversations, can lead to insecurity before the first lesson has even begun:
- Do I know enough?
- How much of the subject fits into one teaching session?
- Is everything prepared so that it is understandable?
- What are the students like?
- What kind of impression do I make on them?
- Do I manage to motivate them?

It is comforting to know that every teacher has stepped into a classroom for the first time. When opening the classroom door, most people without any previous practical experience in handling groups, unless of course they are bursting with self-confidence, will feel the same: nervous. Knowing that this feeling is part of the game and you will do your very best, though, may well help to prevent those nerves from getting out of control. Being well-prepared and changing your own perspective can also help to calm your nerves before walking into class. In that sense, then, everything begins *before* entering the classroom for the first time and focuses on the *how* in teaching, as outlined in the following suggestions:

Prior to classroom teaching:
- have a chat with other teaching staff (within and outside your institution);
- ask other teachers about the students' knowledge level;
- ask other teachers about the students' expectations;
- sit in on the class you are going to teach;
- jot down the targets you want to reach with your students;
- then make a note of the targets you want to reach yourself;
- create an overview of your level of expertise on that subject;
- write a list of everything you want to convey in class;
- then make a note of the portions in which you think that could best be taught;
- write down how your students could do the work on their own;
- then create a semester plan;
- select a mode of teaching that you find enjoyable (solo teaching, tandem teaching...);
- select the type of lecture you feel comfortable with (teaching theory, discussions...); and
- decide whether and how you would like to check your time schedule during class.

In class:
- be authentic and present yourself authentically – there is no such thing as *the perfect* teacher;
- be aware that (most) students learn voluntarily;
- even if the students already know: tell them that this is your first lesson;
- first ask the students what expectations they have;
- then tell them what you expect of them;
- explain to them what your idea of class cooperation is;
- state that you will ask for feedback at the end of class, if desired;
- move around in class;
- encourage the students to move around as well; and
- smile – at least now and then.

Always
interested
in people

At the end of class:

This phase corresponds to the method of getting qualitative feedback from students (p. 77), but is explained here again in single steps. If time is getting tight in the first lesson, you could drop the feedback round. Alternatively, plan to use the last ten minutes of the first session in order to counteract that effect. Not all students need to voice themselves and any criticism should always be accepted without comment, as its actual purpose is to accumulate useful input. Discussions would only be too time-consuming.
- announce the ten-minute feedback round;
- tell them that everything needs to be formulated constructively;
- ask them what was good; and
- ask them what was not so good.

If there's enough time afterwards:
- ask what the students gained personally;
- ask what they missed;
- ask the students what you – and they – could improve; and
- then you can add your own suggestions for improvement if necessary.

After class:
- make a note of the students' input;
- in a summary, capture what you think was important regarding content and didactics;
- jot down what went well in your opinion;
- jot down what did not work so well in your opinion;
- be honest with yourself;
- speak to other teachers about your first day in class first;
- and then consider what you want to improve on your part;
- decide on how to implement the students' ideas the next time in class;
- write down what motivates your students; and
- if necessary, adapt the next teaching session and your semester plan.

These ideas could serve as a starting point for planning and implementing the first teaching units; however, they need to be adapted individually to each situation. That is why the very first suggestion to have a chat with other teachers is crucial. Over time, you will find a way that suits you best.

Enthusiasm

In some places, I have explained the origin of a word or tried to get to the bottom of its meaning. This is due to my wish to communicate things precisely, which is sometimes based on subjective feelings and does not always succeed. Likewise, expressing oneself unambiguously will not succeed in every session with students. However, it can be very rewarding to discuss specific details and differences in our language and our opinions, or in our designs. In that sense, an accurate choice of words is a clarification of the 'meaning of a string of letters', for meaning is the essence of communication. It leads to insights being gained.

In his book *Pedagogy of the Oppressed*, Paulo Freire writes, 'As we attempt to analyze dialogue as a human phenomenon, we discover something which is the essence of dialogue itself: the word. ... Within the word we find two dimensions, reflection and action .... There is no true word that is not at the same time a praxis.'[47]

It is important to encourage students to search for *the* true word, *the* other opinion and *the* convincing idea. In doing so, a discussed design draft might spark an exchange of ideas from which everybody benefits collectively. Or maybe a detailed 3D model of a finalised design could have the same effect. Sometimes one communicates with oneself, sometimes with others. Whatever the case, it is always enriching. It happens at university or in a professional context, when, for example, the necessity arises to present concepts and results to a client. People come together in all those contexts, as do rethinking, *reflection*, and doing, *action*. Curiosity and openness are always highly enriching.

Graphic design is enthusiasm for change.
Teaching is sharing enthusiasm with students.
Always with the aim to learn with and from others.

INTERVIEWS

INTERVIEWS

I have written about teaching based on my practical experience in class. Knowledge and opinions develop through observing, adapting and testing; it is a continuous research process with the aim of discovering new things. For the interviews, I have adopted the same approach – with a focus on the teaching experience in class.

I conducted most of the interviews face-to-face, some in video talks and a very small number via email. All interview partners offer inspiring insights into their method of teaching – into the way they act and communicate with others. While some things differ culturally, others do have a lot in common.

Their answers also provide further ideas for everyday graphic design practice which entails communicating with, asking and listening to people as well as making carefully considered decisions.

Katrin Androschin

teaches Strategic Design

Professor
Programme Director Strategic Design
SRH Berlin University of Applied Sciences
Germany

Co-founder of the brand agency Embassy

Katrin Androschin is convinced that ideas need to be tried out
quickly and that not only the right questions are important, but
also the person asked. She also talks about how she deals with
dissonances and why all students are required to create a toolbox
with methods during their time at university. — July 2022

Thies: You direct the Strategic Design master's programme and applicants always need to have a design background. Where does design end?
Androschin: That's a good question. We have also taken people with an artistic background. But many come from communication design, architecture, fashion and product design. And we have also taken a non-designer on a trial basis, who was then given the task of acquiring design knowledge in a different way. Perhaps in the future we will open the programme to people who do not design.

You teach here at the university and are a partner at the brand agency Embassy. Is it an advantage to be working in both worlds?
I work 50-50, which adds up to more than 40 hours. We are not a purely academic discipline but very practically oriented, which makes it an advantage to have up-to-date industry experience.

How do you teach this practical knowledge to students?
I create a theoretical underpinning for each subject or topic and then explain the theory using practical examples – benchmarks or my own work. And the students also have to apply the knowledge immediately!

Do you follow a systematic approach?
Yes, there are steps that come up again and again which we use to teach the strategic design process. Borrowing from design thinking, we start by trying

to understand the problem. After this, a large part of the process is qualitative research, which is followed by a synthesis of everything you have learnt. Then it's on to idea development. Valid ideas are always tried out right away. However concrete or inconcrete the ideas are, the mandatory test phase then starts with the question, 'Does that have relevance in the outside world?' In all this, we attach great importance to documenting the results and presenting them to project partners.

What types of qualitative research do students learn?
That depends. We create research and test plans and show how to get qualified research results with a huge variety of research methods, for example, through interviews. Because not only do you have to ask the right questions, you also have to ask the right people. These can be experts or users or even 'extreme users' who start off with extremely negative or positive viewpoints.
We teach students to analyse every potential solution for feasibility, viability and desirability.

What types of feedback do the students and lecturers receive?
Students are given feedback in person, in a small team or as a whole group. We have introduced structured feedback to our degree programme by including module reviews. We summarise five weeks of work and reflect on how it went together. For that we often use whiteboards with a feedback grid.

What do you learn from your students?
I learn a great deal about interculturality because the group is very international. And I learn about human behaviour: how this generation argues, or how it lives the uncertainty and volatility of our times. And sometimes you realise that you think you know what they know, but that's not the case at all.

Do you encourage students to hold lectures or to teach others?
Yes, both formats are always integral parts of my teaching, as are other interactive formats, such as short workshops using appropriate methods and peer reviews.

Are design skills taught in the Strategic Design master's programme?
There is hardly any time for that, and I always tell the applicants, 'We teach very few design skills and expect that you will bring them with you or acquire them on your own.' Especially as we don't even know which skills we need when we announce the research question at the beginning of the semester. Our process has to be open when it comes to the results because only this openness reflects the complexity and future-focused nature of the challenges

that we work on in this degree programme. In the end, we might just need music, or just product design, or a combination of various ways of expressing a solution, or a lot of sociology.

What is *the* most important quality a person teaching Strategic Design needs to have?
They need to be curious and enjoy collaborating with people from other disciplines; they need to be open and flexible, and like to manage and shape innovation. Here they also need to have intercultural skills and speak English as well as our students do.

Are lecturers free to choose how they teach and which topics they use?
No, we have a module handbook that defines competency goals: methodological, personal and professional competences following the European educational system. There is some freedom in the teaching itself, but it has to fit the modules.

How are these modules structured?
There are four block modules, in which in-depth content is taught within a few weeks, and two longer modules, each lasting about a semester. One of these focuses purely on theory; the other is called 'Profession and Best Practice' and is basically the connection to working life, to companies, NGOs or experts. There is an exam at the end of each module and, in the fourth semester, students write their master's thesis.

Strategic Design has an interdisciplinary function. How do you teach this?
You have to think and act in an interdisciplinary manner. As a Strategic Designer you need to lead teams, understand the role of design in organisations and help to shape company processes and strategy on a management level. That is why leadership skills are also part of our curriculum. Students learn to lead projects and to take the initiative in changing work processes.

How do you start projects?
With a central research question formulated by the programme director together with the project partner. It's mostly a 'how might we' question to keep things open.

So the students don't formulate the question?
No, because the first question has to be formulated in such a way that it's neither too restrictive nor too broad in terms of time and content.

In the complex projects that we manage, we have to deal with uncertainties and keep an open mind. Many students want to be told exactly what to do. But we then say, 'No way! You have to start thinking. You have to expose yourself to that uncertainty. And we'll show you how.' That's why they are complex questions to which you can't have a qualified answer straight away because they involve too many factors.

Then, when a synthesis is generated, the right things need to be left out. Working on this opening up, closing, converging or diverging, this breathing in and breathing out is part of the process.

How do you open up?
Through our research methods that we use to analyse the topic from the perspective of users, experts, society and companies. In the ideation phase we give the students other tools: How do I come up with new ideas? How do I evaluate ideas? How do I cluster ideas? How do I get ideas from external sources? How can I think out of the box? How can I manage this? They need to create a toolbox – a toolbox that they design themselves and that fills up over the course of their studies. It can be digital or it can be made up of physical cards. From the third semester project onwards, they decide for themselves which methods from their toolbox are the most suitable.

How do you encourage students to be curious?
By being curious myself. They often laugh at my curiosity. Not because I interrogate them, but because of the way I quiz project partners. I ask questions they would never dare to ask, question things in a way that surprises them at first and also ask uncomfortable questions. In doing so, I try to make sure they have a sense of accomplishment because they actually find out something new. These things can be surprising insights that are only discovered through a change in perspective.

How do you get students to have lively conversations, to discuss?
Role play is a good option – students can then adopt different perspectives. But the students are very motivated and already have a BA degree – I only need to ask a question for a lively discussion to start.

Is this also the case with distance learning when everyone comes together virtually?
When we only had remote teaching, discussions were more difficult to get going in larger groups. As soon as there are more than 10 or 12 people in online formats, things take longer and are more hard work.

I've also found the same, although I prefer group sizes of up to a maximum of five people and divide large groups for discussions if necessary.
Really? I find conversations also worked with 10 to 12 people.

But I had to ask more questions and get more involved. For example, I asked the students to physically move, to hold particular objects up to the camera or to write something on paper.

Your students come from different cultural backgrounds and have different levels of knowledge, so conflicts are bound to arise at times. How do you deal with this?
That depends. I always start by saying, 'You are a team. Please don't come to me right away, but try to solve the problem yourself first.' If that doesn't work, we'll help.

This is one reason why we have the subject 'Intercultural Communication' in the first semester. And now I say in the first week, 'There are certain rules and we run on German time. I explain that means being punctual – and that the term 'German time' doesn't actually exist. [laughs]

What do you enjoy most about teaching?
I like watching the individual students learn and develop as people.

How do you encourage your students' personal development?
I am lucky to be able to get to know people in small groups and respond to them individually. This works with face-to-face teaching but also online. In discussions I give suggestions, tips and advice tailored to their personality. I do that automatically.

Do you have an example?
It works well for problems in small teams of four to five students. When there are situations when there are, for example, three against one, it often emerges that one person is more aggressive, one is mediating and two are holding back. Some students aren't aware of it but, as an educator, you have to address it and also motivate the person in a leadership role in order to improve the interaction within the team.

Do you use video tutorials or other digital options to teach students?
I don't because I'd rather spend more time with the students and with answering additional questions than with making videos. This exchange can take place in the same room or virtually.

Was there anything about distance learning that worked better than face-to-face teaching?
There are a few things. It started with the fact that in October 2020, half of the students did not yet have a visa. They were only able to start their degree on the first day because we made it possible to attend remotely. Students were also more punctual. Those who also worked could juggle things more easily because there was no commuting. Another advantage was that we were able to organise international expert talks and agency visits in different countries.

How do you start the first day with the students?
Before the first day they have a Welcome Week where they get to know the library and things like that. On day one, I ask them to introduce themselves and I tell them a bit about the university, and about the degree programme and its structure. On day two, we always do a portfolio day: third-semester and first-semester students introduce themselves and present their short portfolios. That is very interesting because the applicants come from different fields. A few lecturers and I also present our work so that we start off on an equal footing. And student buddies are matched up who will support each other during their studies.

What is the students' last day like?
Certificates are awarded on the last day. I get the students to open a sealed envelope containing their definition of Strategic Design, which I have kept since they put it in there on the first day of their studies. Depending on the situation, some read their definitions out loud during the ceremony or in a small group. [smiles]

How do you keep in contact with the alumni?
We support graduates in their career development by advising them on interviews and on a first salary level. After that, we stay in contact with the alumni informally by keeping them up to date via a Slack channel and inviting them to a meet-up two to three times a year. At the meet-ups I try to introduce people who I think should get to know each other.

What was formative for you in your studies?
Having to organise and motivate myself. I now know that you sometimes need to leave the students to their own devices so they get started themselves and make their own decisions. Because otherwise you say A, and they do A. – It's often not that easy to leave students to do their own thing. [smiles]

How would you describe your teaching style?
I think I'm motivating and you can tell I enjoy sharing my own passion for the subject. I take the students seriously and want them to see me as a primus inter pares – not as someone who teaches 'from the top down'.

I try to be clear and fair, and to be human at all times. I am always well prepared, but I also admit it when I'm improvising.

You lead the master's programme together with a second professor. How do you as a female leadership duo try to ensure equal opportunities among students and lecturers?
We have a very good male-female diversity ratio among our lecturers, and we explicitly support our female and non-binary students. Inequality isn't a problem in the programme itself and there's rarely any need for discussions to sort out issues like this. But I still often tell the women, 'Talk louder!', which on the surface is only about presentation skills, but they are important. Or I encourage them by saying, 'Don't put up with that behaviour from your male peers.' And I add as a sidenote, 'In Germany, you can express more than in other cultures.'

Thanks a lot, Katrin.

Masayo Ave

teaches Sensory Experience Design

Guest Professor
Academy of Fine Arts and Design of the University of Ljubljana, Slovenia,
and Kanazawa College of Art, Japan

Founder of the Sensory Experience Design Laboratory (SXD.Lab)

A room studded with many bright objects. Masayo Ave
teaches the fascination of using all our senses to experience
things. She is doing that more and more online now, constantly
discovering new advantages of working in that setting.
Without pausing too much between her sentences, she explains
why planning is essential, how she puts groups together and
what she does with magnifying glasses. — August 2022

**Thies: One of your previous positions was at the Berlin University of
the Arts where you founded the Institute of Haptic Interface Design.
Where do you currently teach?**
Ave: I am teaching as a guest professor at Kanazawa College of Art in Japan
and the Academy of Fine Arts and Design of the University of Ljubljana in
Slovenia (ALUO), with a special duty to conduct joint workshops connecting
the two institutes online. I am also giving workshops not only for the students,
but also for the teaching staff at different design institutions worldwide.

Why did you stop teaching as a full-time professor?
I have held a full-time professorship at three universities in my life, but I re-
mained in that fixed position only for two to three years each time. I see my
mission as setting up sensory-based new design education in the department
where I am appointed, so once I had built the foundation, I wanted to hand it
over to the next generation. It was tough to handle the academic task and my
design practice in parallel, and I also wanted to practise the programme
beyond the academic framework.

Design is a profoundly multisensory and multidisciplinary subject for all,
possibly to learn from a very young age. To learn the fundamentals of design
is to get a comprehensive understanding of your own living environment
through sensory perceptions. Taking sensorial and imaginative approaches
to basic design principles, I carefully make a starting point of my programme

the activation of senses to perceive colours, textures, shapes and structures in the living environment. Learning design interconnects mathematics, literature, music, science etc. and links them to everyday life; therefore, it would be ideal for practising in the very early learning process. I did it, for example, in a pilot project to bring the new design education programme to pre-schoolers in Singapore in cooperation with the Design Singapore Council from 2012 to 2015.

Regarding your point on handling a professorship and your own practice: Would it be better to have more flexible short-term offers for professorships and for students as well?
To allow practitioners to teach, it would be a good idea to provide shared professorships for two members of staff. That way, they could continue their practice better.

For working students, a one-year course would be easier to handle, for example by taking a sabbatical. Umeå University in Sweden and some others like Aalto University in Helsinki offer one-year courses like that. At Aalto, people with different backgrounds have to solve given problems collaboratively. The assignments no longer focus on profit-making; they are about social responsibility and 'how to read the future' or about management itself. One great consequence is that some of those master's students continue to collaborate after their courses. That is, for me, one of the most advanced ways to make design education lifelong.

Recently, many courses have been offered via online platforms due to the COVID-19 pandemic, but I see online education not just as an alternative, but also as a new way to enrich design education and to make it inclusive in many senses.

Your specialisation is Sensory Experience Design. How did you start doing that?
I started with haptics because that element of design somehow got lost completely. The sense of touch is fundamental to understanding the environment.

However, mothers tend to say to children, 'Don't touch. It is fragile', instead of teaching how softly one can touch something to enjoy its delicateness. It is a misfortune that one loses the chance to learn how to perceive the world with one's own tactile senses while growing up. I carefully incorporate the haptic discovery process into design education to make my students aware of different haptics. However, later realising that the senses are inseparable, all interconnected, I expanded my focus to sensory experience design, including all the other senses: hearing, smelling, taste and seeing, yet also envisioning. I found that the sense of seeing is not only about what you see with your eyes, but also about envisioning what is in your mind.

How does all that work online, in distance learning?
In the case of the five-day intensive summer course, I remotely led 36 architecture students of Hōsei University in Tokyo via Skype before the COVID-19
pandemic started. All the students gathered in a classroom in Tokyo, and I was
the only one there who was presenting remotely from Berlin.

With the support of the teaching assistants who prepared the space and
materials for me, I was able to conduct the course in much the same way as
in the classroom. They actually carried me around in the laptop monitor as
if I were being pushed around the classroom in a wheelchair.

However, the closure of the campus and increasing restrictions starting
in 2020 required the 36 students to participate individually from home without
gathering in a classroom. So I had to re-design the entire process of the course
to best fit the extreme online conditions. I paid particular attention to the
planning of online collaboration time and offline individual time.

For example, the highlight of the online collaboration I plan in the course
as a two or six-person team works in the Zoom breakout rooms. Each team has
to find the best way to discuss and cooperate among themselves. Such an
isolated environment is impossible to realise in the real world with everybody
in the same classroom. For specific exercises, I left each student alone offline,
as being alone is the ideal condition to let each of them concentrate on their
own thoughts. I often focus on hearing, using sound to enter and open the
imagination to activate their sense of wonder and envision the invisible
material. The most outstanding feature of online teaching is that you can
easily switch situations and settings. Online discussions among unknown
participants are peculiar because you face all the participants simultaneously.
Somehow, it has an equalising effect. And they don't know how small I am.
[laughs]

Bringing together the experience of such workshops conducted fully online
in the past two years, I recently conducted a joint online workshop connecting
Kanazawa Art College and ALUO Ljubljana University. The students from the
two institutes joined individually from their homes in Japan or Slovenia.

That is what we can offer as an international exchange experience beyond
all physical restrictions and limits, and I believe that remote teaching is an
enrichment.

**How do you bring the right students together, for example, in groups of
six for projects conducted remotely?**
Before the workshop, I send them an online questionnaire related to the
project's theme. Sometimes I also give a minor model-making assignment
as a warm-up exercise to see the participants' form-making skills in advance.
Then I carefully make a two-person team based on their shared concerns

and skills, then I create a group of six, putting three of the two-person teams together. I also try to ensure that the group is not composed of members with the same skill set, sex and experience or of the same age. When the group-making is done well in advance, the workshop runs very smoothly.

What kind of specific questions do you ask in advance?
My questions are always related to the theme of the workshop. Since 2020 I have been focusing on how to cope with invisible crises, such as a pandemic, global warming, microplastic and radioactive pollution, loneliness, uncertainty and poverty, setting the workshop's goal to envision a new way of living in 2030. In the five-day intensive course for the architecture students of Hōsei University in Japan, mentioned before, I ask them to select the most concerning crisis today out of the list in the questionnaire, then also the most concerning topic for their life in 2030. I also ask them to express their own emotions about the crises they choose in one word, specifically in one kanji ideogram in Japanese. And they get free writing space to express their concerns in life.

How did you structure the day when holding the workshop?
The first day starts with two-person teams. In a breakout room, groups of two students develop a small project merging the ideas of their warming-up exercise. After lunch, a guest architect who is actively involved in the work-shop theme gives an online lecture.

On the second morning I provide a sensory experience design exercise to practise individually offline. The students get a series of kanji, emotional words such as fear, anger, sadness, frightening, isolation etc. collected on the questionnaire. They must describe each word as a colour, smell and haptic texture. After a short break, they get another series of words to work on, a collection of the opposite words, such as relax, joy, safety and solidarity, which are critical for life in order to cope with the crisis well. After the exercise and a break, three of the two-person teams gather as one group. The six members introduce the first-day teamwork to get to know each other, then each group member defines a role in developing the main project, as project leader, creative director, technical director, research director, communication director and project manager.

On the third and fourth day, they work together on a project focused on 'Home', a shared shelter that resists and copes smartly with a specific crisis, proposing a new lifestyle in 2030. The sensory elements they noted for 'opposite words' are to be applied in designing the 'Home'. At the end of day four, they submit their proposal in six panels: two panels with the colour and the smell chart, four panels with sketches, drawings and images, and a one-minute soundscape on an MP3 file.

On the last day, each group finalises the project by providing a unique title and a description of the project. The teaching assistants edit the submitted panels and the soundscape files as one-minute movies, and we review them together to conclude the workshop.

Are there ways to make a group feel more connected in online sessions?
The foremost vital steps are to give a clear mission to each group, leaving the group members alone in a breakout room, and letting them manage the group work by themselves. The members are thus alone in their own virtual space, disconnected from other students and even from me as a facilitator, and this already creates a feeling of intense connection, as if working on their own in a spaceship, finding the best way to discuss and collaborate to realise a project all by themselves. To strengthen the feeling, I often provide each group with a specific background. For example, I give them a background image showing a view from ISS, from space to the earth, to the groups who work on the topic of environmental crisis on the planet; it enormously supports their perception and togetherness, letting them forget that each participant is joining from their own room.

How can I make sure people collaborate without having preconceptions about, say, hierarchies?
The case of one offline workshop I conducted for Japanese professional designers organised by *AXIS* magazine in 2010 might be an example worth mentioning. In Japan, people are used to exchanging business cards and checking their social position before introducing themselves. It is a problematic habit as it easily creates prejudice among the participants. So, I prepared the participants' name tags only with their given names without surnames, commonly used for business, and let them start doing an exercise of sensory experience design, which is new for all, in a small group right away. Exchanging business cards was only allowed after the conclusion of the workshop. Once they start to play through the exercise together as they did once as children, it doesn't matter who they are, because it's about becoming collaborators without any prejudice.

How important is space, the room setting, for teaching?
I plan that thoroughly as well. For example, I prepared a small book for two-person teams who had never worked together before. They would read in pairs to get them physically close while reading it together, or one would read while the other listened. It's an effective way to form a team quickly, you know. And I saw that it worked both offline in class and online in the Zoom breakout room. Another example: when I do an international workshop offline in class, I give

careful consideration to who will be with whom in a team and define the seating plan in the space. By putting name cards where each person sits, I determine the appropriate distance between people. The space setting, including placing the tables and chairs, tools, and materials in the best positions in the given space, I regard as vital to enhancing their learning experience. I think 80% of the workshop's success is due to the advanced preparation of the spatial environment.

By doing that, you help them to find out what they are good at?
Yes, because it is crucial to understand what they are good at or not. I can give some suggestions, but above all, I try to give them a chance to learn about themselves beyond all limits. For example, one of my students was not good at design, even though he decided to study product design, with a dream of being a good designer. But he showed his fantastic talent in project management in a group project. He phoned to procure big sponsorships for a semester project we realised with 16 students without presenting any paperwork. He was a natural at convincing sponsors. That was in 2004. Although project management was not a subject in design education at the time, I recommended that he take a project management course at another institution as a visiting student in the following semester to find a way to apply his gifted ability in design projects. Later on, as his diploma project, he organised an exhibition in one of the major national museums in Berlin in cooperation with other young designers and architects yet without designing anything by himself. It took a while for him to give up his dream of becoming a successful designer; still, he was able to find the best way to go, recognising how his gifted management ability enriched his diploma project. Since then, working for almost two decades in many museums, he has developed his career as a project manager specialising in design.

So, your feedback style is always honest and straight?
Being honest and straight with students is essential for me. I have my own style of giving straightforward critiques without causing emotional complications, and I think the style fits well with my personality. Criticism may not be comfortable for some students, but they accept my critiques quite well, probably because I always point out where I see hope, presenting many other possible ways to develop, while also pointing out where I see problems in their work.

Do you advise your students on how to present their work?
Yes, I advise them not to use pronouns like I, my and me in a presentation. Because if I present it as my work, the work remains a personal matter.

Putting a proposal on a table means it is already a matter of the client or the public. Avoiding I-my-me is a magical technique to let one instantly be an objective presenter. The students immediately realise how this makes the presentation more professional.

You mentioned curiosity. How do you encourage curiosity?
Activating curiosity is the key to perceiving your own living environment and knowing the world with your own senses. Children are curious about everything and unconsciously perceive the complex world by focusing their view, straining their ears and twitching their nose to concentrate on many visible and invisible points. But growing up with an ordinary education, almost all of them start to lose their curiosity. 'I know this already', 'This is not the subject of the exam' and 'This has nothing to do with my profession'; thus, much of the curiosity starts to fade away, and one begins to establish a world of no wonders. Today's educational system, with its super professional aspirations and focus on directing students, makes us lose curiosity. Therefore I designed a series of exercises, which I named Design Gymnastics, to help people to keep alive an inborn sense of wonder and renew their own delight in the mystery of the world. I practise it daily myself and in my workshop for children, young people, university students and professionals.

Fred Rogers, an American TV presenter of children's programmes, who passed away in 2003, said that curiosity is very much linked to our sense of communication. He always said that 'Did you know that?' was the starting point of curiosity. Curious people want to show and share their discoveries.

So I carefully designed a process of multisensory discoveries in the series of exercises as a game to play in a team or group to activate their sense of communication.

I read that you use magnifying lenses for children to let them get new perspectives and that this works well with students and adults alike.
In Japan, the magnifying lens is one of the first tools we use at school beside pencil and paper. Being useful throughout life, it is a magical tool that brings a new world into being for everyone.

Thank you very much, Masayo.

Paulus M. Dreibholz

teaches Typography

Senior Artist
Institute of Design
Class of Ideas, Graphics and Advertising
University of Applied Arts Vienna
Austria

Founder of Atelier Dreibholz

Paulus Dreibholz loves talking. Simply because, in his opinion, language is the best tool for reflection. As he speaks, it is easy to follow his thoughts, which always seek and offer connections. They mirror his international teaching expertise and the need to let the students themselves become clients. This interview is the result of conversations on three different days. — January 2023

Thies: Can you tell me in one sentence what you want students to learn from you?
Dreibholz: To design with empathy. To take conscious design decisions and understand the socio-political consequences of their activity.

In the introduction of your book *Reading Form*[48] you write, 'working without reflection is a wasted opportunity to get to know yourself and your environment better.' Which of both reflections is more important with regard to a design task?
Well, you are part of your environment; it defines you and it is defined by you. So to understand yourself better means to understand your environment better, too. There is a constant interaction between these two concepts.

Do you have any method, any approach to help students consciously reflect on themselves and on, say, the given design assignment?
My method is to provide feedback on their work and initiate an open discussion in smaller and bigger groups. Language is the most accessible tool we can use to reflect, first spoken then written.

Do you have an ideal setting to let these reflections unfold?
My ideal classroom invites discussion. It is bright and has a big table that is accessible from all sides. People need to sit side by side; they have to 'feel' each other.

Does a settee have a place there, too?
No. I think a settee is an invitation to lean back. What we are doing, however, isn't comfy. It's exciting. In the same way, it's also taboo to doodle or even knit during class. I don't know anyone who could formulate a question while doodling.

From whom did you learn how to teach?
I have been teaching for almost 18 years now, and so what has shaped my style are the various experiences I gained, the exchange with other educators as well as collaborative teaching. Likewise, speaking to students is a constant source of inspiration for me.

Did you ever have a formative experience during your own studies?
Yes, a practice session in the foundation course. We had to transcribe music to paper. Like an equalizer, we reacted to what the music did, drawing a line with a pencil on a sheet of paper. When we arrived at the edge of the paper, we raised our pencils and started somewhere else. That exercise opened my horizon and made me realise how boundless graphic design can be.

What shaped me in addition to that were people whose private and professional lives formed a unit, particularly two former tutors Paul Farrington and Peter Willberg. I was working with Paul on a website once when his wife brought their two-year-old daughter along who fell asleep on her father's tummy while we carried on with our work. An impressively powerful amalgam.

I was also shaped by the process-based approach, which was enormously encouraged in England at the time; it was the day and age of studios like Why Not Associates and Tomato. People weren't afraid of designing things without knowing from the outset what it would actually turn out to be, following the principle of: what if? In scientific research, a hypothesis is proposed and then either refuted or supported through experimentation. In artistic research, there is often no hypothesis and sometimes I don't even know which question I am going to ask. I simply do it. However, this action is always accompanied by one's own decisions, which makes it fascinating, because in that way, the project gradually incorporates an ever-increasing part of me.

How do you motivate people to take that action?
By rating the experiment, even the one that went wrong, as a success.

You have two children. Do you encourage their curiosity?
I have no pedagogical agenda. But I always used to ask them random questions or say things that were obviously wrong. During our time in London, for instance, I would casually mention, 'Oh look, a blue bus!', when in fact a red bus was passing by, to see whether my son was paying attention to what I said. That always worked well with my children – I'm not sure if it would work so well with others, though. As a parent, and also as an educator, you always have to adapt to the different qualities of a child or student. While one student will be grimly determined, the other one will be a free thinker. That is a wonderful experience for me.

Do we teachers provoke perplexity like the blue bus in class as well?
Yes, because every question and all of our attempts to observe and treat the world with care and caution are exactly the same, albeit on a different level. As far as design is concerned, the question will not be which colour the bus is, but rather whether we could look at it in a different way.

Is 'teaching' the right word for what you do?
I actually think that 'informing' is the most appropriate word. Far from instructing them, I *inform* the students by providing them with information, viewpoints, possibilities and lots more. I use that expression in my own studio: I *inform* my clients about design decisions so that they can make informed decisions.

How do you teach students how to handle clients?
Since no one client is the same, I don't think that you can teach that. You need to experience for yourself whether to question a project, to say no to it, or how to deal with a client's ignorance or arrogance. What you can practise in class, however, is the ability to argue your design proposal and to let yourself be convinced. For example, if I get the feeling that my argument is no longer cogent because my client presents a valid counter-argument, then I say, 'Great!' Then I will have learnt something.

How do you practise this sensitivity, as regards human interaction with clients, in class?
For me, 65 percent of what we do is psychology: reading, interpreting and attempting to understand other people. You can only do that if you listen carefully to what they have to say and reflect on the content. The same applies to clients too. I try to provoke that by turning the students into clients themselves. In one of my courses, for example, I ask the students to bring along or write texts and then read them to the others. Their fellow students are now required to design something with the texts. In that way, the students, who are both

clients and designers sitting in the same room, learn that their interpretations and statements could even be hurtful to some. That is key in developing and training empathy. If that succeeds, it creates a wonderful atmosphere in which to collaborate empathically.

Do you sometimes play the client's role when you teach?
No, I don't think so. For as a teacher, I am not only motivated to achieve an amazing final result with the students, but also have the educational task of challenging the students.

How do you go about challenging students?
Ideally, you want to bring out the best in that person in order to ensure that they will rise to the project task – both technically, in terms of craftsmanship, and intellectually. The discipline of typography involves language and form, meaning that I can teach technical skills such as spacing, font choice and composition as well as conceptualisation, holistic thinking and reflection. In the best of cases, students will leave my course asking themselves questions, including those of a technical nature, as to how they could improve their designs. And it's not me who gives them those questions; they rather find them for themselves. My goal is for them to know *why* their solutions are good. Because only then will they be in a position to communicate them to the outside world, to explain them to me or clients, to our discipline, to their fellow students and co-workers as well.

Should they leave every teaching session with questions to ask?
The point in time is irrelevant for me. Ideally, seeds are sown that slowly begin to sprout. If someone doesn't want to listen or isn't interested in typography, that's okay by me. That's not my problem nor does it have to be a problem for the person concerned. My responsibility is to deliver sufficient material for someone to find inspiration. What that person makes of it is their responsibility.

How do you sow the seeds to make them ask themselves questions?
I have no particular formula for that. However, I do think that there is enough material to automatically spark questions when you get to grips with it.
    One example of that is 'The New Art of Making Books' by Ulises Carrión in which he compares the old and new way of making books. Based on the design task of expressing the text, the students have to understand his paragraphs and adopt a stance. I do not give them any specifications; they have to decide for themselves what they want to do. The tasks I give, especially to older students, are designed in such a way that students have to contribute a great deal in order to accomplish them.

Do you give the students any criteria to help them assess design decisions?
I would like their projects to have substance. That means to have performed
to the best of one's knowledge and belief, which always involves different
responsibilities: towards myself as a designer and as a person, towards my
client, my colleagues, the target audience and, not least, towards my discipline.
These responsibilities are bound together in a dynamic relationship and
some of them cancel each other out, like when the responsibility towards an
approaching deadline gets in the way of the best idea or design. Students
should be aware of those dynamics and know that their decisions have consequences – not only during the project, but later on as well.

How do you kindle awareness in students for those responsibilities?
By asking questions such as 'Am I a good designer? How do I survive within
my discipline, also economically? Who comes to me? Am I replaceable?
Or do I understand my discipline as culture that will always continue to
develop?' These are questions you need to ask students to ensure they develop
a sense of responsibility. I can always do the same things over again, but if
I do, I will not contribute anything at all to the development of my culture.
Ideally, as a committed designer, I co-develop a visual language as well as
all of its dialects.

**Do teachers eventually reach an age in which they are no longer able to
keep up with the development of dialects of style, form and influence?**
I think we are all children of our time, not only in terms of media formats, but
in our approaches as well. And our knowledge changes with the experience
we gain. Accordingly, we classify the latest craze as what it is, namely a short-
lived trend which we don't have to keep up with because it is superficial.
In this context, age is often seen as a burden instead of a resource. However,
looking back on personalities like Adrian Frutiger, Albert Kapr, Jan van Toorn,
Wim Crouwel, or in the English context, Stanley Morison, they are all individuals who made their deliberations over decades. We can obtain sound opinions
from them – albeit not the latest flavour of the month.

**Should educators consciously demand that students deviate from current
trends?**
Yes, absolutely. I think it's even crucial to let the students know that this
phenomenon will sooner or later come to an end. Having said that, it's no
problem to adopt trending design or contemporary languages and elements.
It is even vital that we – as designers – evolve alongside new meanings.
But the careless or irresponsible borrowing of vocabulary from these new
languages is dangerous. Because if we do that, we and everyone else will be
saying the same things all the time.

What do you say when a design outcome carelessly follows a trend?
I believe in meanings. And meanings were created through convention. That means the significance of serif typeface is a higher aspiration; there is touch of intellectuality to it. A modern serif typeface is rather fashionable, gloss and glamour, a renaissance serif typeface is more book, history and science. Sans-serif typefaces, on the other hand, are often associated with objectivity. All of that also applies to visual style, colours and formats and has inherent meanings. Students have to be aware of these meanings in order to be able to express correctly what they would like to express. The sole key to refining this ability of realising and knowing is to reflect, read and analyse, which you can practise with the students.

What does typeface design teach us in that respect?
In my opinion, typeface design is the high art of composition. For not only must the character be harmonious in itself, it must also be at one with all the other characters. I recall Bruno Maag speaking at the Royal College of Art about the 'good curve' which is hard to define. At the time, I didn't know what he meant by that. One of my theories is that a good curve is determined by three parameters: gravity, velocity at which an object moves and resistance. When we throw a ball, it's always a good curve. And if we throw a washing machine, it's also good. It would be a bad curve if the ball didn't keep to the expected flight path. And if there was a gust of wind, the flight path would be affected only insofar as the ball's inertia allowed. So there are many different good curves and lots more bad ones. [laughs]

How do you motivate students to improve their design skills?
By means of a comparative study. When they repeat their trials once or several times over, look at the results and compare them. In that respect, I am always very wary about working with things that have already been made, because I want them to try lots of things themselves.

Why is it better to experience things yourself first?
Your own experience leads to intuition; learnt experience rather leads to knowledge. For me, the experiences you gain yourself are much more important than theoretical knowledge.

Do you encourage students to gain these experiences?
Yes, because you have to let them go sooner or later. Similar to children. Some learn to walk earlier, others later. But if I always take them by the hand, they will never learn to walk alone.

In your publication *MAtters Transcript*[49], Tom Foley said that students get so accustomed to university structures over the years that they may be scared of stepping out of the ivory tower into the outside world.
I would interpret that as a lack of practical relevance. Is freedom at university something positive or is it a potential risk?
Hard to say, because people have individual ways of coping with rules, formulas and systems. Ideally, an art university allows non-conformist thought and action as long as it doesn't restrict others. To act on an institutionalised basis could certainly indicate a lack of practical relevance because it doesn't follow any conventions outside of it. But it could also mean that I reflect the maxims of the university or institution.

An institution also inevitably forms one's own attitude, which is of crucial concern, not least because the person in question actually chose to study at a certain university, in a certain class.

I know that you and I share maxims that students should develop personally and further make intelligent and coherent decisions based on their motivations – design decisions, but at the end of the day, life-shaping decisions as well.

Does the ivory tower have any other advantages or disadvantages?
If you don't know certain rules, you won't have any qualms about breaking them. That can be helpful, but also painful. I'd rather we teach our students how to fly instead of the law of gravity.

In an inaugural lecture at Central Saint Martins, I showed a photo of Evel Knievel. That's the stuntman who did those crazy jumps with his motorbike – and at the time, people all thought that it was bound to go wrong. I then explained, 'You should have that feeling of losing control at every point of your studies – like walking on a precipice without going over the edge.'

Nice picture.
Well, that's the way I still feel – unfortunately. [laughs]

What is your opinion on the abstract idea that 'listening is crucial to teaching'?
That's something I should take to heart more often. [laughs]

Does that mean other people never have any say when you talk? [laughs]
I have an enormous need to talk due to my enthusiasm for the things I do. But when it comes to the end-of-course student feedback, no one has ever held that against me. [smiles]

Do you nevertheless agree that listening is key?
No. Why not? Well, if I haven't listened at all, I won't be able to contribute much constructively. On the other hand, if I do nothing but listen, my contribution will probably be just as poor. As a teacher, though, I always have to deliver something. I can't just listen and understand.

Listening, then, must always be preceded by something else.
Right. In my case, the briefing is often the sole stimulus. Sometimes even a course title alone will do to get me started.

Do you have any questions you ask repeatedly?
One of my favourites is 'What does that mean then?' I want to analyse a design proposal according to its meanings. It's not only important for me to know what led to the decision, but what it means for someone who doesn't know these decisions and who only sees the final product.

How do students develop an attitude? And do they need teachers to do that?
You don't necessarily need teachers for that. Ideally though, there is someone available as a possible source of feedback, much like a mentor. I think that a lot more happens in dialogue than in monologue. It's great to elucidate and question one's own set of values together with others. And it's not only students who carve out their attitude in that way.

What is the relationship between attitude and values?
I think that attitude is based on values; they are dependent on one another and should permeate both our private and professional lives. Only then will we be able to go to work every day and change the world in a certain direction. It's nothing other than life translated into an activity which you were trained to perform.

So, in your class it's not just about creative attitudes, but also about socio-political topics and opinions?
Chiefly the latter, I'd say. I think self-enhancement and personal development are crucial, for only then will you be able to sensitise people. In class, even for me, design is only a tool to that end.

In a conversation prior to our interview, you distinguished between 'creating' and 'designing' with respect to the design process.
Yes, the design process not only encompasses the creative, constructive part, but also the editing and selecting.

How do you teach students to select, to make their own decisions?
They do that autodidactically by learning how to deal with the freedom I grant them or confront them with in the course.

What do you say to students who ask you whether they should choose A or B?
'Choose either A or B, then.'

And then they repeat their question.
Yes, and I repeat the answer. [laughs] And after a while they get fed up and do either A or B.

What was the biggest mistake you ever made in class?
To have thought that I had to be someone other than myself. At the very beginning – the question as to whether I wanted to teach came as a bit of a surprise to me – when I began teaching second-year students at the London College of Communication, I thought I had to be an authority with a vast amount of knowledge, which made me feel nervous and I didn't enjoy it. But then, I realised that I could also work together with them as partners without knowing so much more, but by showing more endurance. I have become calmer since then and have now reached an age where I've earned a wee bit of authority on account of my year of birth. [laughs]

[laughs] Many thanks for all your insights, Paulus.

Fritz Frenkler

taught Industrial Design

Professor
Emeritus of Excellence
TUM Senior Excellence Faculty
Technical University of Munich
Germany

Co-founder of f/p design

He likes to get started right away. And he wants his students
to think first and then act. That includes reflecting on how
designers can become moderators and interact with other
cultures. Fritz Frenkler talks about all that in his Berlin
office where there is no place for needless objects. — July 2021

Thies: You created the master's degree programme in Industrial Design
at the Technical University of Munich (TUM). Which criteria did you use
to select candidates applying to the univeristy?
Frenkler: We had a questionnaire for that. My team would ask the standard
questions. My questions were more general and personal: 'What are you
interested in? What was your home life like? What motivates you?' In the
end, what counted for me was their ability to tell me something I didn't
already know. We didn't even ask them anything about drawing techniques.
Ability to work in a team and general knowledge were essential for us.

You told me once that you reduced the scope of the master's degree
programme shortly after its introduction because the workload was too
high. However, could a high workload have a positive effect, too, if it were
time-limited or project-related?
Yes, certainly! Because I heard – way too often – that many students were
spending their weekends in the beer garden. On Monday morning, I would
always ask what they had done at the weekend and only very few answers had
anything at all to do with design. They didn't even go and see the latest film
at the cinema, nor did anyone know anything about the new video game.
So, I guess I should have stuck to the workload instead of letting them waste
their time.

Did the students' attitude change after you'd asked that question a couple of times?
My students knew that there had to be more to their answer than just the 'beer garden'. Particularly since the university offered a host of opportunities and many people there came from various different cultures. I would always ask them things like, 'Have you already spoken to your seatmate from China?' 'Um, no', was the answer. Then I'd follow up with, 'Well, why not? Don't you want to ask any questions about China? I'd have a million questions about China.' Or I'd ask, 'Have you had a cooking session together yet? And here at TUM, you can learn Chinese for free!' Back came the answer, 'Well, when am I supposed to have time for that?' 'At lunchtime', I'd reply. 'But I always go to the student's canteen at midday.' 'Well, why don't you meet up in the afternoon? Go to the beer garden for heaven's sake, but just start talking!' General knowledge, or at least interest in it, is important.

Did you just express that in words or establish it structurally?
No, I only did that as an additional aspect, as they did have their freedom, of course.

What should universities do to generate greater exchange in that respect?
At my firm, for example, we have an international meeting of our three studios in Munich, Berlin and Kyoto every Thursday. An employee moderates the meeting and briefly presents all the latest projects as well as something that has nothing at all to do with us. Recently, a Japanese employee presented the most expensive three-square-metre flat in Shinjuku. Someone else spoke about Koala babies having to eat their mothers' faeces in order to develop their body's defences against the leaves they eat, which are actually indigestible.

Universities should foster intercultural exchange, even if it's only mandatory five to ten-minute student presentations.

Did you give the teaching staff instructions as to what and how they were to teach?
The curriculum prescribed which areas were to be covered. In all other respects, I gave everyone complete freedom. If someone asked me how or what they should teach, I replied, 'Just do it! I want *you* to tell me what you have in mind. What do you think will be important for young designers in the future?' Afterwards, we would discuss those matters as a team and that always worked very well.

It was always meant to be life-centred, human-centred – to put it in simply: 'How does your granny see that?'

I know that you always attach importance to doing things, taking the plunge...
Right. Because there is no formula for design. That's precisely what makes it so exciting, but perhaps also vulnerable. It's neither mathematics nor physics. Medicine undergoes change due to technology and research; design undergoes change owing to new social structures. We anticipate social rituals. And we make products out of them that have a subsequent impact on society. That is crucial. That is why an educator should be able to comprehend and respond to all kinds of changes.

At TUM, you are currently involved in establishing a brand new institute that will have a cross-institutional and cross-disciplinary function. Students from different fields of science will attend design-related courses there. Design will become cross-functional. Why is that so important?
At this studio, we are doing projects ranging from a dental chair to catalogues and websites, involving designers, programmers, engineers and other specialists. It is becoming increasingly important for everyone to develop in-depth understanding for and engage in communication with other colleagues. And design will always have an auxiliary function in that respect.

How can we convey that auxiliary function of design to students?
We have scientific disciplines we have to consult which collaborate directly in a project or which need to involve us.

That is why we require engineering, economics, psychology and – what I regard as key – philosophy in addition to function, form and experience to enable us to understand our own and other cultures. Nobody understood why we involved a sociologist as well, questioning as to why sociology was needed to develop a technology. My reply was always, 'Do you want to beat that into society with a baton? We are doing this for society.' In Brunswick, Germany, where I went to university, we used to call all those subjects reference sciences. I think we must prepare students – and that is a major challenge – to understand and create relations and to become moderators.

My idea was always: design represents man. Engineering represents technologies. In company structures with clear tasks in design, engineering and marketing, designers must be in a position to moderate processes and not to appear arrogant. The first design task is then to compile a briefing. What does it say? What are the focuses? And that already needs to be conveyed to different departments.

How did you manage to tangibly convey all those procedures and goals you've just described in a way that your students internalise them?
Well, for example, in projects where ideas would be presented time and again. And every time the thinking process got started, the critical question as to 'Who needs that?' would be asked. Because design is primarily a thinking process, not a sketch or model. What it will look like plays no role whatever initially. As an example, Tesla built in a screen and all of a sudden everyone did the same. [laughs] What an anachronism! The question should rather be: why do we still need this information?

How did you convey and train moderation as a design-related task?
In order to moderate topics, the students require self-assuredness, rhetorical skills, specialist knowledge – and general knowledge.

They acquired self-confidence by doing presentations again and again – in a language that they were comfortable with and which I understood; so it wasn't Chinese obviously. [laughs] You can have an amazing product but present it badly. And part of that is how you behave towards other people, how you approach various different characters and when it would perhaps be better to shut up.

Knowledge is essential. You have read, seen or understood something. Keep in mind where you got it from and tell it to others. Those things will be pivotal for designers in the future. Especially in view of the fact that we are venturing into areas where we designers maybe lack sufficient experience and are naturally dependent on specialist advice. Our job is to ask the right questions. And you can learn that. So that you'll be able to ask again if you don't get the right answers, or offer to research it. And that's how you get into the scientific area where design must go as well.

If doctors or engineers collaborating in the development of an eye robot say, 'We must fix the head here', you need to find out first how the fixed person feels. It's important to question things.

How can you teach students how to ask questions and question things like that?
By asking questions yourself all the time when the students are doing something. And by suggesting that maybe questions need to be asked in a different way sometimes. Between us, we established an understanding that everything could be asked and everything had to be answered.

How did you give feedback? Did you make suggestions or tell them what they have to do?
Always let them find things out for themselves! That's crystal clear. Sure, I very often had different ideas, but I was positively surprised just as often.

Until that point was reached, we often helped by asking, 'Are you sure that this will lead to a result that satisfies you and others as well? Take a second look at the solutions presented by designer A or B.'

The students had to know the 20 best furniture designers and their history – what, when and with whom they did something and why. If somebody did not know the designer, architect or communication designer I named, the next time they'd have to tell us something about that person. Students need to know about the past and present of design because their future might depend on it. Historical knowledge is a kit which they can use to build things – intellectually and physically.

Let's come back to the role of cross-functional design that will be deployed across disciplines at TUM. Is it possible to collaborate with other disciplines without founding an institute? If so, how?
That's quite simple: through human communication.

When I started at TUM, I introduced myself to all faculty colleagues, even if some of them asked me – quite surprised – what it was for. I went to see everyone – even the caretaker, the administrative staff and the president.

And you should always make a point of saying if something is wrong in order to rectify it. I also visited other universities. Because the wealth of universities is their knowledge, expertise and people. I wanted to find new approaches, right through to the administrative department, to improve their printed forms. None of that is doable at a distance. You have to go to the people. Because design is for people.

How did you learn to teach? Did you adopt methodology from your own time at university?
During my studies, I realised how essential a good grasp of general knowledge is and I learnt how to organise projects and to let the students do things themselves, have confidence in them. And if nothing comes of it then you can see that and intervene. I have never read any books about how to teach, but rather learnt from experience in various different phases of my career, amending and modifying things from time to time if necessary.

Did you add anything completely new to your teaching?
Well, from the very start, I connected the master's degree programme to the start-up scene, to the business incubator 'UnternehmerTUM'. By participating in summer schools and joint projects, the students learnt how to start and build up a business using corporate design, product and communication design, but also how bookkeeping works and tax declarations are done. Engineers, technicians and investors were sitting side by side in meetings, which was a thrilling experience.

Have you ever made a mistake in class that you regret?
[reflects] If I was ever gruff, that was a mistake. Even if it had perhaps been a response to a provocation. It's always wrong to allow yourself to be provoked. Or to believe that you're the measure of all things.

My aspiration is to do something for the common good and not for people who need a bigger parking space because they drive a Rolls Royce. That raised my hackles: 'No need for that.' If I had kept my composure, I would have said, 'Let's try and reduce the size of a Rolls Royce.'

Is there any content you would consider worth putting online for students to use?
Yes, that's always worth doing. For example, it's good to post summaries as a follow-up. However, as far as personal relations are concerned, I think human beings are not ready for that yet – I speak differently in video conferences than I am speaking to you now. But things might change if we continue to develop in the same direction over the next couple of generations. And if so, would that facilitate more personal interaction over distances? Or to put it the other way round: would we suddenly require the glazed screen of our smartphones to maintain distance in personal meetings?

Should reading be part of education?
Yes! As an assignment, for a paper or an abstract. That need not necessarily be subject-related but could also be literature. Leonard Cohen's lyrics. Or what style did Rilke use in his poetry? How do I express feelings in writing?

Which word best describes what you did at university?
There are two: speaking and listening.

Did you pursue a bigger goal for and with the students?
Yes, I did. You have to find out what expectations these young people have, as they all come to university with a certain expectation. And then you have to get together with them and reformulate those expectations. Essentially, it's always about having an effect on social development and providing as many people as possible with access to that development, regardless of their level of education.

My goal was to educate my students to prevent products from being made and to get paid for it. Because 25 to 50% of our products on the market are a flop. Whether it be software, hardware, communication or other things. Our mission was to produce evidence based on scientific findings that it would be best if the contracting business did not manufacture that product – and we earned a few per cent of the money they saved. We don't need so many new things anymore.

Does that goal include preventing things related to architecture or communication design?

Yes, of course! Building services for instance. How long did it take to build Berlin airport? 12 years? Why do they need to extract smoke through the ground there? It's common knowledge that smoke rises. So, they could have said, 'That's going to cause problems. Let's discard the idea. It's much too expensive.' [laughs] All of those things are design-relevant.

Or in Japan where everyone's asking, 'Why is the underground so crowded in the morning?' Why doesn't anyone suggest introducing staggered working hours beginning at, say, 8.30, 9.00 and 9.30 am? Then they would only have half as many problems and probably fewer problems with containing the coronavirus now as well. That's what I call design solutions.

What did you tell your students on their first day?

That I wanted to learn from them.

And on their last day?

That I hoped they'd learnt something.

What was the answer?

Yes! They were all well brought up. [laughs]

[laughs] Thanks, Fritz.

Nikolaus Hafermaas

teaches Transmedia Design

Professor
Former Dean, Undergraduate and Graduate Graphic Design
Head of the Satellite Program in Berlin
ArtCenter College of Design, Pasadena
USA

Managing partner of Graft BrandLab

For 14 years Nikolaus Hafermaas guided over 50 educators and
300 students every semester. In his agency's office located in an
old brick building, he replies to the questions, reflecting first on
how to maintain one's childlike curiosity and which educational
models will be necessary in the future. Dogma, he states, has no
place in teaching. Short-sleeved T-shirt. Clear gaze.
— September 2021

Thies: What did your job at the ArtCenter in Pasadena involve?
Hafermaas: During my 14 years at the ArtCenter, my main job as Dean was
to transform that particular specialist area, to evaluate all teaching staff
– 50 professors in all – redefine the curriculum and build new structures.
It was about changing a very traditional graphic design programme with
over 300 students into what I called Transmedia Design, where 2D, 3D and 4D
would come together.
    As a teacher, I mostly did interdisciplinary projects.

What kind of projects do you mean?
Either industry-sponsored projects where we were commissioned by companies
that own major brands to carry out projects, or social innovation projects that
we did for the United Nations and various other non-profit organisations.

Why did you choose that particular kind of project?
Because projects like that had a social impact and were especially challenging
with real clients. But above all because it gave me the chance to let the
students learn from the very start how to interact with creatives from other
specialist areas. In that regard, the entire spectrum of disciplines was available:
product design, transportation design, environmental design, photography,

advertising, entertainment design, fine art and other specialist areas offered at the ArtCenter.

How did you form those groups, put them together?
We primarily put them together for sponsored projects. For example, some organisations would approach the college, saying, 'We need an awareness campaign on Deep Ocean Life.' Then we'd tender that as a communication project and would always determine a host department responsible for it. In the case of a communication project that would, of course, be the Communication Design department. If the project required an additional exhibition, for example, Environmental Design would also be involved as a co-teaching department. For these projects, we would search for students from all specialist areas in order to broaden the scope on a specialist level. Communication projects would often consist of one-third communication design students, while the rest came from other specialist areas. I would then appoint them proportionately to four working groups of three to four people each.

According to which criteria did you select students?
The students applied by providing a link to their portfolios and adding a short statement as to why they were interested in that project and what they thought they could contribute to it. In order to get a concise and preferably complete picture of a person, I would always ask them certain questions relating to their lives outside of college: 'Do you have any other interests? What is your attitude to life?' At the same time, I paid attention to diversity, intellectual diversity and creative diversity. Analogous to a football team, I also always tried to include a few 'disruptive' people who were especially independent and unconventional.

Did you ever make the wrong decision?
Yes, of course. There has been the odd drama. In that case, you observe their behaviour for a while to see who has an A-type or B-type personality, and then you change the composition of the group, if necessary. When it came to projects at our college, however, the risk was relatively low because we already knew many students.

It's quite a different story here at the Satellite Program in Berlin where students in the group spend their whole time together. The social dynamics are much more important because of that and so you step in and provide support more often.

Do the groups compete against each other in interdisciplinary projects?
Basically, the ArtCenter is relatively competition-oriented. First, because it's hard to get into and second, because the tuition isn't cheap. Among some

industrial clients who we refer to as 'sponsors' or 'industry partners', there has been a fair amount of competitive situations. For example, if an invention or design emerges that the sponsor wants to have, there is a buy-out possibility afterwards. The college is the broker, so to speak, and there's quite a lot of money involved. As a rule, one or two results are acquired from the output of three or four teams.

What do sponsors pay as a rule?
The usual going rate for well-established enterprises is 75,000 dollars for a class of 15, 16 students and at least two teachers. That also covers the cost of external experts, excursions and the final prototyping. So two-thirds of the sponsored amount is invested in the class and the rest flows into the infrastructure of the ArtCenter. An additional buy-out of successful ideas can also cost up to 10,000 dollars per student team.

Irrespective of the sponsors, how did you assess the students?
We asked ourselves what characterised a successful solution. The most important thing in that respect is the learning curve. And since there is not only a right or a wrong, achievements were not only assessed individually, the students were supported on an individual basis as well.

Did it ever occur to you to give up helping a particular student?
Not really, at least, not on my part. But some people did give up because of personal problems. Some of them came back again after about two years saying, 'I've solved the problem. I want to carry on now.'

The ArtCenter always inspired me because of its dynamic and energetic atmosphere that one would otherwise encounter in creative professional practice. That, of course, has its dark sides too.

Could you name those dark sides?
[takes a deep breath] Burnout. Not only students, but also teaching staff come under huge pressure.

We were always asking ourselves what value we could offer students who were paying 20,000 dollars per term. At the end of their studies, they often had to repay a 200,000-dollar loan. Some students even lived in campervans on the college's carpark. So it was my responsibility to ensure that those people got a job that would pay at least 100,000 dollars per annum after two years.

It was also an incredible incentive to always think far ahead on which capabilities, beyond purely technical skills, make transmedia communicators indispensable. However, we knew we were on the right track when – straight after presenting their final portfolios at the graduation show – the students were recruited by all the Googles and Teslas of this world who were looking for very open-minded people. We always spoke of T-shaped people who had a very broad knowledge with a strong focus in a certain area.

I first heard of the term 'T-shaped' through Tim Brown from IDEO. Did you try to teach exactly that kind of skill?
Yes. The whole curriculum is built on that. A broad, interdisciplinary scope coupled with connectivity to other disciplines – not only to creative disciplines, but also to strategy, research, science and technology as well as other areas.

How do I learn to work on an interdisciplinary level?
By doing it. By practising it. There are no rules that you can learn. But rule number one could be: 'Don't be an asshole.' And you need a certain readiness to communicate and be open-minded which, in the first instance, needs to be conveyed to people who, as youngsters, rarely voiced their opinions at home. Our job is to change that in a positive sense.

I also tell my students that there was a time when design was the very last thing to come after everything else had been thought out, tested, constructed and pieced together. And that now, design isn't just in demand at the very start of the problem solving, but ideally, at the beginning of the opportunity-seeking process as well.

Are there any specific exercises to help learn this interaction?
At the ArtCenter we had classes on certain subjects such as 'The Art of Idea Generation' or 'The Art of Presentation', which focused on practising individual facets. But in my projects, we concentrated purely on real-life cases. They were practised time and again until the work got better. Critical feedback was given not only by teaching staff, but also by clients.

Which other skills should designers acquire?
I would say you need creative curiosity and to be able to communicate in a persuasive way as well as empathy – by that, I mean empathy in all directions, towards tasks and everyone with whom you collaborate. You also need a certain quantum of self-confidence that enables you to assert your opinion, your attitude – not just to finish a job, but to question what's behind it.

What objective do I pursue as designer?
I would like to put the designer's objective as a question: do I try to be part of the solution or am I happy with being part of the problem?

One example to illustrate that point: when I began teaching, there were classes on sustainability. Eventually, we said that our aim should be to abolish those classes because we should not be doing anything that wasn't sustainable.

It's exactly the same story with social sustainability. In California, one of the wealthiest regions in the world, there is a lot that isn't right, there is social Darwinism, and you teach and learn in a fantastic ivory tower. In that context, the daily question arises as to one's own responsibility towards society.

Is the objective the first thing you discuss at the beginning of a project?
This is not a linear process beginning with a discussion, but rather resonates from the first to the last week. When we make creative decisions in the process, we ask the purpose question – which also includes why something is red or yellow for instance.

Do you encourage discussion and mutual critique amongst students?
Oh yes, definitely! What we really practise intensively is the art of critique. How do people give honest feedback to someone without spawning a negative response? This sensitivity requires training.

And how do you convey that?
A lot of our work, from the very first sketches on, is pinned onto the wall and the students have to be able to speak about what they are doing. They constantly give and receive feedback. And the quality of the feedback constitutes part of their final grade.

Do the students sometimes have to give written feedback?
No, we always do that directly in dialogue.

How does one learn to become a creative?
I create conditions under which amazing stuff can happen. People need to feel appreciated. An atmosphere is required in which provocation is permitted, which is a huge issue in the States because litigious society will sue you for anything. As a student, but also as a teacher, it's vital to know that college is a safe space where you can experiment, voice unpopular opinions and where you learn to wake people up.

How do I learn that?
Well, you don't just design things for yourself and your private bubble, but rather for people who are outside of it. So it's important to expose yourself to situations, other folks, questions and contrary opinions – and to endure that. Besides, you have to cultivate your curiosity and creative hunger and learn to learn. I think that's a crucial point because the environment in which we live is constantly changing.

How do I learn to learn?

This is conveyed here by practical application, too. And that's where the Berlin Satellite Program comes in: the programme is not a mere branch of the college, but rather works like a pop-up creative agency. Here, everything the students have learnt comes together in projects and can be practically applied.

Here, too, I create an environment and situations to coax them out of their comfort zone. One good example of that is the 'Berlin Unplugged' project that we did a couple of years ago. We asked ourselves what the most scary thing would be for us. The answer was obvious: being abroad in a foreign culture and having no internet access. No digital translation tools, no social media, no YouTube videos. You're there. And you're there unfiltered. And you're not just gonna survive, but you're gonna thrive. The project lasted 12 weeks, six of them without access to the internet.

And what happened then?

It was interesting because after six weeks without the internet, which was quite challenging initially, the students wanted to carry on. They had loads of fun and incredibly amazing things emerged from the enterprise: self-confidence communicative skills. Even through small things like chatting to people on the street and asking them the way. They appropriated the city in a different way, for instance, by producing frottages of shot-damaged façades and buying Polaroid cameras and typewriters from flea markets. They went to Erik Spiekermann to do some letterpress printing. At the end of it all, an impressive self-written manifesto was released.

What was the goal, the actual task definition of the project?

To sketch a portrait of the city. To experience the city graphically, artistically and visually, but also analogously, and to translate it. At the end, we set up a gallery in an open shop space – and following that, the American greeting cards company Hallmark approached us and wanted to buy it all. So as a result, the students even earned some money through that purchase.

You fitted a gallery there. How important is the final presentation?

It's absolutely essential. You need a goal in order to maintain the tension.

You said that the social impact of projects was important to you. When are projects successful in terms of their social impact?

Well, ideally, when the projects are used and are effective. For example, we did a project called 'Safe Agua Chile' in which environmental, communication and product designers attempted to solve the problem of the water's 'last mile'. A whole host of innovative solutions emerged from the project, ranging from the first solar shower and water transportation systems to communications around community washhouses.

You mentioned initially that you were constantly adjusting the curriculum. In that regard, to what extent are students' opinions taken into account?
We were able to get lots of impressions in the classes. And I attended all final project events. The actual feedback from students was relatively formalised; they had to evaluate in a fair amount of detail what was relevant, what was difficult, what they had and hadn't learnt, what didn't work quite so well etc. on a platform. Wherever there were peaks in the overall assessment – and not just exceptions owing to the bad mood of some individuals – we had follow-up discussions and made adjustments accordingly.

You also mentioned curiosity, which is – also for me – one of the greatest assets we are born with, coupled with childlike carefreeness. How do I maintain or arouse that carefreeness in students?
That's a very good question. I discovered my childlike curiosity, which I recall vividly, at the documenta in Kassel where I practically learnt to walk.

As a teacher, I think the only thing you can do is to amaze your students to make them long for more. And we should make even more effort to amaze those who weren't brought up that way. We should do everything to open up new horizons for our students. That is why our Satellite project is so important. In that respect, a displacement need not always be spatial. It can also happen on an intellectual level.

What was your biggest mistake as a teacher up to now?
Cool question. [laughs] I made lots of mistakes. I just can't say which of them was the worst.

Well, something really did go wrong once. At the time, we had a first semester class called 'Offensive Imagery'. I organised the most provocative teaching staff for that class and the task was to create things that were offensive, politically incorrect or designed in such a way that they stopped you in your tracks. The objective was to show the students right from the start that the ability to communicate visually can be an extremely sharp-edged tool. Sometime afterwards, I was summoned to my president because of something a student had left in the printer. Frankfurter sausages with the Anne Frank logo on top. And our president was of Jewish origin. That was really awful. Naturally, he was beside himself with fury, why I'd allowed that. I explained to him what we were doing and invited him to class as well. That was a very difficult situation.

Did you still repeat the task definition?
Yeah. We continued 'Offensive Imagery' as a class. One of my professors there was suspended because he had mooned the class just as Facebook and YouTube were taking off. He pulled his trousers down and exposed his bare buttocks in front of the class. Somebody filmed the incident and put it online.

His explanation was wholly understandable. When he was young, he said, students were revolutionary and recalcitrant, and those in his class were so passive. So he told them, 'Right – I'm gonna give you a rude awakening. Even if it had actually been your job to provoke me.' [laughs]

Do you think students are interested in how an older person ticks?
Perhaps not per se. But if you want to be a designer, you need empathy. And if you don't want to just design things that are already overly designed like hip sneakers for hip kids, then you look for so-called 'creative opportunities'.

Design for the elderly is a huge issue, for example – without clichés of having to design something adequate. In many projects, we practised listening carefully and asking the right questions.

Do you think that there is an age limit to teaching?
Nope, quite the opposite. Whatever hipness you may have lost over time, you easily compensate for with life experience, wisdom and the calmness that goes with it. As long as you don't get dogmatic, you are never too old to teach.

In my opinion, dogma in any form has no place in teaching.

You mentioned listening. What do you think of the hypothesis that listening is the most important part of learning? Is that an exaggeration?
Well, I'd say there's nothing wrong with that. Seems almost impossible to refute. Maybe I would extend it by saying: listening and creative processing are most important. If I only listen to what's being said, I may have acquired a vital prerequisite, but it won't be anything new. And I think it's also important to listen to yourself.

What's your opinion on the hypothesis that listening is key to teaching?
For me personally, learning and teaching works in a circular way, like an echo sounder: I receive something and send it back. And every time something is sent and received, it's enriched. The most important thing for me as a teacher is to operate in both directions.

We have spoken a lot about content. So I'd like to change the subject: How do you convey taste?
You don't.

At some point in the creative process, though, you have to find a form – whether it be an advertisement, packaging or an exhibition. Doesn't taste play any role in form finding?

I always tell my students, 'You have to know the rules to break them. If you break the rules without knowing them, you just seem stupid. But if you know the rules and don't break them, then you are missing an opportunity.'

And that, for me, applies to aesthetics and taste as well. I think good taste is eclectic and multifaceted. Of course, I have to learn and teach which compositional and perceptual principles there are, perceptual psychology, great examples of all forms of fine arts, in nature, in technology and so on. But I don't believe in a dogma of good taste. That is terribly boring and doesn't reflect life at all.

That brings me to artificial intelligence, a tool that we could use. Do I have to learn and teach that?

Of course! I regard generative design as extremely important in that context – the same as I feel about raising awareness in students that certain tools and their limitations have a great influence on your own design work. Photoshop and Illustrator make some things incredibly complex, while others can be done swiftly. And the software behind it is not made by designers, but by programmers and engineers. Generative design, in that sense, means that I open the black box by processing, where I write my own algorithms. As a creative person, I should be able to know about and exploit the possibilities of those technologies – whether I want to or not. For successful design is achieved at the interface between the human world and the world of technological possibilities.

Which brings me to blended learning. Did you apply that in Pasadena?

There was always a lot of talk about it, but it has only been practised in recent years due to the coronavirus.

My own experience is that it can make sense to convey certain things in YouTube tutorials. Although, at the same time, it's a challenge for any college whose business model has so far relied on tuition fees and classroom teaching. Blended learning as a term is therefore only the tip of the iceberg beneath which lie quite fundamental and inevitable changes as to how academic models, in fact, will function. Of course, getting direct feedback, learning by doing, in the same space is incredibly important. It is my hope that being physically present with all one's senses will not be replaced in the near future.

However, both blended learning and remote learning are shaking the foundations of higher education. On a different note, does it make any sense to continue with degree programmes? Or should it be an entirely different certificate where degrees are offered in a number of smaller units? Should a curriculum become much more modular for the purpose of quicker adaptation? Lifelong learning that always gives students a boost whenever they need it, while kindly leaving out all the nonsense they don't need? We would need to experiment on that.

Thanks a lot, Nik, for your insights and outlooks on the future.

Brigitte Hartwig
teaches Communication Design

Professor
Department of Design
Anhalt University of Applied Sciences, Dessau
Germany

The key, in her opinion, is what design sparks in our world.
This is true for brand and urban development. Her teaching
projects always focus on the content and the design process,
aiming to seek out new forms of behaviour in our dealings
with one another. Nobody should take their problems home
with them, says Brigitte Hartwig, sitting in a bright classroom
in the direct vicinity of the Bauhaus in Dessau, adding that
this applies to distance teaching as well. — August 2021

Thies: How would you describe your teaching style in a couple of words?
Hartwig: To put it very briefly: intuition, improvisation, empathy, passion
and encouragement. And I always try to create a pleasant atmosphere that is
fear-free and humorous.

Have there ever been any situations that caused an unpleasant atmosphere in class?
Obviously, there are students who will always talk back, but when I notice
the rest of the group rolling their eyes, I just take it as a challenge. Inevitably,
the following discussions go on until we drop. [laughs]

So you don't let a discussion die down then.
No, not if I can help it. I think it's important to address everything right
away. At the beginning of the semester, I always say that nobody should go
home with anything on his or her mind.

**You teach communication design. 'Social design' is a term that also crops
up in articles about you. What do students learn in your classes?**
I try to teach them how to design means of communication that are socially
relevant and have a social impact as well. Even if it's a trade-related task or
building a brand, I think what it will provoke in the world is decisive. Essentially, it's about the content and the how. In that sense, I help the students

find out what is central – not just for them or for me, but also for others. In addition, it's about conceptualising formats, taking action and consistently plucking up the courage to try everything out straight away. And about learning that mistakes and failures are part of the game.

One exemplary project involved revamping allotments. Another project aimed to convert an empty salesroom into a students' café, to establish it long term and manage it. My role in all this is to facilitate and coach.

Do you have any other exemplary projects?
We often do an eight-day project at the beginning of the semester, for example. For one of them, a student came up with the idea of installing a screen-printing workshop in an empty beverage store.

In this project, first-semester students worked together with senior students and international students. It was extremely important that everyone realised that they all had to muck in. They improvised a project room for eight days and began with our brand development process, starting with questions such as 'what's the name of the workshop?', 'whom does it address?' and 'who's allowed to print there?' The whole undertaking was carefully considered: from who was to be responsible for running it to grant applications and various offers that were sent to prospective parties who wanted to hire the space for events.

At the beginning of a short project like that, do you have an agenda in mind?
The core is frequently a brand development project. For smaller projects, I provide plans with project sheets. But in bigger projects where you're not really sure what's ahead, that would defeat the purpose of the students finding their topic themselves. On that level, I teach highly intuitively and case based. This openness often causes many to flounder somewhat in the first third of the project, but, in the end, much more brilliant things emerge because they feel so intrinsically motivated.

Are there some students who require support for longer?
Yes, definitely. Especially when we do major projects, we gather around the table spending a lot of time chewing over what we could make out of it. In that respect, my projects are mostly team projects to enable the students to benefit from one another.

How are decisions reached at that table?
By discussing things. Everyone says what they think and then we decide on our interim presentations and feedback sessions. Only now and then will I steer the discussion in a certain direction if I anticipate that one idea has more potential than others. But I talk about that frankly, too.

How important is the long-term potential of a project for it to be implemented and maybe perpetuated beyond the actual semester project?
It all depends on the students' enthusiasm for the topic. Although continuing the project after the end of the semester is no prerequisite, it does increase the perceived self-efficacy – to actually experience that what I do has consequences. Those projects are not only about aesthetic design, but about using design to change something as well.

How do you start a project?
Well, I always begin every project by asking who has what expectations in order to tune in to the students. More often than not, the ensuing discussion makes everyone aware of the fact that they are all standing together at the beginning of an open-ended semester.

What does such a discussion involve?
I mostly save pictures and thoughts on a flip chart. During the first semester, we also discuss the basics of what it actually means to study at university, defining the differences between school and university and establishing how important it is to take responsibility for yourself.

Are students involved in decisions on the curriculum?
Yes, two and a half years ago we established our working group on that matter called AG Curriculum that consists of half students and half lecturers.
The group meets every Tuesday from 6:30 to 8 pm via Zoom or in person to discuss how we could make progress and whether we could make any changes to our teaching.

How do you teach awareness and a sense for aesthetics?
By talking about it, trying it out and comparing. Aesthetics is about coherence – about intrinsic and overall harmony, fitting together – or about things turning out to be interesting and exciting in their interaction with one another.

How intensively do you engage in that process?
I don't restrain myself in that respect, but I always add that it's my subjective feeling. I prefer asking the others first what they feel. I might ask, 'What would schoolchildren think? And your grandmother?' And if we don't get any further on that score, we go to town and display the draft somewhere and speak to people about it. Or we interview other lecturers in order to get out of our project bubble.

Let's go on to something completely different – to gender equality: design faculties tend to appoint more male than female professors. How can that be changed?
By paying careful attention to the issue when it comes to new appointments. There's nothing much else you can do.

Do you talk about that to your students?
Of course! One student even conducted interviews on that subject, but since we only have three female colleagues working here, the results were not overwhelming.

How do you live equality when teaching?
Well, it's primarily a matter of non-violent communication and empathic cooperation, of being able to slip into someone else's shoes. Today's students don't really have any problems in that regard. It's more of an issue with staff members of my generation.

You started teaching in 2004. Have any changes happened since then?
Yes, but only in the last five years.

At the beginning of the interview, you mentioned that having an impact on society was important to you. What are your reasons for that?
Principally, we were trained to design products, printed matter and other things. However, now we have reached a point where we don't really need any new products but rather new forms of behaviour and new ways in which to treat each other. We need to rethink our consumer behaviour. I'm inspired by the idea of being able to create visible incentives, I mean incentives that could be a designed statement.

For example, we had a student project that involved putting up posters on every house in a rather middle-class neighbourhood of Dessau: Dessau Nord, near Funkplatz Park. These pink paper posters with their bold black letters announced that a picnic would take place in the park the following Sunday; people were invited to come along and bring a blanket with them. That Sunday, the place was packed. People from the whole district were sitting on their blankets and chatting away. This incentive would never have come from the neighbourhood itself. If you take that phenomenon to the next level, there's no end to the potential that other topics would offer.

How do you encourage students to search for topics that trigger socially relevant incentives?
By showing them examples. I often take examples from other cities in order

to show how something like that could work. Or sometimes we go for a walk through town to see what strikes us in particular.

How do you help people to approach the world with their eyes wide open? Do you give lessons in perception or something like that?
Not explicitly, as that is part of their basic tuition. However, that is a good question because it's about important incentives. For example, I would love to do something with the Bauhaus stage, which is an event space at the Bauhaus that was historically used for body awareness. How far can I reach? How are the proportions of body and space related to what we are designing right now? That is the basic essence of any design practice to prevent people from trying to perceive everything on a purely intellectual level.

What you're describing is dependent on a physical setting and helps us to get to know our body, to grasp something. Can that also be realised in the context of distance learning where we find ourselves suddenly separated by screens?
I certainly had reservations about that, but I was pleasantly surprised in the end. The students were much more focused and worked harder as well. Online, we were able to stick to topics and elaborate on them – that's something we don't have time for during the normal course of studies. That was cool, you know. But I'd probably go crazy if it went on and on.

Why?
Because I am not in direct contact with the students. In a physical setting, I can have a few words with anyone privately, if need be. When we're online, though, everyone's involved in everything, and even in breakout rooms everything is much more targeted and project-related. Communication that is not task-related doesn't take place online. Coincidences don't happen either. In my class, however, coincidences play a big role in paving the way for new things.

Is there any aspect of distance learning that is nevertheless worth adopting?
Maybe the Miro board. It creates a space in which everyone can work at the same time and it offers more surface area than a classroom wall.

In your view, which content could be provided online in order to give you more time for joint developments and discussions?
Well, definitely anything to do with software. We had a cooperation with LinkedIn Learning. That worked out quite well.

Some teachers use short videos to explain terms like 'corporate design' or 'branding'. Do you think that makes sense or would it be better to discuss them in class?

I think when explaining these terms you still need a flip chart beside you. I wouldn't feel comfortable with a video, as you never know if that explanation will still be appropriate the next semester, especially in our discipline with its constantly developing terms and buzzwords. Besides that, in my class, we work together on a brand development process – also based on examples and projects presented by students.

Should we educators initiate even more shared spaces?

Yes, definitely. That's also a part of an on-the-spot project we're doing. It's a real activity hub for everyone. One of our bachelor's degree students does joint kitchen projects with an international alumna, for example. One of my colleagues holds lectures or shows a film in the evenings that he puts up for discussion afterwards. It would be a real benefit, though, if that vertical network were permanent in order to unleash the amazing potential that we have here in our department, not only in seminars, but in our teaching activities as a whole.

If you could, what would you change in the teaching spaces at your department?

The greatest thing for students would be to have a project room for the entire duration of a project with their own workplaces, including a desk and their books, where they could perceive what's going on next to them. That would spawn a completely different kind of liveliness and they could spend more time there. It would also be super for them to use the workshops around the clock.

Would you prefer to teach block seminars only?

Yes, that would, without exception, be my preference. I love doing short intensive projects because it allows me to concentrate on just one topic at a time. After finishing one, you carry on with the next. You'd be much more flexible and have time for excursions, or could just spend a week in London, meet people there, do various interviews and come back like a saturated sponge. It would be a hugely different study programme.

Many thanks, Brigitte, for the interview.

Jianping He

taught Poster Art and Visual Language

Berlin University of the Arts, Germany
China Academy of Art in Hangzhou, China
Hong Kong Polytechnic University, China

Founder of Hesign design studio

During a very nice telephone call, Jianping He agrees to the
interview, which then takes place via email going back and forth.
Jianping He's answers are precise and he explains why design
cannot be taught, why he thinks that active self-learning is the
best learning method and the main reason for letting his students
sympathise with their work. — March 2022

Thies: You worked as an artistic staff member at Berlin University of the
Arts, taught at Hong Kong Polytechnic University and supervised students
in their master's and doctoral degree programmes at the China Academy
of Art in Hangzhou. What are the strengths of Chinese students during
their studies in comparison to German students?
He: At Chinese universities, you have set study periods and a regulated
curriculum. A bachelor's degree programme lasts four years, and a master's
three years. Due to their predetermined schedules, students are more goal-
oriented and work harder. During their studies, they remain in the same class
structures and can therefore learn consistent teamwork. This is facilitated
through smaller classes with no more than ten students and a larger number
of teaching staff.

   Furthermore, they learn competitive thinking from the very start, which
motivates them hugely. During the bachelor's degree programme, students
enjoy a wide range of courses covering various subjects without the supervision
of a selected member of staff, whereas in the master's degree programme,
they do have a designated supervisor.

Does competitive thinking in China also have any disadvantages?
I view competitive thinking critically only if it becomes more important than
independent thinking.

If you had the choice, what would you change in class in China that in your opinion works better in Germany?
I would prefer a more individualised education that would enable students to tailor their studies more freely around their own projects and interests.

Does that mean that teaching at Chinese universities is more like school teaching with very clear requirements?
Since Chinese design education evolved directly from handcrafted and decorative art, it has a clear focus on technical skills and practical training in techniques such as drawing and colour theory. Therefore, education structures modelled along similar lines to school teaching have also led to some teaching sessions consisting of pure practical training.

What are the strengths of German students during their studies?
They can organise their studies independently and pursue their personal interests. That, in turn, leads to increased personal initiative and motivation.

In a lecture, you once recounted that, as a student in Hangzhou in 1993, you were impressed by a guest lecture held by German graphic designer Uwe Loesch. What was it exactly that thrilled you?
Loesch's lecture opened my eyes: He understood typography as a visual language. That sparked my great personal interest and ultimately inspired me to go to Germany after my studies.

Did you impart that to your students as well?
Well, no. That's difficult. In my opinion, you can neither impart nor teach design. You can draw inspiration from many other aspects in life and the environment so that you don't necessarily require specific education. In the end, it was that conclusion that eventually persuaded me to quit teaching at university.

I was having doubts as to my own ability to spark enthusiasm for design in my students. There are limits to teaching in that respect, and ultimately, it's impossible to teach students that vital interest in, and passion for, design.

I find that very intriguing. The late American concept artist John Baldessari said something quite similar about art at universities, 'I don't think art can be taught'[50]. However, he nevertheless taught it. – Why is it not possible to teach design?
Designers or artists always convey knowledge through their own experience. That is not reproducible per se. Experiences can inspire, but they should never

be the sole teaching method, for if the focus on the educator is too strong, it inhibits the independent development of the students.

Concrete design knowledge such as design theory, design history and certain techniques and criteria can, of course, be taught.

Let me put the question from a different perspective: Why isn't it possible to *learn* design?
Design can be learnt, certainly, but only if it is connected with one's personal interest. In that case, inspiration and motivation can be drawn from art and design. Moreover, you have to start the process with a problem which is solved by the expertise you have acquired. The best learning method in design is active self-learning.

Can you give me a specific example of what you mean by 'active self-learning'?
German designers like Hans Hillmann, Uwe Loesch and Holger Matthies prove that a so-called graphic design education is not necessarily tied to a university institution. Gunter Rambow, who started as a glass painter, is also a good example of requiring a certain quantum of active self-learning. Hong Kong graphic designer and painter Kan Tai-Keung's life, but also Andy Warhol's and Alan Chan's careers just go to show how important it is to be passionate and willing to learn.

If design cannot be taught – which word would describe your teaching more suitably?
I wanted to let the students sympathise, to involve them on an emotional level.

With whom or what were the students supposed to sympathise?
'Sympathising' is a process that begins with an insight into my projects based on working examples. If you actively process what you've learnt independently, you will fundamentally develop more sympathy for the oeuvre as well as for your own work.

In that sense, sympathy also means that emotions and being connected must go hand in hand. Only by showing sympathy for an assignment or task can we develop a functional solution.

How did you practise that with the students?
I encouraged the students to formulate their own questions and problems and to discover their own topics. I also allowed them to get insights into areas that were not on the curriculum, for example, giving critique.

How did you give critique?
Critique was primarily given in discussion sessions and individual feedback sessions. When it comes to the development and selection of final project results, you not only have to take a critical stance, but also slip into the client's role, which raises the quality of the work.

Were the students allowed to criticise you as well?
Yes, of course. Principally, I was always ready for and open towards critique, because, in my view, the teacher's opinion never reflects a universally valid opinion.

Who decided when a piece of work was completed?
The students always made the final decision.

Can you explain your teaching method?
I used my own works as a basis for teaching in class. To inspire my students, I showed how ideas evolved and decisions were made, including the respective final products. However, I didn't adhere to any particular teaching method; instead I let the works speak for themselves.

What do you mean by letting the works speak for themselves?
Well, good design can speak for itself. Essentially, visual communication is an attractive and aesthetic representation of the content we want to convey. After all, a creative and inventive design will always arouse people's interest.

What did you intend your students to learn from you?
To listen. They were meant to learn to listen carefully, but never to lose sight of their own interests and to represent them assertively.

When should students listen carefully?
Especially when something unknown or unusual is being presented. You require courage to free yourself from your personal expectations and criteria – or from the rules you have set. You should always be ready to rewrite the rules and enrich your own knowledge and working methods by gaining novel insights.

Thank you very much, Mr He.

Michael Hohl
teaches Design Theory and supervises doctoral theses

Professor
Department of Design
Anhalt University of Applied Sciences, Dessau
Germany

*Michael Hohl welcomes me to his apartment. The room is
full of books, but also empty. He searches for precise words,
pausing for a while before he starts speaking again at top
speed. Although his declared aim is to inspire enthusiasm
for learning and to render himself obsolete as a teacher,
95% of what he has been teaching his students is laid
down in no curriculum.* — September 2021

**Thies: Could you describe in one sentence what students learn in your
'Design Theory' seminar?**
Hohl: I attempt to create enthusiasm for learning and acquiring knowledge
about design, including its theoretical and methodological concepts. We provide
our students with a firm methodical and theoretical foundation to enable
them to organise their own ideas, for example, to seek and interview experts
on their particular topic.

   Those interviewees could include, say, a gardener or a scientist from the
environmental authorities. Inevitably, drafts and solutions always require
sound argumentation and are critically scrutinised.

Is 'teaching' the appropriate word for what you do?
Actually, the educator's role is a trick; one is a kind of catalyser at best.
That's because nobody can learn for anyone else, you can only do that yourself. My aim, therefore, is to render myself obsolete. Students should take
the sole responsibility for their learning. And if it gets hard, I'm there
to support them. In my seminars, we are all learners and learn from
one another. Although I know a lot, I usually try to ask questions and get
to the bottom of whatever the topic is in our discussions, practice sessions
and experiments. Interestingly, the students often already know the answers
themselves. I would prefer to describe what I do as 'inspiring curiosity'.
Or as Ranulph Glanville liked to put it, as 'leading from behind'.

How do you inspire curiosity?

By posing questions, I suppose. It's important to let the students go and get on with their work and always be ready to discuss matters when they come boomeranging back to you – reflected practice. That way, many interesting issues arise such as, 'Well, design isn't what something looks like, but rather what it does to us.' Then I follow up on that with a text by Lucius Burckhardt – and suddenly, we're talking about theory. However, experience, attitude and argumentation will always come first. I take a hands-on approach.

Does theory require a practical approach?

Absolutely. There is no theory without practice. Film critics wouldn't exist without films. Which means that practice is the primordial model. Everything originates from that. And theory evolves from reflecting on the practice.

On the one hand, we have hard sciences such as chemistry and physics. People who can build aircraft. On the other hand, we have the humanities. Design lies somewhere between the two, but is something unique. We want to understand the world, how it works, with the intention of changing it in the future. All our methods are speculative and a means to an end. Donald Schön gave us researching designers the gift of 'reflective practice': for design is a research discipline per se. If I go to a workshop and make myself a stool, that's a kind of small research project. Albeit not an academic one. It could become research on the same level as established research, though, through systematic, methodical and critical reflection.

Design is powerful because it is visual – we don't reflect and substantiate solely by means of language or mathematical or chemical formulae. And design also evokes a connection to socio-political problems and theories. As early as the first semester, I attempt to convey to my students that even a teaspoon has a political dimension and we could discuss that throughout the whole semester and never come to an end.

Do we learn more quickly by actually doing things first?

Yes, I think so, because it leads to swifter outcomes than thinking things through time and again. One simple example: I take a look at a poster draft and consider whether the graphics would fit better on the left or right. It would be more efficient, though, if I shifted the graphics quickly to twenty different meaningful positions, printed the whole thing out and experienced it directly, and then carefully selected a few drafts that would provide a solid basis for the next step.

Instead of thinking things over for an hour, I obtain clear and plausible facts and decisions in just half the time. You have to learn when it's time to think and when it's time to act. And to pay attention to errors. Sometimes, it's exactly those errors, accidents and coincidences that can spark new ideas.

How can intrinsic motivation be encouraged, maybe even demanded?
Partly through the independent choice of topics to work on. Partly through
one's fascination for and interest in the topic. Later on, it happens through
the effectiveness which a solution might achieve in the world. Self-efficacy
and autonomy. That's why we find it meaningful to work on real-life problems:
at home, on the campus or in the city.

As a result, the individual projects are rarely comparable with each other,
that is why we spotlight the similarities and comparability of methods and
processes instead.

What do you expect from your students?
Openness, tolerance and friendliness. Active participation; to engage in
practical sessions by taking on tasks such as moderation or timekeeping;
to hand in their work punctually.

**That brings me to your approach of letting the students co-shape their
tuition, a concept which you developed together with Mathilde Scholz.
Could you tell me briefly what's so unique about your teaching method?**
I think what's special about our teaching method is that we take learners
seriously and treat them with respect and openness. We give them responsibility, certainly, but we also offer them a protective bubble where they don't
have to be afraid of making mistakes. Everybody makes mistakes. It's just
important to reflect and learn from them.

In that context, we show them that there are different ways to reflect.
For example, using your workbook, filling in the feedback questionnaire that
we hand out from time to time or by taking a walk with older students to get
feedback.

Do students also have a say in their grades?
Yes. We have a self-assessment scheme which invites the students to state
which grade they would award themselves and why. Their self-assessments
flow into the final grade, and they are often stricter than I am.

Do you let them award grades to each other?
Nope. [reflects] But that's a good idea.

We would like to try joint grading though. Students are asked to write down
anonymously how they would grade, say, a presentation, and their average
grade is worth as much as the teachers' average grade. It would be exciting
to trigger a discussion on that, too: 'How good was the presentation? Justify
and explain the grade you gave.'

Do you initiate cross-course projects in which you start, say, with design theory related to the topic, which is subsequently continued and expanded by a different teacher?
Unfortunately not. What we do have, though, are seminars to which I am invited by colleagues to provide initial input or give feedback at an interim presentation.

Do we as teachers support students in their personal development, too?
Yes, definitely. I always explain the following to my students, 'Look, folks, one of your former classmates is now studying law. In the course of the semester, you will notice that she's starting to speak and think differently. That means she isn't just studying law but she's becoming a lawyer. When she walks down the street, she sees the world through the eyes of a lawyer. And you are running around with a designer's head. Now what does that mean? What sort of perspective is that?'

For me, teaching at university is like an iceberg: the tiny tip of the iceberg represents the abilities and skills that you convey to students. However, what you really teach is the remaining 95%, which we rarely talk about; I am referring to cultural education and what it means to be a designer in Germany in 2021. That is an attitude, a mind-set, a certain way in which to view the world. They are soft skills that neither exams nor an accreditation commission could take into account, like how well a person works in a group or moderates group work, or how attentively and considerately people treat each other. And the socially relevant aspects of teaching are also part of this iceberg.

How can a teacher foster attitude?
You can only do that as a role model. You can't expect students to be punctual if you're not always punctual yourself. You have to set an example of integrity and authenticity. And if you don't do that, you are a hypocrite.

Students know us much better than we know ourselves and often they can look right through us.

What makes you think that?
Because I talk to them and some of them confide in me.

What do you think: is it an exaggeration to say that listening is key to *learning*?
Yes. Listening merely plays a minor role. You can only learn by doing things yourself. It's nothing you'd hear from anyone else. And if so, then it would be something of a reflection, a different perspective, because you ask the other

person beforehand how they see or feel something, for instance. Listening only works if the person who's learning is ready for it. Like in the previous example with Lucius Burckhardt.

To put it the other way round, then: Listening is key to *teaching*.
I tend to agree with you there. That is something teachers need to learn. I also think that observing should go hand in hand with listening. It doesn't suffice to just listen to students, you need to know them more or less well and see how they tick. Listening is vital as a teacher. But it's something that is easily forgotten because, after all, you possess the knowledge and want to impart it to them.

Listening is easier for me when I'm not standing in front of the group feeling stressed, but more in the background, for instance, moving from group to group. Then I feel sufficiently comfortable to put a few questions on the meta-level: 'Look, she said this and you replied that. What's been going on?' Being more relaxed also means listening more attentively. And I've still got a long way to go as far as listening is concerned.

Listening as you've just characterised it happens when you join a conversation passively. But does it sometimes make sense to ask questions actively in order to hear the answers?
By asking questions, you force people to think hard, and that way, they acquire knowledge by themselves. To ask good questions is what students learn from me. They learn that questions are more important than answers because questions will always help us to make further progress. Answers are like a wall you drive towards, a dead end. When I teach theory, I find that discussions and the pleasure of making conversation always emerge from questions that can lead to something new.

In discussions, do you sometimes assume the opponent's role despite it not being your conviction?
Yes, all the time. I think that is essential because it elicits different opinions and views. That's the reason why I frequently play the devil's advocate, asking 'What would you think if ...?'

After asking a question, how long do you wait before you break the silence?
Well, I am tenacious. I don't rush people and it's no problem if nobody says anything for a minute or two. It used to unsettle me, though. But now, the students know that I sometimes stop in the middle of a sentence and take my time to find the right word, as language is really key. Every word is significant. I would say that silence is relaxation for us because we've got used to it. It is our shared thinking.

Do you have any other ways of listening to students?
I like to visit a student space called 'Cloud'. It is a room at university acting as a platform for exchange and projects where students meet to discuss or teach mutually. Often, they strike up intriguing conversations and I sit in the background and listen for two hours without speaking a word. Which festivals are on, who does the washing-up and how they manage their personal budgets. They are so kind to one another. Respectful. Generous. Constructive. They never cease to surprise me positively. We can learn quite a lot from them, too.

Maybe we wouldn't always need to fetch external specialists if we simply spoke to the students.
Yes, they are a shining example. I always thought that as a teacher you could bring your students to the door but no further than that. However, in the course of their studies, they reach a stage in which they are suddenly able to teach me things. That's a really brilliant experience.

What I find grotesque about university education is that we old fogeys are preparing today's generation for tomorrow's world! It's a travesty!

Ideally, older people do stay young at heart anyway.
Yes, but only those who are prepared to learn how to change things and themselves and to remain open towards the students' questions and provocations. In that regard, I hope everyone's understood how essential feedback is – and I mean in both directions. Rule number one is to never justify yourself! Simply accept the feedback. It's all about listening with the aim of understanding. Should a practical exercise not produce the desired results, something needs to be changed. If something doesn't work out, I always ask my students what we could do to improve it.

Many thanks for all your interesting suggestions, Michael.

Gesche Joost
teaches Design Methods

Professor
Head of Design Research Lab
Berlin University of the Arts (UdK)
Germany

Design research, wearable computing and digitisation are
just three of countless areas in which Gesche Joost is active.
In an online interview on a sunny day shortly after lunch, she
talks about the responsibility that goes with her commitments,
the potential of online colloquia, and that it is sometimes good
to cook together. — October 2021

Thies: You call your colloquium at Berlin University of the Arts 'Design Methods'. What's in the name?
Joost: Within this specialist area, I focus on specific subjects; this semester I chose 'Responding to Crisis' as a headline. In my class, we look into the question of how we deal with climate change, geopolitical transformations, social inequalities and many other crises. To that end, we invited a number of international guests ranging from activists to politicians and designers to present their perspectives on those different crises, and to point out possible courses of action and interventions.

So, it's not 'design methods' in a narrow sense, but rather an approach to regarding the world from the perspective of designers and developing our own attitude as a basis for designing. The questions we ask ourselves are, 'What can we change in the world?' and 'What is our responsibility as designers?'

This is part of Design Research, then. What exactly does that research encompass?
Design research is an approach to analysing and encountering societal challenges through design and by using means of design. That frequently occurs in the form of participative design, which is a design process involving various different stakeholders right from the start. It is a process in which designing is understood as a research method, as 'research through design', thereby not only generating knowledge, but often also design artefacts, new processes or interventions which, in turn, change the research object itself, taking effect in society as well.

This also has an effect on one's own attitude to teaching as well as the attitude that students develop. How can we help students to develop an attitude?

Firstly, as educators, we need to be aware of our commitment to doing that and of having a huge responsibility in teaching young people to act responsibly as well – not just in the future but right now. To teach people to adopt a stance and hence take socio-political responsibility is profoundly humanist, which is a tradition I value enormously. How do we best prepare mature young people for their future life? And what can we offer to help them develop their own attitude?

Well, in order to provide solutions, one has to be informed and capable of weighing up world outlooks, and – this is an all-important dimension – make all of that experienceable: make it tangible! It's not just about theoretical concepts that we can interconnect; in our discipline it's a lot about digitisation and technology, which I need to be able to comprehend. In the literal sense of the word: a critical making.

I develop, for instance, an interactive installation in order to understand how a computer works. Or I create a simple algorithm in order to comprehend why and how algorithms make decisions. Once I have acquired my own attitude, I can invariably adjust it to changes in digital transformation and put it up for discussion later on.

As a rule, enthusiasm is prerequisite to developing personal values. Do you define the topics or focus yourself or does your class have absolute freedom of choice?

Well, I'm not keen on telling my students just to get on with their work without providing some sort of framework. Too many possibilities can be quite over-whelming in my opinion. That's the reason why I often propose a topic that is up-to-date and relevant and that intrigues me, too.

Last semester, for example, it was 'Outside the Bubble' coupled with the question as to how we could break out of our own filter bubble, and which other views existed outside the academic bubble, outside Berlin, outside Germany. To that end, we invited a speaker who explained to us why the social credit system is accepted in China, or which role South American tech activists play in digital transformation. Thanks to the virtual format, those international perspectives were well accessible.

As far as freedom of choice is concerned, within the given framework my students are at liberty to define their own questions and approaches in order to tackle the topic from a design-related perspective.

People can only develop values from their personal experience. However, do you intervene if you think someone's attitude does not comply with our western European values?
I could give you a concrete example of a student who was a COVID denier. Of course, in a liberal society, he is free to have his own opinion, but unfortunately, he sent it out via the institute's own distribution list, thus abusing the institution for his propaganda. That was a red line for me. In the end, he left university because, as he said himself, he no longer trusted any institutions at all, which is sad.

Normally though, I rely on my students to negotiate their own attitudes in discussions with other students, the guests we invite and with me. Their opinions can be contrary, such as in the case of a Chinese student who explained to us why he admired the Chinese coronavirus app, which monitors the number of infections on a house-by-house basis. In Chinese society, it seems, security is so valuable that it is worth more than individual freedom.

How many international students attend the colloquium?
Since we've been implementing anti-coronavirus measures, that is, since it's been online, there have been around 40 students in the colloquium. Before that, when it was held here in the building, we had about 15 students attending. Currently, we have participants from Norway, Estonia, South America and many other countries … and that's why I'm continuing the online colloquium.

Is the number of students limited in this virtual format?
No. I have opened the format to anyone interested in the topic – for example, to guest students wishing to participate only occasionally. The yardstick is the extent to which larger groups of participants are willing to engage and pluck up enough courage to play a part in the discussion. If that doesn't work though, I would broadcast the lecture and then invite those willing to take part in the discussion to a separate format.

Can 40 people really strike up a lively discussion?
Yes, certainly. When we began with the open colloquium, I was afraid that people wouldn't talk. But surprisingly, quite the opposite happened. It turned out that people experiencing social isolation during the pandemic were more willing to engage in especially pressing issues and, indeed, address personal questions in the colloquium.

Were the guests you invited mostly educators or professionals, or students from other regions as well?

A good blend, I would say. For instance, we invited a broadcast correspondent who had lived in Beijing for many years, teachers from Germany, but also student activists who had founded initiatives. My objective was always to invite people who could provide alternative viewpoints. In that respect, it's not just about theoretical discussion, but about taking the initiative and being active.

Is a shift in perspective a strategy you use to help students develop their attitude?

Yes. Before I get involved in the actual design process, it's vital for me to go outside and observe – to conduct sociological observational studies, as it were, or just wander around aimlessly, as proposed by the Situationists. To take the client's perspective is to think small. To think big, though, is to leave your own institution and to perceive other realities.

In 2013, for example, we ventured out with my entire Lab to the Berlin district of Neukölln and moved into an empty shop where we opened a Street Lab. The focus was on technology design; mobile technology for people from migrant communities. In the summer holidays, we did workshops together with children and young people from that predominantly Turkish neighbourhood. The website with required registration was not accessed at all. But once we hung up balloons outside the place, the shop was suddenly packed, not just on that occasion, but every day. We learnt a lot as a team, especially about communication behaviour. One good example of that is a 12-year-old Turkish boy who had to share his smartphone with his family. How awful at that age! So I think it's important to meet people on an equal footing in order to understand their needs. Our co-design process began with research and surveys and we went on to develop prototypes for mobile services, for instance, with different access rights.

Sounds interesting. What did it feel like to leave Neukölln, and do you still stay in touch in order to keep the research project going?

Well, the project was over much too soon, and so it didn't seem appropriate to just quit the scene. It had been a typical helicopter intervention: here today, gone tomorrow. We realised very quickly that this wasn't a sustainable form of commitment. We therefore founded so-called Neighborhood Labs as a co-operation with projects in other districts such as a senior citizens' computer club and a neighbourhood shop – always with the intention of offering inclusive technology design to the local community. That went on for quite a number of years and we still have frequent contact. After all, it's not just about troubleshooting, but about comprehensive process design.

Students with varying levels of knowledge, education and motivation are sure to experience this direct contact differently. Do you try to balance out those differences? And how do you encourage students who are rather shy and perhaps feel uncomfortable about approaching people from a community like that?

Again, my approach as a teacher is not to determine the direction. My aim is to build a community of practice. My Lab consists of around 35 staff members who are financed through funded projects. Then, there are the students who become part of that community as well. Only in exceptional cases would I approach a student if I thought he or she was in danger of losing touch or falling behind. But as a matter of fact, a lot happens in our community through mutual interaction, and every single person is welcome to bring in their own competences and learn something new themselves. Group dynamics generate knowledge transfer, too.

How do you foster group dynamics? Could you give me some specific examples?

By cooking, for instance. [laughs] I have just come from cooking. My Lab is centrally organised around a kitchen. Not only because I love food, but also because so many cultural codes are exchanged in the process of preparing meals, inspiring an alternative way of getting together. Everyone takes their turn to cook once and, in doing so, reveals a little more information about themselves, about where he or she comes from and which project they are currently working on. We also do off-sites, which means we relocate to the countryside for two days. On those occasions, I don't define the programme, only the framework, and the teams have to organise everything themselves – from shopping to their evening entertainment. Everything is done with a big sense of personal responsibility, collectively and on an equal footing. Both students and staff are highly motivated precisely because I am confident that they will accomplish all the given tasks.

How much say do your students have in shaping or conceptualising the course of their tuition?

As far as tuition is concerned, I give them a main subject and determine thematic highlights – including the relevant people – in order to establish different positions. However, I will also ask my students or staff members, 'Which people do you find fascinating? Who would you like to include?' With the help of many interactive formats, which can also involve Miro boards in virtual sessions, the students' ideas emerge very clearly, and I am happy to respond to them.

You co-initiated the non-profit project Calliope. This initiative has developed a unique micro-controller and provides teaching materials to pupils and teachers, enabling them to discover the digital world at primary school. In that context, you describe pupils as developing higher error and frustration tolerances through programming. In my opinion, schooling sometimes curbs a child's natural sense of curiosity which normally knows no bounds. On the contrary, a child seeks to explore those boundaries. Do you always allow your students to experiment freely without feeling compelled to achieve results?

We developed Calliope from this critical maker spirit prevailing at our Lab.

One trick is to let disorder prevail – right now I am sitting in our little open workshop where nobody needs to be afraid of breaking anything. The technologies we use are all open, that is, open source and unfinished. And exactly that is one of our approaches: I need to try things out for myself and see if they work. The open-source idea is based on the principle that I can exchange ideas with others on a global level. I search forums and join forces to practise identifying and resolving problems, which is real teamwork.

Importantly, the concept should be well thought out and prototypically representable. Whether built from paper or a 3D rendering or something quite different is up to my students. That way, I think you become aware of the intrinsic aesthetics of every stage in the process and how you move within them. There is no wrong or right here, but only collective process logic.

Do some students feel uncomfortable with this free approach and open encounter?

Yes, definitely.

Some students would prefer closer guidance and more teaching sessions. But I don't provide that kind of tuition. To be honest, I wouldn't want to be in my students' shoes these days – because it's suggested that they can do anything they like and just need to get on with it! I think that's too much to cope with and creates enormous pressure to deliver, which many feel or build up inside. In that case, I try to navigate them through that space of endless possibilities – always together with a community they can connect to.

Do students from different years learn together in your Lab community?

Exactly.

Many of my staff members working in my research projects are alumni who worked as substitute professors at other universities before joining my team; they can be regarded as seniors. But we also have student assistants on a temporary basis or first semester students popping in.

Which criteria do you use to select select teachers, assistants and members of staff?

That is primarily a subject-related question due to our focus on digitisation and digital society. Whether a person with his or her specifics is able and willing to get involved is one thing. The second thing is not to be afraid of technology. Nobody in my team works on a purely theoretical level. You don't have to be a professional programmer, but you should be willing to play your part. And thirdly, it's about attitude. To be keen on working together on a project is crucial. You have to be a very independent person and guided by self-motivation. You should also be aware of the privilege that we at Berlin University of the Arts have in that there is sufficient scope to realise a plethora of designs thanks to funded projects.

What do you do especially well as a teacher?

I think I'm quite good at motivating people. And creating platforms, communities of practice and structures which people easily connect up with. Painting the big picture, providing stimuli and running everything smoothly, basically.

What could you do better?

Minor details, micromanagement. And I'm impatient. I can't stand it when students or staff are not in the mood, or someone tries to fool me or talks rubbish. If I notice that someone is wasting my time, I get grumpy. Or if I miss lunch. So if someone tried to sell me something during my lunch break, I'd be livid. No, that would be a bad idea. [laughs]

Good job we arranged this interview for the afternoon, then [joins in laughing]. Do you deliberately deploy online formats to obtain more time and greater intensity in class?

From my experience, I would say that online formats are very time-efficient, very much to the point. The same goes for our regular weekly meetings with the whole team, which are also held online. That way, we come to appreciate the intensity and quality of physical presence coincidentally emerging from social interaction and informal exchange – fostered through our off-sites, our cooking activities or the physical dimension of prototyping together at university. Pure information exchange and short lectures, however, take place virtually.

Are these your personal impressions, feelings and appraisals? Or are they shared by all of your students?

The students at the Berlin University of the Arts suffered a lot from not being able to access the building for so long. They were craving in-person meetings – I realised that this was a psychosocial consequence of the coronavirus disease that I hadn't noticed online. Building an online community amongst students was very difficult. That is why we have arranged a two-day event with an external moderator in order to share our thoughts and to discuss things, because as a teacher, I do believe it is our duty to scrutinise the students' situation.

You started by mentioning that an online discussion among 40 participants can work well. Now you're saying that the intensity is better in a physical setting. Which differences in quality do you see exactly?
Targeted queries worked very well online, and so did the lectures, that is, everything taking place on the rational informational level. Physically however, I can create an atmosphere, a situation in the room that always has a sensual dimension to it. That could include having a glass of wine together in the evening, for instance, which often ends up with politicians we invited and other guests simply staying on – just like a good party amongst flat-sharers. That often leads us to other subjects, too, and those are the memories that linger most.

I'd like to talk about 'blended learning', a buzzword used for digitally outsourcing educational content, for example, as a video in which a teacher talks about design history. What do you think of that? Which content could be taught online using videos or other formats?
It strikes me that our traditional methods of knowledge acquisition are constantly rewritten or overwritten by students, which I find very positive. I also think it's good to offer shorter sessions on YouTube or as a podcast, teaching specific knowledge as you go along. However, this can only be seen as a complementary offer. Since my teaching does not consist of any concrete units or modules, I hardly ever do that. My approach is to take a holistic view to the subject, which is highly curated and time-dependent, that is, highly topical – for instance, in my colloquium on the filter bubble. In that sense, then, they are complementary approaches.

You said before that your discussions with students were on an equal footing. In my opinion, that should go without saying. Do you think 'teaching' is the right word for that?
That's a good point. In fact, I wouldn't call it teaching – because that would imply the existence of an asymmetrical power structure in which I were the one to convey my advanced knowledge. I try to mitigate this asymmetry. I create an experiential space, providing possibilities to connect and interact.

That is why I prefer to speak of research-based teaching and teaching-based research. What I am doing is more research-related than teaching. I don't mean research in a purely academic sense, but rather in terms of investigating and experimenting in order to gather experience. We always teach manual basics such as coding and prototype building as part of a subject, for example, in a course for machine learning and design.

In a Designing Gender project, you dealt with the question of how to include gender-related aspects in research and development. To what extent are you still involved in that question now?
Gender is a dimension of permanent concern that I always include in my teaching. In addition to the gender issue, though, I focus increasingly on diversity. This is one of my fundamental core values, mirroring my attitude as a whole. Due to Uta Brandes's influence on me as a student, I always point out different perspectives. It is an aspect that should never be neglected in teaching because, even today, people are still pigeonholed into certain roles, such as using pink razors – amazing that nothing's changed in that respect.

In the Calliope project, you say that the gender issue does not exist in children.
Yes, exactly. It is wrong to assume that girls say, 'Technology is only for boys' from early on, as that phenomenon only begins at the age of eleven or twelve. Therefore, teaching technological skills to both girls and boys should begin much sooner as a basis to strengthen their sense of self-efficacy.

How do you persuade your students to drop those stereotypes?
Actually, by persistently drawing their attention to the absurdity of it all. Not by wagging my finger, but by voicing my views. Whether it be on the sole presence of men on the podium or the total absence of female groups in bibliographies. Just one more way to impart your attitude to others.

Thank you very much for the interview, Ms Joost.

Katsuya Kato

teaches Design Basics and Media (Web Design, Coding)

Associate Professor
Faculty of Art and Design
Department of Graphic Design
Tama Art University, Tokyo
Japan

He enters the room smiling, bobbing slightly as he walks.
Katsuya Kato explains why experimenting is important and
that it is okay to fail in the process, and how students make
progress when they notice that there is always a next step ahead.
He also points out why it is essential to transform the invisible
into information. — December 2019

Thies: Can you give me an idea of how you teach?
Kato: One good example of my teaching is the Coding course, which is very
practice-oriented. We only have five weeks' time, but it is just about enough
for all of us to get to know each other a bit. During that time, fairly concrete
tasks have to be carried out, for example, an error-spotting game.

And that works in five weeks?
Well yes, it does. [laughs]

Why did you become a teacher?
Actually, because my teacher asked me to. However, I have always been aware
of the fact that education plays a major role in our society. I absolutely believe
in what they say that there would be no society without education. And in
the process, education enables students to surpass themselves.

What, in your opinion, is the objective of design?
That's quite a difficult question to answer. From the viewpoint of the educator,
design should not only be about earning money, but rather about optimising
human life and human development as well. In my opinion, we should pay
far more attention to issues such as the increasing quantity of media and the
possibilities of living more comfortably and getting information more smoothly.
Unfortunately, design in Japan is often regarded superficially and merely as
a useful means to sell products.

When you refer to information, which information do you mean?
Well, starting with the so-called news, of course, information could also include exhibition announcements or advance warnings and reports relating to a catastrophe. However, there is much more information out there that people are not familiar with and that has not yet been visualised. I think it is crucial to transform this invisible data into generally accessible information.

Which teaching method do you prefer and could you briefly describe it?
Just as you mentioned yesterday in your lecture[51], we should endeavour to let students gather experience and widen their knowledge. In that sense, it is important not to instruct, but to allow students to go into depth independently. I think part of my method is to wait and give them time, not to tell them too much and not to present answers.

Do you ever lose your patience while you wait?
Of course, there are times when I do find it hard to wait. But I try to be patient – most of the time! [laughs]

Can you give me an example of when you do say something?
In some cases, the person involved does not quite understand what they are actually doing, and even if the result is good, it often does not lead to the next step. They do something merely because they were told to, and not because they found out the answer by themselves. By contrast, students who find answers on their own are far better equipped to develop their own ideas further. 'It's okay to fail', I often say, 'simply try out whatever comes to your mind. Take the first step.'

How do you create an atmosphere that allows people to make mistakes?
I attempt to convey that it's fun to try out new things and that there is no use in doing the same things all the time. If we repeat things time and again, we become less motivated, or at best, remain the same. I think there is a common consensus that the purpose of design – or of art – is to let people experience things that they have never done before. I would not want to lose this explor-atory spirit. I see design as an experimental space where we try to do those things that society cannot achieve.

I would not want to see students imitating society or a certain product in their four years at university. I would prefer them to work on completely new ideas, even if the quality may be inferior.

What do you mean by 'inferior quality'?
As a university, we have high standards. However, even if work sometimes does not conform to them, I still consider the work to be good if the concept

and degree of challenge behind it are exceptional. This is based on what you said in the context of Otl Aicher yesterday: that the content counts.

How does that 'inferior quality' come about?
In higher courses such as a master's programme, it's possible to focus and concentrate on individual works. In the first year, however, the course is about fundamental principles and experimenting. There's not much time for anything else. Basically, I can say that students who are prepared to work harder will always excel.

How do you motivate your students to excel?
I think it depends on one's personality. But I also believe that we can make people grow through challenges in their development process. Students who never experience that process simply collect marks and only do things that resemble reference works at art universities. And I think they lead their lives in society in the same way later on, too.

What skills do you want to teach your students?
I don't want them to assume a formal way of thinking, to have preconceptions. I want them to learn to think freely and to question everything, because that is essential to the process of design. Taking a phone as an example, they should ask themselves whether it really needed to be hand-held or not. Nothing new could ever evolve if those questions weren't asked.

Do you choose certain topics to encourage students to think freely?
I don't think that it depends on a certain topic, but rather that any topic could offer similar possibilities. For example, students should be able to do more than just reproduce a text when they hear or read it; they should be able to 'read between the lines'. You have to practise that on a daily basis in order to see other dimensions as well.

How do you bring that home to your students?
I tell them so, expressly and repeatedly, and I always question things. I hate it when students ask, 'Can I do this?' Designing also means defining your own rules. Of course, there are requirements to be observed, for example, to use the right size whenever specified. But within those prescribed boundaries you can do what you want. That is why I very often tell them that they need to be able to make their own decisions.

What do you say to that person asking whether they can do something specific?
I say, 'If that's what you want to do, why don't you do it?'

Even if you don't think it's good?
Yes, even then.

Still, are there times when you need to intervene?
I respect a person's decision to visualise a concept in his or her own way.
The most important thing is to be sure of yourself. However, if that person
keeps on creating illustrations in the same way, I will ask, 'Is that really your
idea of illustration? What about photography or graphics as an alternative
form of expression?' That kind of one-sidedness in a person of about 20
would otherwise lead to a loss of variety in expression.

What if the student doesn't try anything new?
I never use force, but rather point out other possibilities. To put it pictorially,
as if one were to show photos and ask, 'If you were the objective lens and not
the creator, which would you choose?'

From whom did you learn how to teach?
I come from a family of educators: my grandfather was head of a primary
school and my mother was a primary school teacher. As a student, I taught
at an infant school and an art school. I don't think anyone taught me how
to teach, but my background could have had some influence on me.

Do you remember anything specific?
I had lots of bad role models: In Japanese primary schools, you are always
told how to do things.

Were your parents like that, too?
They were very understanding when it came to art books and such like, and
compared to others, they weren't strict. I try to give my students the feeling
that they are not under pressure to do certain things.

Were you forced into anything during your schooldays?
Yes, I was. For instance, the order to 'go to that high school'. What saved me
from that was ultimately my father who said, 'Simply do whatever you want
to', so I thought, 'Oh, perhaps he's a good person after all!' [smiles] And perhaps
I was only able to really appreciate my freedom of choice because I had been
forced into this or that before.

Do we need restrictions in order to appreciate freedom?
That's difficult to say – but perhaps it's exactly that. I'm not sure. I often quote
that myself. Freedom written in Chinese characters means 'to define the reason
oneself'. It's about how to lay down rules, not about having no rules at all.

In our profession, it is important to communicate. How do you foster that in your students?
In our department, there's a lot of individual work to do, so we don't have much opportunity to discuss the works. Despite that, we try to offer our students that sort of option; sometimes only small things like tidying up the tables together or preparing for an evaluation session.

Do you organise sessions for mutual criticism?
Yes, in small groups they can speak their mind without having to raise their hand.

How do you help your students express themselves precisely and present their work understandably?
Students have different personalities – some are shy, while others are very talkative. Since there are things that exist before we speak, I would say that students who do not like to speak should be capable of expressing a lot during their presentation without having to speak too much…

… to show more than to speak, then?
Yes, one leaves it to the work to express what the artist is not able to say.

Does their ability to speak improve the more often they do a presentation?
Yes. That's why I let them do presentations from the first class on. In that way, they learn to use formal language and finally realise how important that is, even if they had initially thought, 'Why must I show people my work at all?'

Are marks important?
They are probably not so important for the students themselves, but I think they're important for the university system. [laughs] An assessment will take place when a person goes out into society at the latest – if it is important for that person.

As an educator, what do you do especially well?
I'm not sure whether I'm particularly good at it, but I do try to communicate with my students as often as possible – after all, I am younger than the other teachers here. [smiles]

What do you mean by 'as often as possible'?
Well, for example, I greet them when I meet them in the corridor. Or I eat a meal with them in the canteen.

In that way intensifying relations with them …
… Yes, I also ask them what they've been doing, and how they are.

What would you expect even younger professors to do particularly well when they begin?
I don't have any overall expectations, as I think it's better to stick to your own style of teaching. I would want to stay true to myself – just as I'd never tell students to do things in a particular way.

What was the worst mistake you made?
I've made a lot of mistakes. The biggest of all was – when my students did exactly what I told them to. That was a real blow.

What would you wish for your students?
To be successful, to go their own way and find what they've been looking for.

For example?
I think it would be a pity to accept a job that one doesn't like. Ideally, they should have a job that brings happiness and independence, and not just work to earn a living. To put it more drastically, I want them to enjoy their lives no matter what profession they choose. It does not necessarily have to be design-related.

That brings me to my last question: What is creativity?
Hard to define – I think one could say that creativity is to build the future that lies before us. Although many designers work with high-tech, normal folks have no access to those things. I think the task of designers is to bridge that gap and make it more understandable for normal people – in order to visualise things, make them visible.

Many thanks, Mr Kato.

Ruth Mateus-Berr

teaches Didactics

Professor
Institute of Art Sciences and Art Education
Center for Didactics of Art and Interdisciplinary Education
University of Applied Arts Vienna
Austria

A room in a university building with a colossal atrium.
Ruth Mateus-Berr offers tea, takes a seat on the colourful
sofa and starts to talk at once: about peer reviews and
didactics, about students who have a say in teaching
formats and about aggression. And she reveals why she
once told a student that she missed him. — May 2022

Thies: Were there any role models who shaped your teaching?
Mateus-Berr: Yes, the industrial designer Ernst Beranek. He was also the one who brought me to the University of Applied Arts Vienna. He very often worked in an interdisciplinary manner and developed, for example, drop objects with pheromones for malaria control or dummies for babies. He was a strong leader who always made his team feel appreciated.

After exciting years of developing my own methods, I then took over subject didactics. The methodology uses pedagogical and didactic topics to connect art with science and transfers this to other spaces – such as schools or extracurricular spaces, museums or social space. I could also have imagined the department being called Design Thinking. In 2013, this method was still something of a rarity in Austria.

How do you manage your team?
Training in positive leadership taught me how to lead while treating team members as equals. You have to communicate clearly and give freedom at the same time.

For example, I involved my then administrative assistant in all kinds of decisions – even when it came to which picture we should hang up in the office. And when there are tasks to be divided up, I always ask who would like to take charge. When it comes to applications, whatever the position, I always take care to involve all colleagues, because they will have to work together.

All the applicants who were not chosen get a personal letter of rejection with at least some brief feedback – that's also part of showing respect.

And I also find a family-friendly approach important. This means that we sometimes do a great deal of rearranging in our team to make sure that women can be given 20-hour positions when they start a family, so that they have the freedom and security they need. We also make sure that mothers can benefit from flexible hours.

I would describe my management style as extremely transparent. I talk about everything and question everything self-critically.

How do you deal with mistakes made by staff members?
When you work a lot, mistakes happen and you have to have the feeling that your superior is behind you. This is something my team can rely on. It's okay to make mistakes and the priority doesn't have to be asserting yourself. Much as Nigel Cross said, there are many solutions and I only progress from novice to expert by making lots of mistakes.

Let's talk about teaching: are there courses where students have a lot of say in the content and approach?
Yes, that was the idea behind the new course format 'Bits and Bites', which we developed together as a team. There, students and tutors can suggest topics, people and formats for classes.

How do you give students feedback?
You only come up with great solutions through lots of discussion, so I always include a critique phase which is actually a re-brainstorming. The phrase 'It won't work' is not allowed at this stage either. Here I want to talk about things that are visible. To highlight this I often do a short exercise with the students. I say, 'Think of a tree and draw it.' We then talk about the trees we thought about and realise that they were all different, which is why a drawing or model of our design ideas is essential to be able to discuss them concretely. I often give written feedback too, for example, on seminar papers. I write down what I find fascinating and what I have learnt myself. But I also write down what does not work at all or encourage them to read more literature on the subject. I often then ask if they already want a grade or want to improve it.

Do you sometimes deliberately provoke mistakes so that everyone learns from them?
I don't think my personality would let me do that. The only thing I use is the Stanford classic: 'Develop the ideal', and I then discuss it with the students to reach the following conclusion from the perspective of constructivist didactics: 'There is no such thing as the ideal. There is only that which you

personally perceive as ideal.' I use this because I want to show what constructivism is and means.

How do you help students when they are despairing about a project?
My interaction with them is like a design brief. They give me a commission and I try to understand what they want. If they despair, they have not explained their commission well enough. Then I try to think out loud with them about what comes to mind, which ideally inspires them or boosts their self-confidence. My job is that of a dramaturge.

How do you encourage students to make careful use of language when they, for example, come into contact with another culture or political opinion? Do you say, 'Watch out for your language that shapes your thoughts', or the other way around, 'Watch out for your thoughts that shape your language'?
That's similar to what Marcus Aurelius said. [laughs]
   On the one hand, I am authentic. On the other hand, I have learnt that aggression against a person or against a person's opinion always has a lot to do with oneself. I then tell students, 'Picture this person who you find incredibly annoying. And then think about who's really behind it.' It's a magical moment when you work out the true reason. My example is always my own art therapy training, during which a woman constantly put me down in front of everyone. On the last day, she yelled at me – and I act this out loudly to the students – 'You get on my nerves so much because you're like my sister. She's so passionate about her job too!'
   That's why I speak a lot about non-violent communication according to Marshall Rosenberg and how to deal with conflicts, especially with the new students. That comes from a very different context, but it's fun for everyone and also helps with situations outside of university.

Many design teachers are self-taught. Should they learn didactics and pedagogy before they teach?
Internationally, every university professor has to prove in the recruiting process that they have done at least a year of university didactics. This isn't the case in Austria, which I find problematic because many don't reflect on how they teach and therefore sometimes break hearts. Throwing an architecture model out of a window doesn't help very sensitive students.

Is there any literature that you should read before you start teaching?
The book that had the biggest effect on me is small and thin, and is a quick read: *Designerly Ways of Knowing* by Nigel Cross. It was this book that made

me realise that design is actually a life philosophy, that design often also involves personal contexts, which is important for the process. Another book that I've read several times is *Opera aperta* by Umberto Eco. It's good to keep looking at literature outside of your own field.

How can we make sure that teachers in the design field receive pedagogical training?

By introducing a form of university didactics, through which one gets to know different methods, to analyse them and to reflect again and again. It's about experiencing and learning through reflection, like Donald Schön's much quoted book *The Reflective Practitioner* says. This means that further training that repeats things I already know is also valuable because I can discover new aspects. You can never do too much further training. The point is that unconscious knowledge is made explicit.

To look at the other side: are there advantages to being self-taught?

Yes, of course. Self-taught teachers have a relaxed approach and think less about requirements than others; they don't have the limiting thought 'That won't work because ...'

Is self-reflection central to becoming a better teacher?

I would say definitely, yes. Often a critical friends group helps, whether this is in private at home or with colleagues who I reflect with.

How can the quality of teaching be improved?

Through peer reviews. That's why I brought the first conference to the University of Applied Arts Vienna where peer reviewers gave feedback. And some of the contributions were then published as a peer-reviewed book. This meant that the content was subjected to a double quality control.

You have also taught in schools. What did you do to get to know the children and to together find topics to work on with them?

To get to know them, I often stayed in the classroom during breaks. That's how I learnt what 13-year-olds are interested in. To find topics, I started in the classic way by asking them what they wanted to do. Once this resulted in AIDS posters, which were even exhibited in the town hall. Others wanted to learn how to organise a fashion show. I helped with contacts to the Vienna Schauspielhaus and a model agency I know, and in this case I, for example, worked on cultural management with them.

What are the differences between teaching school children and teaching students?

In school finding topics was often quite complicated because there were too many pupils and it often took two whole double lessons before we got started. That's why I sometimes worked with what was in front of me – for example, when children had a conflict and also wanted to decorate their classroom. We took the conflict as our topic and created a huge comic strip that reflected the mood of the class. Another example is a project I did in cooperation with Caritas and the Wiener Festwochen: 'Dance the Tolerance' with Royston Maldoom. One of the boys was a bit more solidly built and had a difficult background. Right at the beginning he said, 'No, I'm not cut out for exercise. I don't want to do that', and as a result skipped school and the rehearsals at the theatre. I then asked Royston Maldoom what I should do. He was supporting us and, as a choreographer, had experience organising street theatre in challenging settings. He answered, 'Tell him you miss him.' From that day on, the boy joined in, performed – and later became head boy.

One difference with students is that groups are smaller at university. And whether they are school children or students, I often have them work in groups and come and sit with them; I do this with interdisciplinary projects with other faculties too. This means I can listen in.

However, the students are often not comfortable with this. With the school children, I always sit at eye level with them at the table and talk about personal topics as well. This creates a very different type of relationship. University isn't like this.

Why is that different at university?

It does happen, but much less often. Students open up to me too and I'm able to support them in all kinds of situations, but I don't go 'drinking beer' with them like others do. I make sure that I keep to my role, responsibility and authority as a teacher.

An abstract thesis: listening is the most important thing in teaching.

I believe that we teachers enjoy talking too much [laughs] and I'm convinced that listening is the most important thing. I learnt a lot about this in the schools. You learn how to listen, for example, in non-violent communication. That's where you practise just listening for 15 minutes.

These are things that we have totally forgotten. Yesterday, I asked a student to formulate a problem. He chose, 'On Sunday, the supermarket was closed.'

A student who was supposed to solve the problem said, 'Why don't you go shopping on Saturday?' [laughs] She didn't even ask how he was! And then it was great how the whole group of students reflected on it. We just don't listen at all. We don't ask any questions. This is also incredibly important in the design critique phase: how can I ask a question that will help someone else make progress and express that in nuanced language? You should be empathetic to every person who you are entrusted to teach.

Thank you very much, Ruth.

Kei Matsushita

teaches Visual Communication

Professor
Faculty of Fine Arts, Design
Tokyo University of the Arts (TUA)
Japan

Founder of Kei Matsushita Design Room

*Kei Matsushita always appears to be on the go. Both physically
and in his thoughts. He also expects the latter from his students.
He talks about personal responsibility, the value of money
and why his students like discussing the whole night through.
The sound of his hearty laughter often fills the room.*
— December 2019

Thies: Why did you become a teacher?
Matsushita: Because you can look for the ideal design.

What is the ideal?
Starting with the current directions in design you can try to find out what
design in its pure form should be like.

**Is it necessary to become a teacher to do that or could you have done
this as a designer as well?**
It is easier to experiment if you don't have any concrete commissions.

Can you give an example?
We organised an exhibition with the students about the world-famous
photographer Robert Frank, who died this year, and the German publisher
Gerhard Steidl. The students did everything, from the planning to the
budgeting, to the presentation and design of the exhibition location, even
the publicity work. They also planned workshops and lectures held by
Mr Steidl during the exhibition.

Designers should be able to pursue their own ideas and not only when
they have a commission. We let the students do everything themselves;
the key terms here are initiative and bottom-up. This is typical for Tokyo
University of the Arts.

So they should think independently?
Exactly.

Did they have to look for sponsors as well?
Yes. I gave them advice and showed them past examples. Then they had
to go to companies and explain why the exhibition is important for Japan,
get their support and acquire funding. I did go with them to the companies,
but I made sure to stay in the background.
　　When the students can explain the social value of what they are doing
to the people providing funding that's a sign that they will be designers
in the future.

Who did the students get funding from?
From companies – camera manufacturers and cosmetics companies such as
Shiseido, which donate a great deal of money to cultural projects.

How detailed is the students' planning of the budget?
They create a cost estimate and calculate themselves how much they need
for which purpose: production costs, publicity costs, catering costs for staff,
costs for parties, operating costs, everything.

**And what is the decision-making process like when, for example, one
student wants to use the money for a party, but another student would
rather organise a workshop?**
A leader is chosen who is allowed to make the decision. There are various
teams, for example, for publicity work or for the design of the exhibition's
location, and every team has a leader.

And the leaders discuss the topic with their groups?
Of course. And they then have to discuss it with me.

Are you always present during the discussions?
Not during all of them; I just listen to the reports. This already puts the leaders
under enormous pressure.

That means the students learn how to motivate themselves and to discuss?
Yes, throughout the whole process. They also sometimes spend the night away
from the university, rent accommodation and have a work session because
they want to spend the whole night discussing. In that case, I watch over Skype.

Do you sometimes get actively involved to get a discussion going?
I leave that to the students. I only give them the task of reporting back to me with the result.

How do you then give feedback?
I'm not usually able to give the okay. 'It's not perfect; you need to improve this part' is something I say a lot. Or that it doesn't reflect the concept. Or that it's only decorative.

Do you also show possible solutions?
Yes. I say what can be expressed in words, but ultimately I often draw it – I follow the principle of 'say it, hear it, do it, show it'. But a feature of working with students is that when you show them a possible solution, they are bound to do something different.

Does it prompt the students to think more when you or they draw the possible solution rather than describing it?
Yes, I think so. Design work doesn't just happen in the brain – it is also physical work. In that way it's a bit like sport.

Is there a type of 'logic' that designers understand without needing to put it into words?
Logic – thinking logically – is a big topic at the moment. But my approach is the very opposite.

What would you describe as the opposite of logic?
Thinking with the senses. Going your own way. Thinking for yourself. Doing marketing without looking at numbers. The students can do that later – train their thought processes to work with logic and numbers.

Would you call it creativity?
Yes, exactly – using the senses, thinking independently. Globally, this puts me in the minority in today's design world. Most universities promote logical thinking.

Why do you pursue your route?
When society uses logic it becomes homogenous; everything becomes the same. For example, company A and company B put a lot of effort into developing something new, but it results in the same product at the end of the day. I think the only right way is for individuals to bring ideas to the companies.

For example, I go to companies and tell them that more importance needs to be placed on individuality and personal orientation.

How do you support students in thinking for themselves, in approaching others with their ideas?
With what we refer to as the 'first sketch'. There are two main aspects: the first sketch itself and its refinement. The purpose of the first sketch is to decide what you want to do. If you don't know that you will have difficulty drawing it. That's why I train doing first sketches with them.

What is this first sketch exactly?
There is a topic of course. Doing a sketch is then a first small realisation. It's taking an idea from your brain to the outside. It makes an argument or expresses criticism. At this point we're still in the phase where there is no concept yet. I draw *to create* a concept.

Let me give an example: a large Japanese cigarette manufacturer wanted to renovate its laboratory and asked me for advice. There were lots of bottles standing next to each other in the laboratory. We took that as the starting point and drew some initial sketches. [Shows abstract sketches illustrating combinations of lab rooms and bottles.] You can't really implement this but it's important to have drawn it.

How do these sketches develop?
The students just start sketching, but we also collect ideas and suggestions from people outside the class like employees and external parties. We discuss the topic. And then all the topics and ideas that emerged in the course of these discussions are translated into sketches. There are then lots and lots of sketches.

And who makes the choice?
The group chooses. They have to do a presentation and tell me what they discussed. After that, the ideas that aren't needed anymore are ruled out.

Why are these first sketches so important?
Students tend to create copies of their own work, to not develop further. Their newer work is similar to their earlier work. I then explain to them that they need to learn the skill of sketching. Otherwise they are, for example, very good on the computer, but they don't do anything but call up 'past data'.

How do you counteract this tendency to focus on past work and not move forwards?
I can't expect this of bachelor students, but master's students definitely need to create many sketches, several hundreds of them. Collages, nature studies … other things too.

Can hands do something better than the head?
Head and hands are both used at the same time.

Is it always head and hand or would other modes of expression be okay as well? Can I discuss these first thoughts, for example, or express them through dance?
That would also be an option...

So, the main thing is it's not just in the head?
Yes, anything goes; legs are important as well, but hands are the most important. Because hands offer the most options, and finding fundamental and new things is easiest that way. If you're drawing with a pencil, you draw lines that you hadn't imagined before and, in the process, you can make different mistakes. In contrast, on the computer an overwhelming number of variations is possible. It's also better to use your legs, to go to something and look at it instead of researching online. You can get more information that way. This is what I encourage the students to do. For example, they go to rural areas and research in situ how you can bring the places to life again.

Do you encourage students to critique one another on these excursions and in class?
Yes, I do encourage it. But the Japanese aren't very good at this.

Why not?
It is the mentality. For example, I have visited universities in England. Debates are fundamental there. The courses were very good and when you clashed with someone you drank coffee together afterwards and got along again. You couldn't do it like that in Japan. There is a famous Japanese saying 'reading between the lines' [in Japanese 空気を読む – 'reading the air']. You don't express something in words, but you read the air. Important things are decided that way.

Is it possible to read the air?
Of course. That's what I do most of the time. It has advantages but also disadvantages. However, if you want to work internationally you have to learn to criticise as well.

Are students allowed to contradict you?
Definitely. When it comes to design I have an advantage because they are all very young. But outside of this area I make sure not to take the lead and that my presence doesn't make itself felt too strongly. So you won't see me in the canteen much – I don't want the students to get nervous. [laughs]

What do you tell the students on their first day?
I tell them clearly that we will be using our hands.

And what about on the last day?
'Don't rush! Take things slowly.'

Does taking things slowly also apply to design?
Yes, I think so. It takes time to understand design properly – you need until you're 30, 40. I tell them that they should continue with design at least until this age. That's the difference to sport.

Having this patience is the big picture. Does it also apply on a small scale, to one individual project?
Yes, I tell them clearly that they shouldn't expect to find a solution for their project straight away. You first need to plant the seeds.

What do you want to enable your students to do by the end of their degree?
To be able to think independently. I want them to understand for themselves what is needed. In general, they all have too passive a relationship to their environment at the moment.

Will the students become specialists or generalists in their working lives?
Both. I don't want them to start as designers in a company, but as managers, on the board, as presidents. As generalists, as people who lead the organisation. There have been a few examples of this recently, but I want this to be much more common. Specialists are important as well. The interesting thing is that both study together.

Let's talk about you: what are you particularly good at as a teacher? It's hard to say that yourself. [laughs]
I can only say that in terms of the university – design is returning to art. Companies need the artistic approach. As a university we try to sell this way of thinking as a package. This is what I'm working on. American universities like Stanford, Harvard or MIT do it already.

Do you believe design thinking, as shaped by Stanford and IDEO, is part of this?
We offer two-week-long courses on design thinking, but we don't see bringing artistic and independent thinking to companies as part of our approach.

What do you call your method?
I call it 'proximity to art'. At Tokyo University of the Arts, we don't differentiate
so strongly between design and art. I think this sets us apart, even though
many others take a similar approach. There are many paths to design: logic,
engineering ... What makes us unique is that we use sensuality, the senses.

What does this sensuality create?
Something new and essential.

What is this essential aspect?
The ideal state. How something should actually be. A lot of what we take
for granted in our world doesn't reflect this ideal. And so we need to be able
to imagine something that doesn't yet exist but that should exist.

What has been your biggest mistake so far in class?
There have been a lot. For example, when I've given someone advice that
I thought was good but that made them worry unnecessarily.

Which you also admitted to later?
Of course. For example, a student's work and its dimensions became smaller
and smaller. And I said, 'Make them bigger, freer.' I didn't mean physical
size, but to consider lots of different options. They should make the most
of all these options out there. But some become smaller and smaller without
even noticing it.

Who shaped your teaching style?
Teachers who taught me. And my own experience as a teacher – I've been
teaching here for 15 years now. A lot of what I say isn't understood. I have
to look carefully at the times we live in and the students and keep adjusting
my words.

Thank you, Kei, for your intriguing insights.

Johanna Pirker

teaches Game Design, Game Development and Social Media Technologies

Assistant Professor
Institute of Interactive Systems and Data Science
Graz University of Technology
Austria

Johanna Pirker wants to know what the questions are for before she answers them. This sunny December day, she explains why she sometimes plays games with her students, why they learn more in distance learning chats than she could teach them by herself and what she brought to Graz from the MIT in Massachusetts. — December 2021

Thies: How would you classify the subjects you teach?
Pirker: We are a faculty of computer science. That means my subjects 'Game Design and Game Development' belong to the field of computer science and 'Social Media Technologies' to computer science and mathematics.

As a name, does game design always imply creating something?
All my students have at least a bachelor's degree in computer science or software development and therefore they have quite a strong technical focus. With 'Game Design', however, I endeavour to introduce them to a subject that is very interdisciplinary and hardly manageable on one's own. Because, in order to develop a game, you need programmers, artists, composers, and for games like 'Assassin's Creed' even historians – people coming from various different areas.

I try to provide the students with an overview to help them understand principles like which mechanisms there are and which possibilities we have to interact. So, I suppose you could also count it as belonging to the area of interaction design.

Is this interdisciplinary action a part of your teaching?
Yes and no.

Due to the fact that we're a university of technology, our courses focus on game engineering and programming. After finishing their studies, the students will therefore not be game artists. Nevertheless, we try to teach them the basics, for example, 3D modelling and using 2D as a means of expression.

In that context, we cannot really offer an interdisciplinary working environment. But we do motivate students to take part in hackathons, which are events in which students develop a game within 48 hours together with different people from other disciplines.

Besides that, we do a lot of group work to enable the students to achieve their goals together. Ever since the coronavirus has been around, we also encourage groups to exchange feedback.

Do you make specific suggestions when it comes to group work?
Since I mostly have more advanced students, they can usually manage that very well themselves. However, I do show them communication tools that we use for game development ourselves. For example, we use Discord for the whole course and we set up a voice channel or a text channel for every group in advance.

Do you moderate that? Or do you let the groups work on their own?
The groups work autonomously. And luckily, in courses with 140 students I have tutors who support me. We have regular meetings to check whether a group is working well and is on the right track.

Are they always face-to-face meetings?
Right now, we're trying to do everything online, but we also offer hybrid events in order to enable our numerous international students to join in.

How do you evaluate the groups when, especially nowadays, they work independently and entirely detached from one another in different places? Do you solely assess the final product?
When evaluating group work, I not only take the group's final product but also their intermediate submissions into consideration. In addition, the students have to hand in individual assignments so that I can assess them individually according to their different levels of knowledge and talents. We also check with the groups regularly whether all group members are contributing equally. That is one of my main concerns, because after all, they are in the final stages of their studies and inability to work in a team in professional life would definitely not be tolerated.

You have courses with varying numbers of participants. In which setting do students learn the most? When they're together with 139 or only nine other people in the course?
That depends entirely on the model, so there is no general answer to that question. I know lecturers in America who teach a thousand people at the same time and do a good job. It has a lot to do with imparting theory and somebody

being at the front and presenting. Research has revealed that this can also be hugely important and successful. I think both are good for the students.

Conversely, would one-to-one teaching really work perfectly? If I were to teach just *one* individual at a time, that person would imbibe nothing other than a copy of what was in my mind. Probably even less. What I try to do during my online course with 140 people is to keep them writing to one another all the time. That may sound completely whacky. But it works extremely well.

Can you give me a concrete example of that?
Well, I use a streaming platform called Twitch, which is actually designed for gamers who play games while other people watch them. These viewers can chat with each other in the process. I have already had some experience with Twitch in my research and in private too. That's why I knew how to use the medium and was able to hold all my lectures on Twitch. At the same time, I tried to utilise the benefits of the platform; it features a small window where you can see my slides and a little image of me, similar to WebEx or Zoom, but with no focus on the presentation. Next to that is the chat that users, including those holding anonymous accounts, can log in to and write their messages in. So I rarely know who it is. It's a permanent stream in which the topics change constantly. Private chats are hardly used.

While watching gamers on Twitch, you write to other people all the time. In my class, I encouraged my students to do that as well in order to get them interactively connected. I regularly asked questions such as 'Who thinks that it's like that now?', motivating them to post their answers in the chat. And that's perhaps the most exciting thing about online teaching: the interaction. For example, I describe a concept for about ten minutes that we then discuss or I give them small tasks.

Does Twitch have any other effects on your teaching?
Twitch is mainly used for sending messages on a continuous basis and so there is much more interaction between the students and me, and above all, amongst the students.

For some of my lectures, I normally need roughly half an hour to explain everything. With Twitch though, it took me over an hour because so many questions, comments and ideas cropped up. Moreover, ever since the first coronavirus lockdown, so many students from other universities or other people who were just interested in the topic joined my course. So all of a sudden, the number of attendees exploded from 140 to 400 people from all over the world. And all of them began to discuss interactively. When I told them about a certain tool that could be used to develop a game, for example, comments immediately came in saying that you'd need an update for that, or recommendations came in for other tools and lots more. They did assist each other.

And sometimes professional game developers joined us and gave the students even better hints than I could have ever done. This kind of interaction could never take place in a real setting. And, at the same time, you receive such a lot of helpful ideas to enhance your class teaching.

What sort of ideas do you mean?
Well, in a real setting, I try to lead discussions. However, the disadvantage of that will always be a certain inhibition threshold. It's much easier to ask things anonymously in a chat. One ought to transfer that anonymity and encourage people to engage more strongly in offering one another assistance. I also find it nice that I myself am subject to a certain critique. Let's assume that I posited in front of class that the earth was flat. Who would dare to contradict me if I argued the case convincingly? Now if that were to happen online, hundreds of comments would come in refuting what I had said and citing sources to prove it.

That must be awfully challenging: you speak about something online and maybe expect to comment on reactions, but also to lecture in a focused way. How does that feel? And how do you manage to avoid getting distracted?
I wouldn't have been sufficiently confident if I hadn't had some experience with Twitch before. And I wouldn't recommend it to anyone who has no previous experience. One could try a setting like that with WebEx or Zoom and then encourage people to post more comments. But that works much better on Twitch because it offers lots of emojis and voting. You can motivate more interactively.

However, Twitch has its disadvantages as well. Colleagues who tried out streaming on Twitch were suddenly confronted with loads of trolls. You need to bear in mind that anyone can watch your online activities, so you are virtually in the public eye and you might even get some nasty comments. You need a good moderation team that can monitor, respond swiftly and delete things if necessary. My tutors also help me to delete bot messages like spam that suddenly pops up or even Nazi symbols and so on. But you can slow things down a bit if you talk for ten minutes and then interact in the chat again. Or I ask my moderating tutors whether any questions have arisen. You should practise that on a smaller scale to start with.

We still use Zoom or WebEx for smaller seminars, though.

Do you record it and put it online?
Yes. It's automatically available as a video for at least one week. And I mostly upload it to YouTube as well.

Do you have a final ritual following a Twitch session?
Directly afterwards, I switch to a voice-video office hour. I simulate the situation where people come to see me after a course and ask questions. The coronavirus has caused some people to suffer from loneliness and real psychosocial problems. We have tried to mitigate that through the community, for example, by simply playing games together after my course.

Which advantages does distance learning offer if I don't interact in the same space?
The most obvious advantage is that people can participate in the course even if they are sick or in a completely different place.

One big disadvantage of distance learning, though, was that the students weren't able to use our cool new equipment in our lab. That's why I tried to find some other goodies and had international guest lecturers coming to the course every two weeks. On those occasions, famous game developers showed us other perspectives, which we would have only been able to afford perhaps once a semester under normal circumstances.

Which group sizes, if any, are particularly suitable for online discussions?
I love using breakout rooms, especially in seminars, for more often than not it's terribly difficult to discuss with even only ten people at a time. That is why I form groups of three or four, or groups of five sometimes. That way, people get to know each other and start a discussion. In that setting, it doesn't matter whether only ten or a hundred people are attending the course.

What do you think about recording lectures on a video and putting them online instead of the course?
That has its advantages and disadvantages as well. Some videos are high-quality productions, but they certainly take a lot of time to create. So first, the video needs to meet certain quality standards, and second, it should provide additional content that is compatible with the video format. If that doesn't work properly, I will probably only take the odd look at it and possibly become inattentive. Apart from that, I use videos to provide a deeper insight into topics which I do not specialise in, or simply to save time. Then I refer to the videos, and we watch some of them together. In a course, whether distance learning or class teaching, I can always activate the students by interacting. A video cannot do that.

Not every topic will enthuse people to the same extent. How do you motivate your students to be curious?
In general, I think that it's very motivating to show people how to put what

you've learnt into practice. In one subject, as an example, the focus is on graph theory. In that context, it's not the mathematical theory that is so great, but what you can do with it. If I take a multiplayer game, say, with three million players, I can use a graph to find out whether I play better with or against other people.

Is it more about showing an example or doing an example together?
Well, it varies. Frequently, we do an example together. It is important that the students engage really actively. It's certainly no fun holding a one-hour keynote speech, nor do I regard it as teaching. The same goes for a Ted talk. If it were merely about conveying knowledge, I could send people book recommendations. In our engineering field, however, it's about calculating and executing. And if I am present, I can show them where the errors are and we can do the corrections together. I try to include collaborative action regularly in theory sessions. Even if it only involves short discussions or queries.

One nice variant are the concept questions, which I also use in my face-to-face courses quite often. I have blocks of 10 to 15 minutes in which I teach theory. One variant is to first ask a question like 'How many of you know the concept?' or 'What is the answer to this equation?' and to offer four possible answers. In our courses, they can respond with a tool called Feedbackr which functions via a smartphone. If they all have the right answers then I know that I can shorten my explanations drastically.

Otherwise, I take care to convey the concept especially well. At the end, I ask one further test question to check on whether they have understood or not. If not, then it's probably my fault because I explained something badly, and so I go through it again. The pedagogical model I mainly use is Technology Enabled Active Learning (TEAL).

What are you not so good at in teaching?
Oh, quite a lot, I think. That's a good question, actually. I always try to get evaluations from my students in order to improve myself.

Well, I always find group work and its evaluation challenging. How do you manage to detect individuals in groups who have not done their fair share and assess them accordingly or even fail them?

You wrote your master's thesis at the Massachusetts Institute of Technology (MIT). Is there anything in particular you picked up there, teaching experiences for example, that has since helped you enormously?
I didn't attend any courses there. But I learnt things like the concept of TEAL. For that purpose, MIT provides a 1.5-million-dollar auditorium and online tools for students of physics. Another thing I got acquainted with there were game jams and frequent events for students such as hackathons.

Was there anything at all that was not so good at MIT?
No. I was very impressed with everything, including what I myself try to live and regard as immensely important, namely to offer free access to learning content: open content and open source. That is why I put as much as I can online. At MIT you could walk into almost every class and consume lots of learning content, as simply as that. That's a very different culture.

Were there any other cultural differences?
Well, I'm not talking about our university, but in general about other educators. You often hear things like, 'Oh no! That's my slide set, and I don't want anyone else to see it.' I'd never do anything like that. Of course, I have spent a lot of time on my slide sets. But then again, other colleagues have also helped me out with the slides.

Sometimes we are afraid that other people might steal our ideas when we talk about them – be it an idea for a game, an app, or a business idea. We all have the best idea right now. However, I don't think it's likely to be stolen because you mostly have a long list of ideas yourself that you haven't found time for yet. The best thing that can happen to you is to talk to loads of people about it and that way your idea will get even better.

You are also responsible for human resources. Whom do you recruit?
At present, I have 13 staff members and am about to recruit two more. From students who have almost completed their bachelor's programme and who assist in projects to PhD students or postdocs. Various different people.

Do those people hold their own courses as well?
My aim is to partially integrate them into teaching practice. That's something you need to grow into. It's not a good idea to say, 'Hey, let me take over the course for a bit!' from one day to the next. We do that step by step beginning with minor courses. Or smaller tutorials that you can simply try out. I supervise all that.

Can you describe any typical mistakes that everyone makes initially?
Typical things like being nervous or not incorporating enough interactions. But that's just a matter of practice and comes over time. Or that you should have more faith in the students so that they actively collaborate. If I ask them, 'Does anyone know that?' for example, it's likely that no one will raise their hand because they are afraid of going to the blackboard. A typical mistake would be to do the calculations yourself. To avoid that, you only need to reformulate the question and ask, 'Who's going to calculate that for us?' which involves the students more.

Which criteria do you use to select someone who is going to teach?
That person should have a certain inclination because I don't force anyone into teaching. If you want to go for research and development, then that's okay by me. There are specific positions for that. Most importantly for me, the team needs to consist of the right people. Although I value excellence greatly, I will always favour someone who fits into the team on a human level. Everyone here is willing to help other people.

What should an educator be able to do well?
In the past, I have seen a whole range of different teaching styles and I make quite a lot of mistakes myself. Ultimately, everyone has to find their own style.
    I believe it's crucial to be fairly enthusiastic about the subject as well as about teaching. That characterises all the good educators I have experienced.

How do you and your colleagues improve your presentations?
All of my team colleagues do an informal presentation at a weekly meeting to sum up what has happened since the last meeting, what is due next or even private matters sometimes. Each presentation lasts only three minutes. Those who are doing a bachelor's or master's thesis with us also do a weekly presentation in English. That way, they overcome their nervousness and it helps to boost their English as well.

As in other subjects, the majority of staff teaching computer science, in particular, is male. What can be done to achieve a more proportionate balance?
That is a huge question and I find the issue extremely important. It's about having role models and beginning early on. In my view, it would be best to begin with computer science at primary school and to counteract widespread preconceptions. In the process of developing a game, I don't sit there all day playing a shooter. But it's also a fact that 45% of all players are not male, for example. I often give talks or keynote speeches including many press interviews and see myself as a multiplier.

Why do you enjoy passing on knowledge to other people?
As a computer scientist in my specialist area, I could take my pick from a host of very attractive and lucrative jobs. I'd love to develop games that millions of people would play and enjoy. However, by teaching others I have a greater impact. In an auditorium, I teach 140 students how to develop games. Consequentially, 10 or 20 games emerge instead of just one from me. I think that's more worthwhile.
    And I feel that everyone working in the sphere of pedagogy or academia wants to leave a footprint, even if it's just a toeprint.

You are co-organiser of Global Game Jam, an online event involving groups of participants who develop a game within just 48 hours – that is, they find ideas, plan and implement a prototype. Does time pressure change the way people learn?

The most interesting aspect of time pressure is to understand what can be realised in such a short time. You learn what it means to deliver a finished product and quite different things than you did in one of our four to six-month projects. And you also learn to prioritise from the very start: what's the most important thing? What comes first? Does the pony need to be beautiful or should it be able to gallop as well? How do I work in a team? Collaboration, communication, sharing files, time management. Time pressure that you face later on in the games industry, too.

I'd like to ask quite a broad question: why are games ideal for learning?

Unlike classical media, games can convey empathy, understanding and complex situations. We can learn things that would otherwise be hard to learn. If I watch, say, a documentary film about refugee families, I would certainly find everything sad, but maybe I'd just sit there munching popcorn, thinking, 'Boy, they've got a hard life.' It would all seem so distant to me.

In a game, though, it's different. For example, 'Path Out' is a game where you play a Syrian refugee on his way from Syria to Austria in 2014. Initially, I see myself as a carefree little boy and his parents still living at their lovely home. Then the war begins. What do I do? Of course, I have to run for my life, and so the day comes when I have to say goodbye to my family without knowing if I will ever see them again. All of this seems much more realistic to me and triggers various thoughts and feelings inside.

Another quite different example is our Maroon project, which is a virtual physics lab that explains physical phenomena by means of a virtual reality headset or web browser and allows you to perform experiments that would be too dangerous in real life.

What do you think: would it be an exaggeration to say that listening is key to teaching?

Yes. [laughs]

Why is that?

In our discipline, it's hugely important to try things out yourself in order to understand them. An old saying goes: 'I hear and I forget. I see and I remember. I do and I understand.' Sure: listening is the first step to understanding anything. But it's not the only decisive factor. The second step is to take action and try things out to see if I've understood what I heard.

Is it also important for teachers to listen?
Like in a 'flipped classroom' – a concept that I personally find very attractive. The idea is that I can give content to my students as homework. Then they come to me with their questions and we work together on examples, instead of me teaching them in front of class. However, I think a good blend is often the best method.

Listening means engaging wholly in what has been said, doesn't it?
Correct. What we have identified as a problem right now, and which will continue to cause us a headache in the future, is the lack of concentration. There are so many distractions everywhere, be it a smartphone or other things around us.

At the same time, motivation is vital: why should I learn this or that? Today's generation doesn't know a world without information at your fingertips. So how do I teach people that it makes sense to remember things despite being able to look them up?

That is why it's crucial that we begin to rethink with these new generations. Sometimes listening for five minutes without distraction is a luxury. A virtual reality headset can give you a direct learning experience and prevent you from getting distracted by other technologies. [laughs] And that gives you focused learning.

I couldn't agree with you more.
Thanks a lot, Johanna.

Rathna Ramanathan

teaches Typography and Graphic Communication Design

Dean of Academic Strategy
Central Saint Martins (CSM) and PhD Supervisor at the School
of Communication, Royal College of Art (RCA), London
Great Britain

*It so happened that this lively online video interview crashed
the very moment the discussion turned to remote teaching.
One week later, Rathna Ramanathan goes on to talk about
the enlightenment she got from peer reviews, why you should
pay attention to your energy level when teaching, how to
educate educators, and how thinking, making and feeling
relate to each other. — January 2022*

**Thies: Your statement on the *university website*[52] says you were delighted
to address the urgent challenges of social justice and anti-racism
at the heart of your mission. What does the Dean of Academic Strategy
do every day?**
Ramanathan: Beyond attending lots of meetings? [smiles] I like the job
because it is focused on the future and how changes in the present can make
a difference in the student journey. How our students come to us, how they
are with us and how they graduate from us.

So there is a wide range of people in the team I manage. We have, for example, someone who looks after the student experience, someone who focuses
on pedagogy, teaching and learning, and someone who looks after knowledge
exchange, which is about, 'How do we connect industry or organisations from
the outside to the university and give our students opportunities to work on
live projects and gain work experience whilst with us?' Also, digital delivery
in terms of how we learn online, and digital platforms and environments as
well as student recruitment also sit with me. And then we have Academic
Development and Quality, which is how we design processes and structures
so that our courses can work within the UK higher education framework.

So my work is both thinking about the course development and about
future courses. In all that, I am a practising graphic designer; it is the way I
see the world, my life and my work, whether I'm a mum, whether I'm a teacher,
whether I'm a researcher or whether I'm doing my job as dean. We always
have an audience we are serving; we must always consider who it's for.

In my work, strategy and delivery are equally important. It is critical that we consider how this might make the lives and experiences of our students better. So it can't just be words on a page, it can't just be policies. It has to change our student experience in a way that's meaningful to them, right now.

You mentioned student recruitment. How do you ensure getting a good mixture of students?
There is a saying that education is about mutual benefit. I think this is really important because, at the end of the day, it is about chemistry and a community that we're building as well as the work and processes that students bring to us. We interview students as a first part of this process. We see education as being transformative, and that may not suit everybody. Being here is quite intense and it is important that we let students know what to expect when they come to Central Saint Martins. And when you ask any of our students, 'What did you enjoy the most?' they talk about their fellow students, and they forget about us as soon as they leave. [laughs]

So it's ensuring that this chemistry is there, and that we bring together a community of diverse and different people, not just people who are like us.

Before leaving, what should students learn from you?
Having taught both undergraduate and postgraduate, I think it's important to remember what's required on these different levels. I'm uncomfortable with the teacher–student hierarchy, especially as our students, both at CSM and the RCA, come from different walks of life and professional backgrounds. I'm more interested in creating a community of practice where people from different parts of the world can learn from each other.

As to what I bring to the table, I would say my approach is a research-led practice that is grounded in publishing. I'm really interested in how research can ground and anchor a concept, and where graphic design and typography can function as a voice, in addition to the text and the image.

How do you help them to learn from each other?
One thing is to create intentional spaces for collaboration and conversation, which is an essence of an art school because that's really where the interesting relationships start happening, rather than just in the taught delivery.

Going to university or to art college means these spaces should happen everywhere: in the canteen, in the studio, in the workshops with people from different disciplines being alongside each other. For example, a graphic designer meets a textile designer in the workshop, and there starts an interesting conversation.

The second thing is to create intentional learning. We call that the 'collaborative unit' where every student in an undergraduate course comes together with other students to work in interdisciplinary groups on one challenge, for example. They gain experience of working with others in art and design, but not in their discipline. There they realise they need to function first as a human, connecting with people, and then focus on their practice, whether art, design or performance. When you ask our students what they want more of, they want more collaborative opportunities with students outside of their own discipline.

Another opportunity at the RCA are the self-organised studios. You rock up and you go and find a table in a little room that can accommodate 10 to 15 people at the most. The animator sits there next to the graphic designer, who sits next to the typographer, who sits next to the filmmaker. And then you find the collaboration starting to happen.

So you create an interdisciplinary space where students live with each other, work with each other, and that's where the real learning happens.

Those are collaborations between students from related disciplines. Do you also provide opportunities to work with people from other disciplines, say, an engineer or a social scientist?
There are two ways in which we do that. One is knowledge exchange. You might have a company or an organisation who comes to us and wants us to look for new ways of engaging and thinking. Or, for example, it might be about global health. These projects look for creative solutions to global issues. At a postgraduate level we're increasingly seeing that we have economists, scientists, engineers, historians, business people – people from very different backgrounds who are very interested in a creative approach – bringing along their previous disciplinary backgrounds. That is more organic rather than intentional. At CSM we also have courses like Bio Design or Material Futures, which intentionally involve other disciplines like science, anthropology or climate studies. Those courses bring lecturers and teachers into the design departments who come from non-art and design disciplines.

And the other way of doing it is through collaborative degrees. So for example, we have collaborations with business schools, jointly providing degrees like MBAs at CSM or at the RCA Global Innovation Design or Innovation Design Engineering or MRes Healthcare Design. That's when really exciting and innovative ways of thinking about the world and ways of working start to happen.

In my experience, you need to find the same language to talk to architects or economists, for example. How do you support that in class?
I think collaborative units help do that. At CSM we call ours Creative Unions. At the RCA there was this one week where students would work 'Across RCA'. Basically, it's about students offering projects across the college, located in

183

different departments. And you could pick one to work with over a week in an intense, detailed manner to learn a new way of thinking and making. I think that sort of gives you a sense of the limitations of your own language, but also mechanisms that you need to find out. Such as what are your strengths and how do you build on them? And then students often sit and make together rather than just speaking together. I think it's quite interesting to think about how we use form as a language, and not necessarily spoken language, in ways of building that bridge of collaboration.

Can you give an example of using forms instead of spoken language?
It was a conceptual project run by one of our tutors who asked architects and graphic designers, 'What if books were buildings? What if buildings were books? What would they look like?' We wanted them to have little models, using nothing more than paper. So if the book was a building, or the building was a book, it still had to function in a way that it's both. And as both objects have certain rules, it's about a balance between structure and system as well as about being able to break rules.

What is more important in teaching: the thinking or the making?
That's a very hard question.

I am very glad to be the person who's asking. [laughs]
[laughs] I think that depends on the context and the stage of the work.
    There was Richard Guyatt, who came up with the term Graphic Design at the Royal College of Art. He believed in the hand, the heart and the mind. He said the three need to be linked in order for us to practise meaningfully.
    What we're talking about is a critical practice, and for a practice to be critical it has to engage with the context, it has to have a purpose that it is anchored by. If there's a constant rhythm and a narrative between head, heart and mind, then the work has purpose, it has resonance. It also begins a conversation with the people, because the work isn't finished when it leaves our hands.
    As a book designer, for me the work only comes alive when it goes to the reader, and then I learn from readers and bring what I've learnt back into practice. I'd say there's thinking and making, but there's also a sense of feeling of connection with others, which is our purpose. Making is very implicit for us, which goes back to your point about languages. How do you discuss making with someone who's neither a maker nor a practitioner? I believe that the easiest way is to begin the conversation through objects.
    For me, the word 'practice' brings together the head, the heart and the mind. The idea of practice is both, the English word 'to practise', which is regular,

daily connection, but also 'a practice', which means you're building something. Practice is something that is quite unique. I always refer to it as being like a sponge. You could take the practice and put it into a situation, a context, and it absorbs that situation and comes to life, based on that context. It's ever changing in some ways and yet consistent. It is wonderful when you get it right.

Have you ever had a situation where a student does a presentation, and it feels like everything is perfect, but the heart is missing. What do you do then?
That's a fascinating question because I sometimes think it's the fault of the brief, which isn't designed in such a way that you could bring the heart in with the mind right at the start. Because once the heart is activated, it will continue to provide the thread or the logic. Particularly if you're connecting the heart not to yourself and your purpose, but to the outside world and a larger purpose. That can be transformative. It is a very difficult thing to bring ourselves to our work in just the right way. For that, you have to be vulnerable. You have to put yourself at risk. And your ego matters less. In my experience, not everybody has the courage to do that. But to me, that is the only way your work will have soul. It has to touch, connect with somebody.

What happens when it's impossible to create that heart part with a student?
Especially in master's level education, there's a point where you must step back and reflect, 'We have given you everything that we can give you. And now you need to lead us.' The relationship of the tutor and the student then changes. You can't give someone heart; they need to find it themselves. Your job as a tutor is to facilitate their journey to that.

What are the most important skills teachers should bring to the classroom?
I would say there are five important skills for me.

First, an ability to listen and reflect with our students. There is never just one approach to any subject, and by listening and reflecting with our students, we learn how to guide them in a way that is appropriate to them.

Second, two fundamental skills that are crucial to graphic design are knowing how to read and write. Our work in typography is entirely word and language-based, so it is the first step to becoming productive designers. I see reading as a kind of listening activity as well.

Third, as teachers, we need to understand the limits of our own knowledge and experience. There are many diverse typographic and design traditions, and the worst thing we could do is to limit the approach of our students through the boundaries of our own knowledge.

Fourth is teaching by doing – through practice, and in practice with our students. Whilst theory is important and crucial, you only learn our craft through regular practice and by doing and making mistakes.

Finally, as one of my students at the Royal College of Art, Eugene Noble, once said: The best thing about the whole experience was that students left with questions that they would pursue for the rest of their lives.

If we can guide our students to this critical approach – or question – that is fundamental to how they practise, then this, I would say, is our most important task.

What is the application process for teachers like, and what is important to help you decide 'this is the right person'?
I think it's the same as when we look at students. It's someone who the community can benefit from. Someone who brings in a different voice. In recent interview panels, it was also someone who had the expertise, but was unafraid to challenge themselves and other people and suggest new directions.

And of course, there's practice. At the end of the day, we're an art college, and you've got to be doing the thing that you're teaching. That's absolutely critical. Otherwise, I don't think it resonates with students.

And then finally, like with any partnership or collaboration, it's really important to have chemistry and community. 'Why do you want to do this and how?' You know, that commitment someone wants to make, and why they want to join the college.

If we don't find that right person, we just pause it and open it up again. It is an important decision and important to get that sense of community right and to support it.

So what would be the best answer to your question, 'Why do you want to teach?'
That's a really ... oh my God, Ingmar! I might have to send this back to you.

So people who have answered why they want to teach were saying because they wanted to make a difference, to make a contribution. And if you ask me why I want to teach, I'd say I benefited greatly from education, and would like to pass some of that benefit on. Ultimately, I teach because I learn from students.

Tough question. [laughs]

[laughs] I'm still lucky to be the one who's asking. Do you have teachers who are not practitioners?
No, actually everybody is, but some might be part-time practitioners.

How do you form and lead a group of teachers onto the right track?
That is interesting because it goes back to the idea of a community of practice.
Sometimes we're led by the curriculum, because there's a level that we need
to teach our first year's, or second year's, or third year's, or master' students
on. But within that, I think that it's important to show diverse views. In India
we have this saying: 'Unity and diversity.' When you build a community
of practice, people lead each other together.

**Do you reward teachers for doing a good job in class? If so, what kind
of rewards do you have?**
Not enough probably.
　　The university has teaching fellowships, for example. You also have this
higher education academy in the UK of lecturers, senior fellows, fellows, all
of that. And the students' union does reward; students nominate teachers
every year. But I think we should do more of that rewarding.

**You mentioned the teacher's ability to listen and reflect. Putting listening
into a slightly different perspective, my hypothesis is that listening is
the most important ability when designing. What do you think?**
I think that's absolutely right. There's something that I'm interested in called
active listening. Active listening is when you're not just hearing what that
person is saying, in words, but you're actually really – again – heart-connected
to the context of what they're saying. You're then trying to understand it
from their perspective. When we listen well, it guides us as to how we design,
and who we design with. You can listen to people, to objects, to history, even
to culture.
　　And I think the design process starts first by us listening. From listening
there comes understanding. And from understanding comes the drafting
or the sketching and the thinking through. All quite wildly, and in the end,
listening leads to ideas.

**I agree with you there. But shouldn't we always ask a question before we
start listening?**
Let me think about that. [reflects] … no.
　　I'd say no, because I think that if we ask, we sometimes limit the brief
by shaping the questions ourselves. But if we just listen – by openly or actively
listening – then the questions might come to you from the people themselves.
Otherwise we're just having a conversation where I'm waiting for you to stop,
so I can interject. I think we should teach more across all cultures about
how to listen.

Since I also believe that listening is one important ability when teaching, can you tell me a bit more on that?

I am going to give you a short anecdote on that. I was very, very lucky that I did my Postgraduate Certificate in Teaching and Learning at Central Saint Martins. The person who was teaching our group was James Wisdom, who had been in education for about 30 to 40 years. James had seen education go from an art college to a university, which I think provides a very broad perspective over time. He was doing a teaching observation of me. I normally went into a session, let's say, of 12 students, having a limited amount of time of about half a day. Everybody wants feedback, wants 100% from you. And you think the way to do that is to sacrifice yourself. But actually, the most difficult thing is to listen and to get that person to then reflect and understand, so that they provide the answer themselves rather than us providing it for them. And that takes time.

James Wisdom just said, 'Pay attention to your energy when you are teaching, because when you dip and you start to feel tired is often when someone is pulling at you really, really hard.' What I realised was that a part of me is listening, and I'm not paying attention to the part that's listening. So for me, you are absolutely right. Listening is the most important ability, but it's very hard. It's easier not to listen and to give in to what's actually being asked of you as a teacher, which is: *tell me what to do*!

But genuine teaching is when we become less and less important to the student because they are finding their own practice and growing in the confidence of their own voice, and how we facilitate that from the start.

I think active listening is the hardest part of teaching. And when done very well, it can be quite exhausting, because listening happens in a different part of us, rather than in the front of the mind. You're sort of going to your creative mind in a sense, and working with your intuition, which comes over time with practice.

Does the word teaching express what you do in class?

If I had to label myself, I would say I am not teaching, I am practising with students. It means empowering, reflecting and listening. Sometimes it also means it is frightening. Most of us teach to learn.

How are your peer observations organised?

It's a university mechanism, of which there is one every year, but it's organised on a local level. You could choose your partner and usually your partner is someone who teaches in a different subject area.

For example, coming from graphic design and typography, I did it with somebody who was teaching photography. We were looking at the relationship between the tutor and the student.

Do you follow any particular process?
We do have a process; you get some guidelines.

It's like colleague-to-colleague support. The observation is sort of that we meet, discuss things together and talk about some of the challenges. 'I have tried this experimental type of teaching', for example. We then choose the parameters and organise the observations in different contexts. We might just do two short ones. So you come and see me twice, I come to you twice, and then we write a couple of things to each other. Actually, that written stuff is intended for each other but it also goes back to the university in terms of documenting process and good practice so we can all learn from it.

How do you educate educators before they start to teach?
This is a chicken and egg situation.

At the RCA, a lot of people came to learn visual communication and then went on to teach. There was a real interest in teaching. So I started running a teaching workshop and exercises for postgraduate MA students and giving them projects that they could do. It was really popular.

At CSM, where you have a BA and an MA, you could potentially give interested MA students a pilot project for the undergraduate students. Or PhD students teach MA students. So it's sort of enabling that practice whilst they're with us, rather than saying 'This is how you teach.' It's interesting to ask people who are being taught what good teaching might be. It's a more reflective and really discursive exercise about what teaching is. Actually it's more an exercise about learning than it is about teaching.

The other way is the postgraduate certificate of learning and teaching I did at CSM. That's a reflective one. You've got to be teaching while you are doing it or preferably have taught for two or three years. So you've got a sense of your own practice, and then you have something to refer back to.

I shouldn't forget to mention PhD students. At the RCA, PhD students might be doing a project on typography and might be able to set up a project for MA students. Then young people are talking to young people, which is very different from our generation talking to them.

But I think again, we mentioned it earlier, it's about building that community of practice. And I think that I've been blessed very much with generous teachers who have shared their practice with me. So you learn from watching them, in that sense.

Last question: What are the advantages of blended learning, the combination of e-learning and space-based classroom methods?
One advantage is that someone is situated in the context of their work and of their practice, which is really important in design, and they're working with an education that helps them translate to and from that context.

I did my BA in Fine Art in India as we didn't have design degrees. Then I came to CSM to do my MA in Communication Design, and then my PhD in Typography. I went back and forth. I sometimes imagine how my degree of Communication Design would have been if I had done it blended with me situated in India and learning online. It would have been richer in my own context that was around me, but at the same time in London I was sitting next to people and working with people and I would have lost out on that in some way. I learnt by just watching them working and making and not even having a conversation. So I think we're too focused on the screen, the foreground of us, instead of on the background. I think blended learning gives us an opportunity to rethink that balance, to consider situating design in different places around the world.

Another advantage is time. You can't teach for hours on end online. So you have to be really choosy about how you teach, and also how you use the camera for design. For example, is showing drawings just turning on the camera? I think we need to explore that much more: what is a studio online? How do we share practice?

Finally, one great advantage for me is, personally, that I've been able to give lectures across the world. Likewise, I have had people from across the world come and talk to us.

Great suggestions, Rathna!
Many thanks.

LeeAnn Renninger

lectured at Columbia Business School, Princeton, MIT, University College London and the United Nations

PhD in cognitive psychology
Co-founder of LifeLabs Learning, author of *The Leader Lab*
USA

LeeAnn Renninger is interested in people and their behaviour. She is infinitely curious. In an email interview, she explains, on the basis of her own mistakes, what she thinks is essential to keep in mind in class, the significance of movement for our learning processes and how movement helps when teaching. She answers some questions by suggesting to adopt an active role oneself.
— November 2022

Thies: First-hand vs. second-hand experience: do I learn better when I experience something myself, or is it enough to hear it from someone else or read it? What are the differences happening in our brain?
Renninger: Right now, I have an option to answer this question by writing a fact for you to hear or read. I could simply say, 'Learning by doing builds expertise faster.' I'd be correct, but I'd be making an error by answering like that. I'd be depriving you of the chance to learn the concept faster, to create more insight, more gamma waves, more of an 'ah-ha!' moment.

Better option: instead, I could ask you, the reader, to name three things you've learnt in life. Then, articulate how you learnt them. It likely involved three components: hearing, doing/practising and repetition. The things that we learn forever, such as riding a bike, can only be transferred into the muscles by doing. Same thing with learning a language, maths, etc. The reason for this is that the brain is made up of neural pathways. You could draw a neural path along with me right now, as you read and learn about this. I'd ask you to draw a circle, with a squiggly line as a tail, and then connect that tail to another circle and tail, and then draw a few squiggles on top, layer after layer, and you'd have a neural pathway, like a path that you create when you walk over a field and your feet make a groove. We create that neural path by treading over it again and again, by experience and by repetition.

What you describe is also called 'active learning', right?
Yep.

How do I teach creativity, the search for ideas?
I'd say first define which aspects of creativity one wants to teach, and
then break it down into a discrete set of behaviours that can be practised.
Then create practice exercises. Then get and give feedback. Then redo.

For example, there are dozens of behaviour sets connected to creativity.
One I think that isn't taught well are the 'problem definition skills' – to come
up with creative solutions to a problem I have to first understand the problem.
Learners can practise this skill set by thinking of an everyday problem they
face. Have them write it down. For example, they may write, 'My partner and I
have fallen into a boring daily routine.' Now, before trying to come up with
creative solutions for this problem, we see that there is a skill still needed …
the skill of defining this problem better. We'd teach students to 'deblur' each
work they wrote to get a cleaner problem statement. Maybe the cleaned version
becomes, 'My partner and I don't laugh enough.' Or better, a creative solution
to 'I want to laugh daily with my partner.' Now we've given some bounds to
the problem and within those bounds we can be more creative. To teach this,
students would practise writing a bunch of problem statements and cleaning
them to make them more precise.

**I want to create ideas for, say, a poster. What is happening in my brain
when I get inspired via Instagram posts, looking at them and swiping
to the next, in contrast to when I'm trying to find ideas in my head, scrib-
bling them down?**
Oh that's hard! I'm not sure if I can answer well. Here are a few thoughts
but maybe not what you are looking for:

In both cases we are being a curator and recombining ideas we have seen
before. In one case we work from external stimuli (the posts in front of us)
and in the other we work more indirectly, from memories of other things
we have seen over time. Both are what we call 'generative' in that we are trying
to build something new based on what we know. One type of generative work
is 'gradual' in that we take something known and build on it (e.g., creating
the next model of a car – builds on the old). Another type of generative work
is 'disruptive' in that it departs from all old models (e.g., a flying saucer).

Most people think that creating something from scratch will lead to a more
disruptive or unique idea, because it isn't being 'primed' to fit what is in front
of us. But I'm not sure. If we have good creativity skills then it doesn't matter
where we start from, because we can use good techniques to be more disruptive,
like 'inversion' (what is the opposite of this thing I'm seeing?).

In all cases: what we are doing cognitively is branching across neural
networks and schemata.

Manual sketch vs. using an electronic device: Let's assume we want to find first ideas for a new logotype of a university. 'Manual sketch' stands here for drawing something with a pencil on paper, while 'electronic device' stands for doing sketches on a tablet. Does anything work differently in our brain or body when we do things without electronic devices?
The brain is mostly made of motor cortex. The more we move, the more we learn. I don't know of any research that looks into differences between sketching on paper and digitally. I'd guess that both have the same impact, as long as the hand is moving.

What I love about design thinking is the concept of iteration, because it means prototyping (get out there and do it!) and then systematic repetition, which is what the brain needs to grow the neural pathways needed.

I remember learning the Japanese syllable alphabets Hiragana and Katakana by also drawing them as big letters into the air, moving my whole body. Do you have examples of how 'body work' can support designers, say, in idea finding?
This is the field of study called somatics. As mentioned before, the brain is made mostly of motor cortex. The more we can anchor concepts into motions, the more easily we move it literally into 'muscle memory'.

This also works well for ideation. Let's say I want to be creative in my field, which is inquiry skills – teaching people how to ask better questions. If I want to come up with unique terms for questions, what can I do? Well, I start using different areas of life and asking myself what 'movement' is a question-asking one (e.g., maybe 'stepping' – I step into question mode vs. stepping into answer mode)?

Or does question-asking work like football for instance? Now I get up and try it. Maybe I kick the question and see if it gets received. Alright, are there any offside questions? Are there different types of question dribbles, players, etc.? I can stand up and move like a football player, and see how the idea feels.

Basically what I'm doing is borrowing ideas from other cognitive schemata to be more creative.

Are there any books you'd recommend on how to train students to speed up their idea-finding processes?
There are lots of books on this with great exercises and ideas, like these two I like a lot: Sarah Stein Greenberg's *Creative Acts for Curious People* and Michael Michalko's *Thinkertoys: A Handbook of Creative-Thinking Techniques*.

You've taught at different universities. What was your biggest mistake as a teacher so far?

I'd say in a few areas:

a) Balance – not providing enough balance between structure and adventure. As a learner, our brains want to know what is coming next. The craving is for scaffolds like, 'Here is what we are doing, here is where we are right now in today's plan and here is what we are covering next.' And lots of numbering: 'There are three things to know here. They are…' This creation of structure is ideally balanced with adventure, which comes in the form of adding stories, inviting learners to add their stories etc.
   When I first started teaching, I leaned too far in the direction of structure. I was stiff. As I got used to teaching, I leaned too far in the direction of adventure. I allowed a little too much chaos. Finding the balance between the two became a craft that I've enjoyed a lot.

b) Not allowing enough silence – the brain needs time to process. Many professors are afraid to pause, though. They'll ask a brilliant question and then talk over the precious thinking time their students need to process. For example, if I ask you what's the most exciting thing you've learnt in reading this book so far, you need a moment to think, to rifle through the pages of your memory. I, as a professor, though, might forget that and think – when I see blank faces of the thinkers – I need to repeat my question. In fact, what I need to do is be quiet and let the question grow.

Great insights. May I ask for two more mistakes you've made?

c) Not clarifying the question – when students ask questions they often don't entirely know what they are asking. A good fix is to help them clarify by saying, 'Can you give me an example?'

d) Not adding enough story – once I was on a panel and the moderator was terrible. The crowd was getting bored and there wasn't much we as panellists could do because the questions we were being asked were simply boring. Nevertheless, I noticed one guy on the panel, named Didier, who succeeded every time in getting people to lift their eyes from their phones and pay attention. What did he do differently? He answered every question with a story.
   Like what I'm trying to do now. The story is far more interesting for the brain than just the pure answer.

You have studied professors at Columbia and Yale over the years and found that the best professors make more of what you call 'PBS statements': P for passion, B for benefit and S for summation. Do you have some examples which would help design educators in practice?

Try it now. What would you all say is the PBS of this book? Finish the sentences below:
- Passion: what I love about this is...
- Benefit: knowing this will help you to...
- Summation: the key takeaway/thing I want you to remember is...

This is a great way to activate everyone reading our interview. Do you also have some examples of PBS statements professors have already given to you?

PBS is a life habit. It should be done every day, all the time, even when talking to yourself. For example, P: I'm excited about helping out with this book interview. B: it helped me think through things I'd forgotten about and am taking as second nature. I hope sharing them benefits others too, to make teaching more of a fun experiment and adventure. S: and I hope, if nothing else, the key takeaway here is to ask more questions, create practice opportunities, use the body and motion, and share more stories.

What are the most important soft skills teachers should bring to the classroom?

One's own curiosity – start each class by asking yourself what am I most curious about my learners and the wisdom that they bring to this topic? What will excite them? What will confuse them? What can I learn from them today? What conversations would I love to catalyse in the room?

How can one train curiosity with students?

Role model it yourself. Get curious about their lives and on your own daily life. (Quick! Right now spot the weirdest thing in the room you are reading this book in! Now ask yourself three questions about it. When we live in curiosity space, anyone who sees us gets infused too.)

My hypothesis: listening is the most important thing in teaching. Is that correct?

I'd say questions are the most important thing. If we ask better questions we get better thinking.

I wonder if our job is not to teach a subject, but to catalyse better thinking skills, which can be applied to the subject. Questions help guide and nudge and role model ways of thinking about the info.

My second hypothesis: listening is the most important thing in learning. What do you think?

Hmmm – I think listening means a bunch of things:

Creating a habit of curiosity. Like today I was wondering what the most frequent taste we get to taste is, in life. Then I realised … maybe it's toothpaste! Since we get that every day. That's a funny idea! Then, that led me to look up the most popular toothpaste flavours and I learnt about how toothpaste is made and the history of it.

Creating a habit of questions – why is this like this? How does it connect to other things I know? How can I use this info in everyday life? What's useful about it? What shape can I picture it as? What other questions can I ask myself about it?

When people talk, listen through to the foundations: what matters to this person who is talking? What need do they have? How do they think? What is their mental map?

On your website lifelabslearning.com you invent the term 'Tipping Point Skills'. Those are skills that matter most and which spill over into countless other domains. Your eight TPS areas are: Coaching, Feedback, Productivity, Effective 1-1s, Strategic Thinking, Meetings Mastery, Leading Change and People Development – 'Feedback' seems to fit into my topic of 'teaching'. Can you give us two or three TPS examples which help to give good and constructive feedback?

Please take a look at my TED talk for a summary.[53] Good feedback should:
- name what we call 'deblurred' data points. A blur word is something that means different things to different people. It's not 'clean'. An example would be feedback like 'This is too simple-looking.' Better would be to just name the data around what looks simplistic to you: for example, 'The images don't have shadows.'
- include an impact statement: 'It matters because …' or 'The impact is …'

Your own description on LinkedIn says 'with a specialisation in idea transfer and rapid skill acquisition – the ability to learn skills quickly and deeply'. Is there an underlying method to learn quickly and deeply?

Quick: apply it. Ask yourself, 'What did I just learn, why does it matter, how does it connect to things I already know?'

Deep: repeat it at a spaced interval. Come back to it later (take a look at Ebbinghaus's Forgetting Curve to read more on this).

Different topic: how do I silence a student who talks so much that other students don't get a chance to express their thoughts?

- Use your body as a turn signal, like in a car. Indicate that you want to pivot the talking time to someone else or a different topic. Make a change as they talk. Either turn and start walking toward the board, move closer to the student, or go point at your screen, or hold up your hand making an interjection gesture or stop signal.
- Before you ask a question, declare that you want to hear from several people – including voices you haven't yet heard.
- Interrupt gently, saying something like, 'Oh, just one second (person's name) – just noticing the time, can you share the Twitter version of the answer so that I can make sure to fit in the other topic?'

You always have a positive attitude, also posting these nice little habit notes on Instagram @leeann_renn where you analyse our behaviours to improve communication with each other. How do you maintain this positive approach to life and in interaction with people?
See everything as an experiment in the art of living, everything as a chance to learn and to be one notch better than your previous self.

Regarding interaction: Is there 'a best practice' or workshop method to learn how to interact with people?
I think communication is what matters most in life. If we improve it by just one notch, our world can change. A tip: When talking with someone, always know where you are located in the conversation. Think about it like a three-dimensional space:
- Where am I landing in terms of talking vs. listening ratio?
- Am I asking questions or making statements?
- Am I talking about the past, present or future?
- Am I focusing on the content or the relationship?

Lots of different perspectives.
Thank you very much, LeeAnn.

Ichiro Saga
teaches Typography and Design History

Associate Professor
Faculty of Art and Design
Department of Graphic Design
Tama Art University, Tokyo
Japan

*Education and life are full of twists. Ichiro Saga explains
how these can be used and talks about very personal
decisions he has made and of those that his students must
make. He chooses his words with mathematical precision and
explains how the eye and hand work together, about death
and what effect laughter has in class.* — December 2019

Thies: How do I teach graphic design sustainably?
Saga: Well, in my opinion, the difficulty lies in the fact that graphic design
is a complex interplay between functionality and expression. In order to
achieve functionality in design, you should try to view society objectively and
perceive the way it interacts with design. Expressiveness, shaping your ideas,
however, is always subjective and will also always reflect my subjective
thoughts, perceptions and feelings. To make all of that work together well,
you need additional technical and logical skills.

    Therefore, I always discuss everything carefully with the students, then
I analyse their topics and objectives, what they aim to achieve and the
specific challenges involved. In addition, at a university such as Tama Art
University, which is some distance from town, one's personal motivation
plays a crucial role. If you have external clients, you don't necessarily have
to be concerned about motivation. But as soon as you take matters into your
own hands, first of all you have to review your motivation carefully and then
independently divide it into subjective and objective elements.

How do you convey that to your students?
We talk about what I've just mentioned. [laughs] I let the students think
about what challenge they want to take on. Although it is almost impossible
to be objective and subjective at the same time, I try to fathom that out with
the students. Sometimes it works out, sometimes not.

If things don't work out, what do you do with the students?
First, I just wait a while. [laughs] If nothing changes, my only option is to have
a discussion with those students who aren't making any progress in order
to help them find their own motivation.

Do you do that in group discussions or on an individual basis?
Mostly in individual tutorials, especially with third or fourth-year students.
During the master's degree programme, we even have them on a weekly basis.

Why not during the bachelor's degree programme?
Because their choice of topic and motivation are not yet sufficiently clear.

What do you do if someone is too shy to discuss with you?
I will start asking questions.

Does that always work?
Occasionally. [smiles]
   Or I wait until I have the opportunity to comment on the work during
the final presentation. It's a matter of finding the right time. Sometimes
– interestingly – they start to talk of their own accord. Because they want
to all of a sudden.

Were you ever in a situation that really annoyed you?
Yes, I was. One student, for example, had enormous talent, but didn't show
or make any use of it. I told him to his face how much he was harming himself
by not taking himself seriously. I got really angry and loud with him. Later on,
he told me that this had really helped him because other teachers had already
given up on him. And he delivered a wonderful final piece of work. Well, that
worked the first time – but it didn't the second time round. So I just left it
at that, because I felt I may have offended the student by giving him a piece
of my mind. I guessed there must be some other ways to achieve the same
results.

Which ways do you mean?
I haven't found them yet. [laughs] I'm still thinking about that.

Is there a higher goal that you want to achieve in teaching?
Yes. To keep in tune with society while remaining true to oneself. That applies
to my students as well as to me as a teacher. That is the ideal that we should
aspire to.

Are you speaking from a typographer's point of view?
I think that typography is very closely associated with what I have just said.
That has to do with the fact that I have always regarded typography as
a complex and conflicting topic. Language has no form. And neither does
typography. It is versatile. Sometimes it has to be unobtrusive like text in
a book, and sometimes it has to be ostentatious like a heading on a poster.

Good typography is the outcome of a combination of excellent handcraft
and expressive technique. In my opinion, there's nothing more challenging
for the interaction of eye and hand than font design. Equally challenging
are the choice of font size, typesetting or the ability to create a distinct print
image – all these things demand a high level of technique. Hence, all typography is shaped by man. The same characteristics are typically present in
design too.

Does that apply to western and Asian writing systems?
Yes, to both western and eastern ones.

What abilities would you like to teach students?
The ability to realise that the quality of every piece of work will increase
if you apply the trial-and-error method. Even after completion, you should
continue to check it for any mistakes and try things out.

How do you create an atmosphere that allows for mistakes?
I try to make clear that there is always something that needs to be done,
a next step. That creates an atmosphere which gives you the confidence to do
something better if you only try it out. We do our best to see making mistakes
as part of the process and not to see it as a failure.

Do you convey that attitude through tasks or by explaining it?
I speak about it.

During my studies in Switzerland, we had an interesting task on that
subject in our introductory course. We had to work one whole week, eight
hours a day, on one and the same layout. Our task was to constantly create
new variations of it.

What exactly was the task?
It involved designing the front page of a summer course booklet. The text was
predetermined in terms of size and font. We were only given sheets of paper
in different sizes, plus a pair of scissors, and were required to cut and lay out
everything by hand.

Have you ever done that in your course – eight hours a day, five days long?
Unfortunately not. I'm afraid it isn't suitable for larger classes – in Switzerland there were 24 of us from 12 countries. Maybe I'll do it sometime when I have a voluntary study group that is keen on in-depth research.

What are you especially good at as a teacher?
Everyone has strengths and weaknesses. [laughs] I think I laugh too much. It creates a relaxed atmosphere but can also lead to a lack of concentration. And I think I'm good at providing suggestions, although too many of them can be quite daunting for students.

Could I conclude from this that too many proposals reduce one's motivation?
Yes, right. It's important to propose specific ideas, but it's far, far more important that students find out for themselves what they're looking for. On the other hand, leaving them alone too much would only jumble the subjective and objective parts of their motivation. It's vital to find the right balance. I wish I could do that. [smiles]

Would you describe yourself as a teacher? Or use a different word?
Essentially, I would say that I am a teacher. I've been pondering on that a lot recently, because something happened that had a big impact on me personally. My teacher, Kei Mori, died last year – he was 40 years older than me. I was so sad and felt that a piece of my life had been taken away from me; however, not a part of my past, but of my future. Because if I am successful in the future, I won't be able to show him the results of my work anymore. And that has caused me to reflect: on what educational institutions are, what a teacher is. It's made me realise that a university is basically a place where the future is of overriding importance. We are standing with the students in the present, but we're not looking at our feet, at where we're standing right now, but always into the future. Now I feel that my teacher who was standing next to me was my future self. That's exactly what a teacher is for me. It's as if he were standing next to my future.

To lose a teacher is to lose one's future. With his death, the present has gained more meaning, while the meaning of the future has decreased. For the first time I look down at my feet, at where I am standing right now, and think about all the different relationships that I'm part of. Also, I see my students who maybe regard me as their future.

I perceive the university as a special place. For there is no better place than this to leave the present behind you. Here, only the future counts.

Do your students know all that?
I don't think that it's important for them to know. But sometimes I mention it in a personal discussion, albeit after thoroughly reflecting on how I want to put it.

Did you learn how to teach from your teacher?
Yes. From Kei Mori.

Do you teach like him?
Partially.

What do you do differently?
I don't have his acumen, power of observation and comprehension. Instead, I spend more time on theoretical concepts. One thing we do share, though, is that I want to support students on their personal and academic journey.

What do you mean by comprehension?
The ability to figure out with the students what they really want.

Ideally, if you found that out and accompanied students on their journey, how would you grade their work, then?
Actually, I think grades shouldn't be given. However, I have to award them and to do that I only take a look at the final results. I explain that procedure to my students from the very start. Although discussions and suggestions are important, they merely serve to optimise the final result.

What do you wish you could change in your teaching?
I'd like to be able to motivate my students at the touch of a button. I haven't found that button yet. [laughs] But I'm in search of it.

Do you have other ways to motivate students?
I always take a person's characteristics and personal feelings into consideration. Because that personal feeling, the subjective, is the first thing that comes to mind. If you manage to motivate them, you can tell that by the look on their faces.

Maybe their facial expression shows that they are immersed in a creative process. That brings me to the next question. What is creativity?
I think creativity is the ability to live the way you want to. If we take a closer look at the term 'creativity', there is much more to it than just 'designing'.

What should creativity be used for?
For ourselves. Only then can creativity be of use to others, too. Of course, we require a philosophy for that. And democracy as well. It is the ability to grasp the existence of minorities as diversity.

What advice would you give to a person just beginning to teach?
I would say that person could do whatever they wanted – but that they should bear in mind that a university is a special place for students.

Mr Saga, thank you for all those insights.

Stefan Sagmeister

teaches Graphic Design

Graduate Design Department
School of Visual Arts in New York (SVA)
USA

Founder of Sagmeister Inc.

*Stefan Sagmeister ends his email response with '1000 greetings
from 14th Street'. Short are his answers and concise his thoughts
on perseverance and enthusiasm and how his way of teaching
has changed. He also talks about things he is not so good at.*
— November 2021

Thies: Do you still teach?
Sagmeister: Yes, I've been teaching for more than 20 years.

Can you tell me in one sentence what students should learn from you?
The class is called 'How to touch someone's heart with design'. This is what
they should learn. Many of them do, which is shown when they create
projects that touch their audience's heart.

Do you prioritise the idea or the design in class?
Why one or the other?
When I was a young teacher, I prioritised idea over form. Once I had much
more experience, I found that projects with good form worked much better.
So now, I would see them as equal. When in doubt, I maybe even find form
more important, especially as most of my colleagues favour ideas over form.

How do you judge an idea or design?
I would judge an idea by asking, 'Is it original? Surprising? Appropriate?'
Judging design, I would ask, 'Is it an original colour combination? The appro-
priate material? Or would a different materiality be better? Is it the best form?
A good shape?'

Do objective criteria exist when judging a design?
As far as functionality is concerned, of course! This website, brochure, IG post and poster works better than that site, brochure, IG post and poster, because it sold more widgets or had more views or whatever…

As far as aesthetics are concerned, we do have a – somehow – shared view of what is beautiful, original and good.

You can clearly experience this phenomenon at art school, and the students themselves always seem to have a good sense of who is really good in their class and who is not.

Can one teach design criticism, and, if so, how?
I have not taught it, so I have no personal experience. SVA has a graduate course on design criticism, and I've seen very good writing emerging from it. So yes, I think it can be taught.

How do you convey curiosity? How do you train curiosity with students?
I am not sure. My students are usually already curious when they come to me.

How do you convey critical reflection on the briefing?
I sometimes receive briefings that do make sense for the client, but don't make much sense for the much more important client of the client. If this is the case, I bring it up and we change the brief. I sometimes receive briefs stipulating goals that are impossible to achieve. I'll bring that up too. In rare cases, I completely rewrite a brief and see if I can get the client to agree to start from that.

What should communication design do away with in order to reduce its ecological footprint?
Layers of packaging.

My hypothesis: Listening is the most important ability when designing. What do you think?
It's certainly in the top three when designing for a client. All of our clients know their business much better than we do.

In most cases, we know how to communicate that business better than they do. In order to be able to do so, we have to listen very closely and learn as much as possible about their business.

How can I as a teacher provoke failures that students can learn from?
I feel students fail enough, completely unprovoked.

On your website, you state, 'I recently thought about why learning (or simply getting better at something) is so inherently pleasurable, and came to the conclusion that it probably has evolutionary roots. Evolution might have made learning enjoyable because it wants us to grow – it is in its own interest after all – in the same way it made sex enjoyable because it wants us to reproduce.' How can you instil this kind of enthusiasm in students?
By being enthusiastic as a teacher. Enthusiasm is contagious.

Which teaching-related experiences enrich your studio practice, your own work?
Being forced to explain things clearly to students often makes things clearer for myself, too.

What are the most important skills teachers should bring to the classroom?
Enthusiasm and common sense.

Which skills, knowledge and experiences can only be acquired when practising design?
Tenacity.

What is the most challenging aspect of design to teach?
Beauty. Because it takes a lot of work for the student to become better at creating it.

How do you motivate shy students to engage, to express their thoughts in class?
I am sadly not great at that.

Which is more important: experimentation or the methodical approach?
Both. I switch from one to the other all the time.

What do designers need in order to stand out in their profession?
Common sense. Tenacity. Enthusiasm. A desire for beauty.

How does one teach these abilities? Is it about attitude?
Common sense might be unteachable. Tenacity I can talk about. As for enthusiasm, students have to bring that with them.

Is beauty the same as aesthetics?
Basically, yes. But I must admit that I have little interest in defining the two and searching for differences.

How does one sensitise students to aesthetics?
By talking about it, taking it seriously and having your students make beauty a goal in their work. Things don't become beautiful by themselves, you need to keep making demands on the students, which is something many are not used to.

A current (already past?) trend is the so-called 'anti-design'.
What does your wish for 'beauty' say to that?
I am not against deliberate ugliness in design; it can be rather interesting. What I hate is unconsidered form.

On your website, your answer to the question 'How would you describe yourself as a designer?' is: 'I am interested in creating an emotional connection to an audience. I have always been jealous of our music clients who can often achieve this much deeper, quicker and more immediately.' How does one teach this depth to students?
I don't know how to achieve the kind of emotional connection many musicians achieve within visual design myself, so sadly, I cannot teach it either. Unless I design a movie that incorporates music.

Have you ever taught using Zoom or other video platforms?
Yes, like many of my colleagues, all of last year.

What advantages did you draw from distance teaching?
It seemed easier to get otherwise quiet students to participate. Individual sessions were more concentrated and I felt it was more helpful for the student.

On your website, your answer to the question 'What is some bad advice given in the design industry?' is 'That our work is all about solving problems. Solving problems is for accountants and engineers. We can do so much more. We can delight!' How can you guide students to achieve such results?
That should be easy. When a student shows their work in class, does the rest of the class breathe in with delight? Or not?

Delight can be brought about by a particularly original idea, by unusual beauty, by extraordinary ugliness, by surprise.

Many thanks, Stefan.

Kashiwa Sato

teaches Design Thinking

Visiting Professor
Keio University and
Tama Art University, Tokyo
Japan

Creative Director and CEO of Samurai Inc.

*Kashiwa Sato enters the large longitudinal room furnished
only with a very long table and chairs. One wall of the room
is entirely made of glass, overlooking a courtyard. Both earnest
and laughing, he talks about the role of design in society and
of what oversized assignments do to students. The sun comes in
through a skylight.* — December 2019

Thies: Why did you become a teacher?
Sato: Because I believe in the power of creativity.

How would you define creativity?
Big question. Well, I don't think you can describe it in one word – I teach
Design Thinking at Keio University. So what I would describe as creativity
there is the ability to solve problems.

What kind of problems does this ability refer to?
To all kinds of problems. In my class at Keio University, we work deliberately
in areas that haven't seen much progress on the level of design. One topic,
for instance, could be disaster management – ways of thinking with regard
to catastrophes. This year's topic was Earth Reset.

What was actually reset?
Well, we assumed that if we moved to Mars, we would ask questions like,
'Would we have countries there? How would we deal with languages? Would
we need money?' Essentially, we reset the system that we live in now right
back to square one. In order to reshape everything.

Do you specify the topic only or the tasks as well?
I propose a topic such as Earth Reset, Catastrophes, Health or Happiness. Only then do we begin to identify the tasks. The students decide for themselves what they want to focus on. They decide on a certain concept and afterwards – since the solution is also theirs to find – they can do as they wish. My students have to present their work to me and the other students every week throughout the whole semester – very hard work. [laughs] And I give them feedback.

What sort of feedback do you give?
For example, 'This concept is only average and not really interesting.' Or, 'This way of thinking doesn't make any sense, logically', 'This idea wouldn't have any specific effects', 'With this idea, you have not solved the problem you wanted to.' Or, 'This idea is much too like the other team's idea.'

So it's not permitted to have a similar idea?
No, because in that way, I guide my students to their own unique solutions.

Do you also initiate discussion?
Yes, for instance, I ask, 'I'm afraid I don't understand exactly what you mean, could you explain it to me more precisely?' and then we begin to discuss things. Finally, I tell them which points they need to improve by the next week. I do not give them any solutions.

Do the employees at your design studio have the same freedom?
At work, I determine an awful lot of things! However, when I teach, I think it's vital not to voice your own ideas. I prefer to say, 'I've just had an interesting idea, but try to fathom it out for yourself!' [smiles] Apart from that, I think it makes huge sense to teach design at a university like Keio, which is not an art university. SFC – the Shonan Fujisawa Campus – at Keio University is a special place, the newest campus, despite being about 20 to 25 years old. Design, technology, business – different disciplines collaborate there to seek innovative solutions.

Do students from different degree courses get together, then?
Our students can choose and put together their courses themselves. At SFC, much of the staff teaches disciplines such as IT, economy, architecture and – like myself – design.

Do the students see themselves as designers?
I don't know. Those who earn a degree at SFC strive to create start-ups. Our endeavour is to open up new professional fields of creativity.

How would you describe your occupation?
Creative Director right now.

And what is your job as Creative Director?
I decide on all creations generated in an overall project. I really have the big picture. As part of those projects, I forge partnerships with other companies and create their branding for them. Not only for businesses, but for regions as well. I collaborate, for instance, with Imabari Towels, which is an industrial enterprise based in the Imabari region.

That means a project like that can be an extremely complex process. How do you convey that to your students?
The complexity of the process is always the same irrespective of whether you collaborate with a company or a region, in order, for example, to respond to social problems.
   The main thing is always to get the gist of things, the essence.

How do you identify this essence?
Through interviews.

If it's a company, do you always interview the CEO of that company?
Well, that depends on the project. But as a rule, I do begin with the top management. Having said that, to get a full picture, to understand the details, I interview many other levels as well.

Do you then present the essence you identified and come to an agreement that it is *the* essence?
Yes.

And how do you teach this to your students?
Since that is very difficult to teach, we at SFC offer workshops in which I invite my students to search for the essence.
   How to interact with businesses, however, is almost impossible to convey to anyone. That's the reason why this subject is so complex to teach – much more complex than my work as a designer.

Why, exactly, is it so complex?
If a company boss is also the founder, then he or she will know exactly what they want. If I understand this or that correctly, I will almost always come up with the right answer, find the essence. In class, however, we don't have any-one like that, because it's mostly about social problems. And it's simply not possible to bring along a company boss.

Why not?
No particular reason. I guess you could do that in class, too, but I think it's better to deal with social issues.

I'd like to get back to those complex design processes again: How do you teach your students how to collaborate with many different specialists?
First, I always stress that acquiring abilities to cooperate with different people is essential, especially nowadays. To bring that home to my students, I talk, for instance, about case studies in which we succeeded in implementing the process.

Do you invite other specialists to your class as well; for example, an architect?
When I talk about the process, then I usually do so on my own. In class at Keio, however, if it's about issues such as a catastrophe, I sometimes invite a colleague specialising in earthquakes, for instance, as a guest.

Do those specialists participate only at the beginning or at the end of the course as well – in order to assess the results?
At the beginning and the end.

Who decides when a project is finished?
Time decides when. [laughs] At the end, the students hold a presentation, which is open to everyone: anybody can come and see it. And the students have to do their presentation for the audience, not for me.

And what if you're not satisfied with it, but running out of time, is the project still done?
Yes, because it's not my own work.

Do you tell them expressly that the project is not actually finished?
Yes. That's what I tell them.
     At the end, I invite colleagues from other disciplines to give their feedback in addition to mine. Finally, we always vote on which presentation went down best and award points, one, two, three, and so on, down to the last place. Both the teaching staff and the audience cast their votes in the process. The best work is then number one!

Do your students also have to write a paper, a synopsis of their work?
No, the final presentation replaces the paper. However, the students are required to provide a written description of their impressions and what they learnt in class. As an essay.

How lengthy?
Not that long, one page at the most.

What role does all that play in your final assessment?
Since this course makes no sense if you don't participate in the discussions, being present is the most important factor. Because if you are absent just once, you are no longer able to follow the process. The second most important factor is a person's ultimate output. To that end, I ask my students to write down the name of another team member who contributed the most, who was proactive. In that way, I find out which of them were active outside of class, and who took the lead. This is in addition to the teacher's assessment. Two other assistant professors are involved, as well, so there are three of us to decide.

You mentioned before that your students are required to do a weekly presentation. Is that to foster their expressiveness as well?
Expressiveness – to be honest, in half a year we focus on concept making and planning. I would need to add another half a year to train a person's expressiveness. Admittedly, I made a conscious decision to end the course after half a year, because what students should learn during that time is not expressiveness, but ways of thinking.

From whom did you learn how to teach?
When I was a student at Tama Art University, I learnt the most in the class where you had to develop everything from scratch yourself. A topic was given, but after that, you could work freely and do presentations. And there was also an advertising class where we were required to concentrate on concepts all the time. Those are the things that left a lasting impression on me, and that is why I like to use them in my teaching.

What was the biggest mistake you made in class?
[reflects] Have I ever made a mistake? Rarely. [laughs]
   Since I am merely guest professor and not a typical academic professor, and my teaching consists of special lectures or workshops, I can't make that many mistakes.

What kind of students come to your class? Do you select them?
Fortunately, my class is very popular. There are 24 places available at the moment and 150 students applying for admission. So they have to do an exam first, a simple test, and then I make my choice. After selection, they need to be organised into groups. Mostly, groups of six are formed. Since first to fourth-year students are eligible to participate, I try to balance things out a bit, mixing ages and avoiding groups consisting of female students only.

What do you tell those students on their first day? What do you consider important?
Instead of talking about the topic itself, for example, design strategies for uncharted territory, I explain the concept behind the subject I teach. I tell them why I believe this subject is essential for society right now. I talk about the role of design in society, about what it requires.

When it comes to specific topics such as Catastrophes or Earth Reset, I invite guests to join us and we begin to reflect on that topic in a panel discussion. First, the students listen to us and then it's their turn.

What are students frequently unable to do initially?
I feel they cannot think out of the box.

And what do you think is inside the box?
Common sense, I would say, as a healthy asset, but also less positively, as a fixed mindset.

And why can't those students think out of that box?
One reason, for instance, could be a lack of dynamic change in their lives, which means that their ideals have never fundamentally changed, or that they have not seen this in others.

How do you encourage them to change their perspective?
That's hard. [laughs]

Through discussions?
Exactly. Alternatively, when my students are stuck with their ideas, I give them some examples of my own work or some other story of success. I say, for instance, 'You see? That's the way it was, that's how the project was finally solved.' I speak to them as plainly as possible and give them tips. That way, they have no other choice than to grasp the opportunity.

Many, many thanks, Mr Sato.

Yasuhiro Sawada

teaches Graphic Design

Professor
Faculty of Art and Design
Department of Graphic Design
Tama Art University, Tokyo
Japan

Founded Yasuhiro Sawada Design Studio

At first, he only looks in at the door; and then comes a hearty
'Hello!' followed by Yasuhiro Sawada himself. In the conversation,
he talks about rivalry and concentration and why it is better
to ignore students using their smartphones in class. Finally,
he reveals why two students fainted in his class.
— December 2019

Thies: How would you describe what you do at the university?
Sawada: I wouldn't necessarily describe what I do as 'teaching', more as
collaborative thinking. Experience has shown me that you learn what is
missing by studying and researching, and then you try to reach a desired
level. After the first two years of the foundation course here at Tama Art
University you have a certain fundamental understanding of design.

   The most important thing for students in the third and fourth years
of their degree is to think things through together. The most important thing
for us teachers is to take the teaching very seriously. That is why I work with
the students – although there are so many – on a one-to-one basis and don't
give them tasks but rather take on board their suggestions and react to them.

How do you react?
I'm a little embarrassed to say this, but I think I deal very mindfully with
the students, whether the topic is good or not. There's only this one way I know
of having a positive influence on young people who love design. I've followed
this approach since I was invited to teach at the Tama Art University.

Why are you convinced that this sort of mindfulness is a positive thing?
I think it comes down to what you said in your lecture.[54] You also talked about passion and that students feel when you work conscientiously. The younger generations embrace this and act in the same way. And they sometimes surprise you with unexpected thoughts.

You leave a lot to the students. Do they also determine when their project is completed?
I leave it to the students; they decide everything. But I do speak with the students about the perspective of the first step in terms of the development of the project and also about its completion. In the third year, for example, we spend six months on one project, one task.

Who assesses the work at the end?
I do the evaluating.

Do you need grades to do that?
I don't think that grades are necessary; I even find them to be a bad idea, but this is the way things are done at Japanese universities. We have to give the grades A, B, C or fail. Five percent of the students with an A are awarded an S as an additional distinction. But there are so many young people who put their heart and soul into it, meaning that basically everyone is given an A.

So you don't only assess the final result but also the involvement in its development?
Yes, of course. A good result of high quality never comes from nowhere – without a process, without willpower and hard work.

You mentioned that you discuss with the students on a one-to-one basis. Do you sometimes involve other students too?
Yes, because students benefit from the one-to-one constellation as well as from discussions about their fellow students' work, which they maybe don't have a personal connection to. In my class there are normally 50 students and we form a circle. I stand in the circle facing one student and we are surrounded by an audience.

Other students of the same age often see things that we teachers, often from an older generation, don't notice. It's not so much about what I say but rather about whether or not their friends are interested and I think this is a good type of assessment for the students. Rivalry between students is horrible; because then you don't see what you don't want to see.

What do you do when you're standing in a circle like that and have the feeling that a lot of students aren't listening, that they're not concentrating on the task in hand?
I don't do anything to force them to pay attention. Nowadays people might be playing with their phones, but Japan is a polite country. [smiles]

So it doesn't bother you if someone uses their phone in class?
Ignore it! Just ignore it.

And that helps?
I think time is better spent giving all my attention to the people who are really present and talking about them, even if they're not good. Getting annoyed is a waste of time.
    When students have friends who are interested in them, they stop playing with their phones and get involved in the work.

You said that you have 50 students. How do you manage to make sure that each person has their turn to speak?
If I really need to hear an opinion, for example during a presentation, or if I want to talk about something specific, I use my position of power. I determine the length of time and order and have them speak one after another. But I don't force anyone to speak in the middle of a project if they don't want to talk. I think that when you really want to speak you will say something. It is desire that makes us put things into words, isn't it?

Maybe it takes time for this wish to emerge. Do you actively encourage it?
To stay very general: Japan is not a very religious country, but it is a Buddhist country. In Japan we have a teaching according to which the highest level of human life means having no desire or craving. It is vulgar to ask how much money you earned with a project. The Japanese virtue still applies that you need to be patient when you are hungry or you are not to say anything even when you want money.
    But if you want to be creative and bring something into being you have to show yourself to other people. This is where there is a gulf between Japan and the rest of the world. Around 15 years ago, there were many young people who had an approach different to that of other people in Japan and who made themselves heard in this unique space that is the art college. But now there are a large number of very cultivated young people.

Are there any further differences between before and now?
I think that today we all have many different opportunities to, for example, publish information. Even if you don't have much confidence, you can publish

the music you like or come into contact with women and men more easily, if I may say that. When the world was less comfortable you sometimes had to make a conscious decision to start and assert yourself to get something done. But now you can hide yourself and still do what you want. Maybe we don't have to be as confident as before. My opinion is that today more students focus on their internal feelings or specific issues.

There are people who can express themselves very well. But the will to spread their ideas is often missing – even though there are so many different media. Others make very conscious use of media. For example, one student created portraits of people who use their body as a canvas, and she found words to accompany it – words of teenagers. Very beautiful words. In a way there are now many young people in Japan working with design but with a very artistic approach. And they are not interested in the effect on society.

Should designers return to shaping society more?
What do they want to achieve if they don't want to have an impact on society? What are they aiming at?

When I was young there was design and art. I studied design after the end of American pop art and during the period of neo-expressionism. There was a big trend that encompassed the world, one single ism that could bring together people who were interested in this type of energy and people who weren't interested in it. But if you look at the individual skills of young people today, they are doing very good things but it is narcissistic.

What do you want to enable your students to do? What should they be particularly good at by the end of their degree?
I want my students to have the confidence – even overconfidence – that allows them to see new perspectives. They need to be given recognition by friends and people who they respect. During their limited time as students, they should do as much as possible and discover new ways of looking at the world.

What do you say to students on their last day when you say goodbye?
'Let's go for a beer together' [laughs] – really.

What should a young lecturer or a young professor be able to do?
They need to ask themselves who and what they are. Again and again. To stay quite general: you need to be authentic when teaching and be able to talk about your own experiences in research or your working life. From a student's perspective I think that who you are learning from is more important than what you learn. Meaning that I should study with the person whose statements I like – even if I'm maybe not interested in their subject.

Does a young professor need to bring their own convictions and ideals?
Definitely. Based on their own research or their own work.

Are there examples of people who didn't bring this with them and who left the university?
There are a lot, at Tama Art University as well. People who attempt to get by with basic knowledge and a couple of well-chosen words. But they are decreasing in number because students are looking for quality.

What are you particularly good at as a teacher?
What I'm good at? I'm good at getting motivated students to take my courses. It's not something I'm totally aware of, but perhaps the students sense my wish to have a dream and a vision for design with every word that I say.

Which vision do you have? Is creativity a part of it?
In my opinion creativity means doing and creating things that other people can't. Even if it's only a small difference. That's what I try to achieve in my work, even though I'm close to 60. There is a difference in value. I think that a person who has something that only they can do is a true creative. This is my understanding of professionalism. The other thing is to have lots of fun and to really get involved. It is a process. It's about enjoyment at work and at home, and it's also about having a sense of joy in the results.

What is the biggest mistake you've made when teaching?
Are you going to write this down? [laughs]

In my 24 years as a teacher two students fainted. There was no violence involved. But when I gave a particularly sharp critique the two students collapsed. – I was in my mid-thirties when I started teaching. And I came to the university with the same approach and strictness that I was used to in my office. I think I really was too strict. I was called 'Sawada the devil'. Now I'm 'Sawada the angel'. [laughs]

So you're an angel at university … Are you still a devil at your office?
I'm a human being now, so totally normal. [smiles]

But you used to be stricter?
Yes, I was very strict. But my approach to my work is that it is a difficult job and only those who work hard and do very good work can survive. There is no finishing line. There is no end. But the good thing about the design industry is that there are deadlines.

What happens when students don't hand in their work on time?
Basically, I forgive them. But one of the most important rules is that design
has a purpose and one of these purposes is keeping to deadlines, and when
you don't manage that, the result, however good, is useless.

Do you still grade their work?
Yes, I do. Some people are just not capable of keeping to deadlines or something
can have got in the way – it's a relationship based on trust, isn't it?

Should you accept mistakes, setbacks?
Yes, I think so, even when mistakes make things more cumbersome. There's
a saying in Japan: 'Forget to eat and sleep.' Eating and sleeping are the joys
of life in Japan, but there are moments when you concentrate on something
so much that you forget those things. I find something so much fun that I
forget everything else… that's what graphic design is to me.

Where does this dedication, this love of teaching come from?
Teaching is not only about the exchange of words; it's also about finding
yourself, about interaction in class. And it is a great opportunity to get
to know people.

Thank you very much for the interview, Mr Sawada.

Mathilde Scholz
teaches Integrated Design

Lecturer, Teaching Assistant
Department of Design
Anhalt University of Applied Sciences, Dessau
Germany

A quiet talk in the room of a music school in Leipzig. Mathilde
Scholz probably teaches her class in exactly the same mindful
way, encouraging her students to take over the teaching themselves.
Together they decide what to do and check their activities in
feedback blocks. She also explains why it is helpful to follow
a predetermined process while doing so. — September 2021

Thies: You coined the term 'transformative education'. What does it mean?
Scholz: I understand education as a form of collaboration. It is transformative
because, structurally, it is permanently adapted to internal requirements and
external conditions through feedback and reflection. By internal requirements,
I mean the group's needs, which can change anytime. External conditions are
changes to the environment that I have no influence on such as a pandemic
and the inevitable switch to online teaching that it entails.

   I try to teach content with a sense of direct experience and tangibility,
sometimes even playfully. One further important element in my approaches
is to change perspectives, whatever the topic may be: even when it comes
to research.

   Whatever the case, I never do front-of-class teaching, but let my students
do something themselves instead. I want them to get that 'Hey! I've learnt
something' feeling afterwards. In order to achieve that effect, I sum up our
activities and ask them to reflect on questions like 'What have we been doing
here just now? What did you experience?'

   Many of them have told me that my course had also helped them personally in day-to-day matters, for example, in situations related to their shared
living arrangements.

   And that's exactly what I want – to help them develop in their personal
life as well, which is an inseparable part of their life at university.

In transformative education, students structure the course of their projects themselves. Are there recurrent phases in all processes?
In our workshops, there are five recurrent phases: definition, action, reflection, evaluation and modification. We integrate them as a kind of design process in our teaching concept. We begin with the definition, the agenda. This is followed by the action, the part in which I carry out the agenda and the methods I have decided on. The next step is reflection, which involves a discussion with the participants on how everything was. Then we do an evaluation: what do we need to change the next time? And the modification is the change per se, which means putting a new agenda in place.

What crops up repeatedly is the question of team building, role hierarchies, purpose, what outcomes we expect to see, elements of mindfulness and a documentation. And we always have a check-in and a check-out.

What happens at a check-in and check-out and what effect do they have?
When we have a check-in, we form a circle of chairs at the beginning of each session. Everyone recounts briefly how they're doing, for example. That could include trivial matters such as whether you'd slept well or whether you're just looking forward to the day ahead. Another check-in question could be 'What's preventing you right now from engaging fully?' It's a super method to help people get settled. When we check out, it's much the same: each of us says how we're doing or how the class was. In that way, we round off each session nicely.

As a matter of fact, rituals like that are all the more important when we're online, because everyone is isolated in their own bubble and you actually have no idea in what state of mind other people are when you speak to them.

You also describe that in *perMA*55, a book that you wrote together with four fellow students. In the introduction, you say that teaching also needs to be designed. What do you think is the essence of well-designed teaching?
In my view, well-designed teaching enables all participants to work and learn well, while having fun and making personal progress at the same time – that applies to teachers and students alike, because to me, they're both learners. I want them to reap the benefits beyond the class, too. In line with that, some students ran workshops themselves, even inviting teachers to attend, in that way reapplying and passing on what they had learnt.

Where do you get your inspiration for teaching from?
I look into lots of other contexts, taking a bit from everywhere that could help, and then I combine it in a new way – for example, at coaching workshops: which methods and exercises are used there to build a team? The team idea is one of my most elementary concepts because we learn together as a team.

How do you put a team together?

My aim is to break down the traditional professor–student hierarchy while still providing a clear form of communication. If need be, we form a new team every hour. The question is: which of those people will do the moderating, take care of time-related matters and finally give the feedback? Depending on the team's size, the number and types of roles will vary. And if the assignment is a book, that team will differ from a team doing mental work where the focus is more on input. At the beginning of a course, I usually make a few proposals. But from the second week on, the team can independently develop the structure they need to proceed further. In that regard, it helps enormously to reflect and provide feedback at the end of each session. There is always someone who is even willing to carry out the rather unpopular task of taking minutes.

And what happens if a person is tired of their role and no one else is willing to take it on?

That often happens to people taking minutes [laughs], but only at the beginning really. In that case, I always say, 'Okay, if nobody wants that job, we'll leave it out.' Then we wait a bit to see what happens and maybe decide that we don't really need the minutes or that keywords will do instead. After a few sessions, though, someone will often do the job after all because the minutes are sorely missed.

As a teacher, one sometimes needs to motivate students. Does that play any role in your methods?

I certainly give lots of praise, but in the course of their studies, the students require less motivation because they moderate their projects on their own. During the first one to two weeks, I demonstrate how moderation can work. Afterwards, in the first and second semesters, I motivate people to take over the moderation, and in higher semesters, moderation roles are a matter of course. I then assume the role of an expert for the content and keep a careful eye on the participants, paying attention to things like 'Are the moderators too dominant? Are they too strict?' I think it's vital that they develop awareness of what their team needs.

My experience is that the students motivate each other to an extreme extent in everything they do. They even take their classwork home with them although they weren't told to, because they have a completely different attitude to work than if I had given them orders.

How do you teach the students how to moderate?

Well, I never learnt how to moderate, but rather act on intuition. So I watched other people to see which things worked. And that's exactly what I try to do with the students: I just let them have a bash at it for a start. My only requirement is for them to compile a very detailed agenda split into steps of up to five minutes, enabling them to time things well and therefore to know what needs to be done and prepared. They are allowed to try everything throughout the entire process. As regards learning, the students get their biggest boost through the final feedback: what worked well and what didn't? The feedback comes from two other students who have the moderation and feedback roles, from Professor Michael Hohl and myself. Feedback is always given in a reflection phase in the last five minutes.

My job is to ensure that everything is understandable and on time.

What do you do if someone is too timid to give feedback?
I approach the person and address the matter. As a rule, people who have moderated once and motivated others begin to flourish in those roles.

Do you address matters like that in the bigger group or individually?
When I teach in class, I mostly discuss matters individually while moving from desk to desk or afterwards when the students leave the classroom. It's a challenge when we're online, but we always manage to quickly build an honest feedback culture. They learn that everything only works well in a team. And should any personal uneasiness crop up once in a while, it's my job to show them that I'd been in situations like that myself before, that they are just part of the game and how to deal with them, and that it's probably better to give honest feedback than just positive feedback all the time.

In the feedback session, do you merely address what needs to be improved or are suggestions welcomed as to how to improve it?
Both. Principally, there are only four relevant questions: What was good? What was bad? Which questions still need answering? What do I think can be improved? You could add a fifth item of self-reflection as to what you can improve yourself, but you can leave that out if everything goes well. The students are asked to give written answers to those four questions individually.

And how did you collate the feedback during distance learning?
With the aid of Miro, which is an online whiteboard tool that has the additional advantage of providing direct access to what other people have written.

Let's get back to team building again: do you have any specific method that always works?
Firstly, I'd name the role-assignment method. And a detailed agenda which clearly outlines everyone's tasks is also helpful, just like the check-in and check-out.

How do the students experience those different methods in class?
By doing them – by defining an agenda and distributing roles. At the beginning,
I don't refer to it as a 'method'; I only say that we have a problem to solve,
which we shall attempt to tackle using the proposed means, and that there are
thousands of other useful variants besides.

Why don't you refer to it as a method?
Because I want it to surface intuitively so that they get their own ideas on how
to solve a problem without having to learn specific methods. Because methods
can appear abstract and narrow and I want them to be able to adapt their
approaches flexibly.

Can you give an example of what you mean?
One example of that is when I try to explain to the group the principle of
'doing and improving'. To that end, we form a circle of chairs. The first chair
next to me is chair A, the last one is chair Z. Since they don't know each other
well yet, some names will be unknown to them. Then they have three minutes'
time to switch seats according to the correct alphabetical order of their first
names and are not allowed to talk to each other in the process. Then they'll
exclaim, 'Huh? How is that supposed to work?' [laughs] And I reply, 'The clock
is already ticking!' And amazingly, they always find the right order in the
wink of an eye. When I ask them how they managed to do that so quickly,
it seems that some students just sat down while others who knew some of the
student's first names discussed which chairs to take with gestures and facial
expressions, correcting each other in the process – so that it wasn't a matter
of individual people having to bother about their own chairs. They sort of
assumed responsibility in a joint effort. That way, they realise that there are
other ways to organise yourself than just one person deciding everything.

How do you motivate shy students to participate in discussions?
In cases like that, again, it helps to keep on reflecting or to discuss things in
a different role like that of a teacher or Harry Potter. That applies to distance
and class teaching alike.

How do you ensure that the students maintain their curiosity?
I think that the students' curiosity is aroused automatically as soon as they
have to take responsibility for the overall project, and have the chance to
co-create and co-shape an exciting structure. In that respect, I try to connect
the tasks they have with something personal – not a problem in Africa whose
cultural references they are not familiar with, but perhaps the problem of
waste disposal at their student residence.

Do you think it would be exaggerating to say that listening is crucial to *learning*?
Listening might be key to learning, certainly. But it could also be watching.

Is it an exaggeration, then, to say that listening is key to *teaching*?
Definitely not. I think that listening is even more important in teaching than in learning.

Can I even listen before having asked a question?
I can imagine that one could start with listening – without having asked a question and without taking any specific direction. And from that, questions could develop.

When I do sociological research, I sometimes start without a question, too. Especially with respect to other cultures, I observe things first and listen for a while until a question crops up. – But something has to happen sometime; I have to take action at some point. [laughs]

How do you train people to listen?
Again, I think reflection is a key element. To reflect time and again on what one has heard and what one should be aware of. It's like learning to see in visual communications by sensitising the students' sight. Initially, they just listen to you, as they have always done. And over time, they realise that there is more to it than meets the ear: noises inside and outside, noises that they never took any notice of before. For example, a sound that changes pitch when you walk alongside a wall. You suddenly realise that on a 'sound walk' where everyone wanders around, eyes shut, in a soundscape.

With listening, it's primarily about the words we hear, but it's also about subtleties, about what happens when we pause or emphasise things. And eventually you come up with an interpretation.

And now, on a completely different note: how do you let your students know that everything's allowed in the conceptual phase?
Well, it wouldn't suffice to merely say that. I suppose role-playing could help to break down existing barriers. Or trigger questions like 'How would you tackle the problem if you were a millionaire?' Everybody assumes that there are rules. Sometimes, however, there may be two or three who think differently straight away and, for example, don't allow financial aspects to curtail their ideas. You have to address that then. To have no rules does not mean that you automatically think there are no rules whatsoever.

What would we have to do at the end of this interview if it were a transformative education project?
[laughs] We'd both have to reflect on what we'd done for about five minutes. That would also include proposing ideas on how we could improve things.

[laughs] Mathilde, thanks a lot.

Matthias Spaetgens

teaches Conception

Professor
Institute of Design
Class of Ideas, Graphics and Advertising
University of Applied Arts Vienna
Austria

Chief creative officer and partner of the communication agency
Scholz & Friends

Matthias Spaetgens's responses are uncomplicated and precise.
This reflects his aim to be able to express any idea in just one
sentence. He explains why benchmarks and humour are vital
and how he puts together a team of teachers, and about which
teaching experiences help him as Chief Creative Officer of one
of Europe's most renowned communication agencies.
— January 2023

**Thies: You lead one of the largest advertising agencies in Germany and
a university class. What are the differences between the two?**
Spaetgens: I'd first like to highlight what they have in common. Both are
management tasks. In a university class and at an agency you're managing
a team. It's about defining common aims, creating a shared culture, promoting
it and defining processes and rituals. At the university you're leading students
with the aim of encouraging their personal development; in the agency you're
leading creatives through their daily challenges at work.

How do you lead Scholz & Friends?
Scholz & Friends's most important asset is the team. And we're very much
shaped by our culture – we are firm when it comes to business, with a friendly
approach and respectful way of dealing with one another. We're currently
sitting at the university in Vienna at a round table, something which I also
have at the agency in Berlin. It symbolises that it's not about a hierarchy,
about the seating arrangements, but about the best idea. This is very important
for concept development. The main thing is not who had the idea, but how
effective this idea is.

How do you try to solve the problem if someone at the table still thinks in hierarchies?
By getting them a coffee [laughs]. You have to create an atmosphere in which the nuances also communicate that we are serious about being on an equal footing.

How do you lead students?
I try to take students to their personal limit – but not beyond. I make an effort to be empathetic, to understand where they're currently at. And at the same time, I want to sow a certain amount of discontentment and of course encourage a desire for personal growth.

What do you mean by limit? Is this about time pressure, a deadline?
I want to take them to the limit they trust themselves to reach. The essence of outstanding creation is entering new fields that no one has set foot in before. Like walking on a sheet of ice and not knowing whether it will crack or hold your weight. This is the path I want to take with them. So that they leave the much-quoted comfort zone again and again.

Many students have great portfolios but their designs, done with the highest accuracy, appear very predictable and controlled. So I often tell them to do something they've never done before, something that surprises them and that they are not confident that they can do. That's the only way to progress as a creative individual.

You mentioned that you purposefully sow discontentment. How do you do this?
One way, for example, is – and here comes the management slang – benchmarking. I confront the students with outstanding creative work, talk about it with them and then encourage the students to compare their own work with these examples. These reference points are always international – so we don't only look at exemplary Austrian or German communication.

What do you say to motivate the students when their own work is far away from the benchmarks?
It is important that students feel that they are making progress in their personal development. That's why we make the aims we agree on as individual as possible. In portfolio talks I pick out what is particularly good, encourage the students to further develop their strengths and point out deficits or weaknesses. At the end I try to motivate the students to follow the new path we have agreed upon.

Does that mean there is a type of target evaluation a year later?
This is very individual. Of course you could make it into even more of a tool, maybe creating a protocol, but I don't do that. Instead I ask the students to show me the work from the current semester and, as a comparison, the ten best pieces of their entire creative career. Choosing the ten best is important so that they learn to differentiate the good from the mediocre and how to make a choice. If work from the current semester is added to the 'best of' list, this shows their creative development.

Do you criticise indirectly via the benchmarks or do you sometimes also say, 'I find this piece poor because …'?
That depends. Some students are best reached by talking about their weaknesses very carefully and diplomatically. Others need the most direct and clear language possible.

Another question about leadership: How do you manage the team teaching your class?
I hope I show them a great deal of appreciation and trust. There are of course regular meetings during which we define common aims for our class. Apart from that it has to be fun! Many teachers at the university teach because of an intrinsic motivation and in no way for financial reasons.

What do you take into account when you put together a team of teachers?
It's important that each person has a specialisation, an area in which they are outstanding – whether it's in typography, corporate design, advertising concepts or in other fields. And ideally, they bring their own network with them, which they make use of when teaching.

I also find it important for teachers to take up social and political topics and incorporate them into their teaching.

And the third point is quite simple: there has to be the right chemistry between the teachers.

Do teachers need to bring something particular to the table when it comes to dealing with students?
Yes, openness and curiosity towards what the students bring with them and a respectful approach.

How do you determine whether someone can teach respectfully and well?
When they create an atmosphere that makes our classroom a fear-free space where you can open up, where you can express crazy ideas, where you can talk about weaknesses openly and where even failure is allowed and sometimes desired.

Are there limits when it comes to weaknesses? What do you do when the students' topics become too personal?
Basically, you should differentiate between working life, in this case university, and social life, so private issues. Of course there are situations where it is good to be aware of students' problems. University promotes not only professional but also personal development. This is why we offer courses ranging, for example, from typography to acting training.

But don't private matters always have a major influence on personal development? Where do you see the boundary?
When students notice that there are things standing in the way of their personal development, for example, involving their upbringing or their family history, this ideally leads to them working through this for themselves. Everyone has topics like this. But these issues can't be worked through in class.

Why do you sometimes invite external specialists to the class on a short-term basis?
First for an egoistic reason: because I learn a great deal from them. And it is also great for students to experience different personalities and therefore different perspectives, styles and approaches during their degree.

Is it stressful to both manage a large agency and lead a university class?
It's mainly stressful in terms of the amount of time needed for both jobs – my diary is always full, but I enjoy doing it.

What are the advantages of your 'double life'?
My practical work means that I know pretty exactly what is happening in the market, what clients are currently demanding, how agencies work and which challenges they are confronted with in the constantly changing world of media.

I'd now like to move on to a different topic: What should students learn in your class?
That they need a simple and yet unusual idea for every creative task. And they shouldn't rest until they have found it.

How can you teach this motivation?
In that students experience how great the moment is when they discover this idea – the famous eureka moment. Anyone who has experienced this feeling several times wants to feel it again and again.

Is this strengthened by a sense of satisfaction or by pats on the back, recognition?
It is strengthened by the students' experience of competence and through the realisation that this central idea they have come up with has an impact.

Simplifying somewhat: is it important for advertising and design to have a positive impact on society?
As creatives in the world of communication we have a great deal of responsibility. The tools of our trade are very powerful. And I want the students to be aware of how and where they use these tools – ideally, they use them to facilitate positive change. This can be in a social-political field but also in communication for companies. Because now, fortunately, companies are also increasingly measured by their contribution to society.

Which word describes best what you do in class: 'lecturing' or 'teaching' or something totally different?
I think different words apply. One I would definitely add is 'coaching' – accompanying but also guiding the students.

Is listening the most important thing for students learning in class? Or are there other things you find more important?
I don't know if that is the most important thing. But listening, understanding is very central. I believe that only empathetic creatives are also good creatives because, as a communication professional, you have to put yourself in other people's shoes. We have to reach people with our work and these people are very different and not usually identical to us.

What do you do to make students good at putting themselves in other people's shoes?
First you have to make students aware that this is important. And then in discussions you need to keep comparing whether the end product is just something you like personally or whether those you want to reach also like it. For example, it is useful to create what is known as a persona, so a person that you describe in detail and who helps you to understand the target group.

Would students learn even more from going out and interviewing people in real life?
Well, of course, I think that's enormously important. After all, a one-to-one conversation is a particularly intense experience.

Another question about listening: is listening the most important thing when you teach?
[reflects] Well, if you only listen, you won't be able to convey anything yourself. So I don't think it's the most important thing. But it is very important during discussions because this is the only way you can respond to the person you are talking to.

How do you support students in developing their own convictions regarding design?
Having a conviction means that you have made decisions and that you support a certain viewpoint, which you also defend. For me, it's also a question of personal development, and this takes time.

Not everyone has the confidence to advocate for their position. How do you encourage shy people to become braver and thus more confident?
I always try to make it clear to people of a quieter disposition that there is nothing to lose in our class and that you benefit greatly by contributing your own thoughts. Students also always have to present their own work in front of the class, which promotes self-confidence, too.

What experiences from your teaching help you in agency life?
I have learnt to be even more precise when it comes to formulating a task or giving feedback. Many students often don't understand nuances. You have to give very concrete feedback and that's something I've taken with me to my agency work. And that you look at the first results early on. Because this is the only way you see whether someone has understood the task or not.

Another point I've taken with me is how much is possible in a short period of concentrated working. In one hour, you can come up with ten ideas for big campaigns. Power brainstorming sessions like this are very valuable.

How do you practice these ideation processes with students?
I talk to them about how a successful, collaborative ideation process happens as a team. As part of this, we also sometimes try out brainstorming methods. You soon see progress if you do this very frequently and also mix the groups differently so that students have to adapt to people they don't yet know very well. Again this means getting out of your comfort zone.

How does the space influence brainstorming? Does a particular interior help you come up with ideas?
I believe that the space has a tremendous impact, but do not know the ideal environment. However, it's helpful to keep trying out new places and to change surroundings when brainstorming.

Do you become impatient when students don't get to the point?
Not usually. But every so often I try and give them the opportunity to realise for themselves that they're not getting to the point. [laughs] That's when it also helps to keep a sense of humour while working together.

You studied graphic design in Munich and later did an executive MBA in Berlin. How do these qualifications help you in your teaching?
In Munich, I often thought that there could be more variety to the teaching, and I learnt there that discipline doesn't do any harm. My degree was very school-like in its structure.

The MBA allowed me to get to know myself even better, to get a better understanding of my own agency, the market and the industry. I also met many impressive people, and I now invite some of them to class.

How do you get feedback from students on your teaching?
I very often do a feedback round after a session. The students aren't allowed to leave until I get at least three to five pieces of feedback. And I also use the university's evaluation tools, questionnaires.

What do you think works well in distance learning?
What works well is the integration of large groups to communicate information to a lot of people. Breakout sessions can also be used to add a great deal of variety to the class.

Do students have to leave their video on when they are in large groups?
Not in the big meetings where there are several hundred people. But otherwise I do find it important.

Have you ever been nervous in class?
Of course. I think that if you're not nervous, you're not as focused as you should be. It sometimes also depends on your mood or how well prepared you are.

How do you motivate creative, sensitive people?
First of all you motivate by preventing demotivation. Everyone who begins a new job or degree starts off extremely motivated. Otherwise, the person would not do it. The trick is to ensure that this natural motivation is maintained. – When does it decrease? When you don't give feedback, when you don't show an interest in the students, when the workload is too high or too low and when you're not valued.

Thanks a lot, Matthias.

Erik Spiekermann
taught Information Design

Professor
University of the Arts Bremen
Berlin University of the Arts
Germany

Co-founder of MetaDesign, Fontshop and Edenspiekermann

*Erik Spiekermann always speaks fast. He always has an anecdote
to tell or an analogy to make. A conversation in his experimental
Letterpress Workshop p98 in Berlin: what he experienced on his
first day teaching in London, what hurts in the ideation phase
and how to prolong thinking processes in a natural way, and why
practice and teaching are dependent on each other. — July 2021*

Thies: When did you begin your teaching career?
Spiekermann: I began teaching at the age of 27 in the 1970s in London where
people knew far more than I did; I had the practice but not the theory.

My first class at the London College of Printing was Layout and Printing
for working journalists, and I was only a small step ahead in that respect.
It was only a tiny step, but if there was something I did not know, I had
the wonderful possibility of saying, 'We call this something else in German.'
Then I would run home and tell my wife, 'Joan, I have no damn idea what they
are talking about', and then I would look it up. In those days, we only had
books to refer to. The next morning, I would play the nonchalant German guy,
exclaiming, 'Of course … obvious!' I felt pretty awkward about it, but they
believed me. So it was a bit of a bluff in those days.

And today, I still use a similar method when I don't have the faintest idea
about something, or am just too lazy to bother researching: I simply assign
tasks in the group. Years later in Germany, for example, I wanted to give
my class some work on infographics. As it happened, we chose the Olympic
Games as a major event; then it dawned on me that I had no idea what was
on the Games' schedule. So, I delegated the task directly to the students,
saying, 'Come on, folks, let's see what happened there in detail', and they
all came up with Otl Aicher and Mexico and all that stuff. That was great,
of course, because it's also quite fun to do research. We all learnt from it.
And then it turned out that those who were good at researching were not

necessarily good at leading the group. You know, the kind of people hovering in the background who suddenly come to the fore and perform like world champions, bringing tons of books with them – or do the googling nowadays. And in about one or two weeks' time, you discover the talents. To encourage them without letting them know … that's the secret. You just ask, 'Could you …?' It has to be voluntary on their part.

How many students usually attended your class?
Well, I held weekly seminars or two whole days a week, mostly small courses with 16 people. Of those, six participated, six sat around, and as for the other four, I often wondered what they were doing in the course at all.

Those students who didn't participate actively …
Losers.

… didn't you still try to motivate them?
Yes, of course I did.

How did you do that?
Obviously, all of them were required to participate and accomplish their tasks. I spoke to them personally on that, praising them now and then to motivate them. The six students who were active turned out to be top project leaders who took on tasks, encouraging one or two other students to join in.

Did you actively push group formation?
No. I always advised them to work in groups of three or four; it's crazy to work alone on such complex topics. Why should all of them do the research, for instance? Anybody could volunteer to do it. If not, they would be given a task. A group of three consisting of a leader, a co-worker and someone who just sat around usually worked best. Additionally, I had an assistant, for example Severin Wucher, which was an enormous help.

How extensive were the tasks you gave?
The briefing was 'Design Time in Typography', which in those days, in the early 1970s in London, meant designing with the resources metal typesetting had to offer.

Was the briefing so short? Did you just let the topic unfold?
Yes, simply 'visualise time' was intentional. At first, you see jaws dropping. They gaped, then they panicked, then they went home and started to prepare themselves for next week's lesson. In those days, there was no such thing as googling … we spoke about chronometers and tried to find out more about them.

That was very interesting. The briefing began to unfold. That had partly to do with my laziness, to be honest, but there was also a method in it: put the cat amongst the pigeons in order to rouse the pigeons. By doing that, you get approaches that are quite different from those that would have emerged from a detailed briefing.

In a diploma course, on the other hand, which would be a bachelor's degree programme nowadays, you have to be more explicit in order to get quicker results. You can't just let them faff around.

All the same, why is this 'faffing around' important?
Because you need self-confidence to rely on your own idea. – And that can sometimes hurt. It's like staring at a blank sheet of paper and not knowing how to begin. The much-feared *horror vacui*[56] of anyone working creatively, not just writers. Well, I begin somewhere at the top left of the screen where nowadays the cursor blinks and in those days the pencil lay on the desk. That's the biggest problem – and there's a variety of methods to solve it. Brainstorming was not a familiar word in those days, and my method primarily consists of collecting and avoiding. You know, putting something off for so long until you can't bear the pressure anymore. Then you start to iron your shirts and wash the car or clean the bike – all sorts of things – just to steer clear of that specific task. I'm really good at avoiding things, but I've meanwhile realised that it's my method. Far from avoiding, I rather prolong the thinking process until the deadline looms large. In the meantime, I know that I am a quick worker when it comes to concepts. I only need one day because of having carried it around with me for two weeks. That obviously wouldn't apply to technical skills. You sometimes have to let the students cope with that difficulty on their own.

Later on, you are constantly faced with challenges like these in your professional life: tasks from clients who don't really know what they want. Who say something like, 'Could you do a draft, maybe like this…' In the USA they call that 'blue sky'; it's about the worst briefing you can get: 'Just, you know, you can do whatever you like.' Your first thought is, 'Oh dear, I don't know, I don't like anything. You damn well pay for it, tell me what you want.'

It's crucial to question briefings and make decisions.

In the case of 'visualise time', the students got into a panic. They thought, 'What the heck?', and came back, some of them still panicking, with one of them waving the face of a clock, a pie chart. Well, he was right! Task done! An ideal representation of time boldly reduced to the basics. When it comes to the details, though, that's where they need your support.

To go home after delivering the briefing and to turn up again after six weeks to evaluate the results, as many teaching staff do nowadays – that's scandalous, it's just not right.

Were there any other parameters concerning the tasks?
As a professional, I always assigned professional tasks. Sometimes even proper commercial tasks which I would present afterwards…

With real clients?
Yes, mostly things that weren't budgeted for normally, such as the programme for the adult education centre. So I said, 'We are going to spend one whole week working as if we were in a professional design studio', and it was really from nine in the morning to six in the evening, six days a week with a coffee break and lunch break. I always wrote down the briefings clearly to avoid confusion, adding a name, title, date, structure, tasks, time schedule, a list of terms, selected literature and so on. Mostly limited to one A4 page, and distributed in good time. In that way, students learn to pay attention to deadlines, to share tasks and achieve quicker results.

It was a privilege for me that I didn't have to work academically but was able to bring in my professional experience to class; at the time, we had 70 people at Edenspiekermann.

Why didn't you focus exclusively on teaching?
I loved working on a practical level because that's where real problems are solved.

I have no formal qualifications as a teacher and can actually only work in groups, preferably on an equal footing with everyone else. The hierarchical gap between teachers and students or front-of-class teaching is not my cup of tea.

Were you on first-name terms with your students?
In England that comes quite naturally and in Germany, being a fairly cool guy from alternative Berlin, I asked first if it were okay to address them informally, which they always accepted.

Nevertheless, students often perceive the given hierarchy as an inhibition. How did you go about eliminating it?
By sharing tasks in the project, which put us all on an equal footing. We all had our own work. In a certain sense, I was the client, but I also passed on my knowledge and made corrections the next day or looked at the results. Basically, we were an autonomous working group. I held a proper lecture about once a month, an hour or so, talking from my own experience on some subject or other. But it was mainly teamwork because other teachers such as Eckhard Jung, who came from the Ulm School of Design, already practised that kind of collaboration on an equal footing.

How did you initiate the teamwork in particular?

You can really only work effectively with seven people in one group and since I had a maximum of 12 to 16 in my course, I always divided them up into three or four smaller groups.

At the University of the Arts Bremen, for example, where we wanted to design a new logo for the public transport services there, we drafted three concepts on the first day, three different directions, with each group working on one direction. At the end they were all realised. Of course, I intervened a bit, just as I did in my business, because I already know from experience what is likely to turn out successfully.

Do you have any tricks and tips for effective teamwork or did you just let your students get on with it?

Team building is only problematic if you don't know the group. First of all, I used to pin my conditions on the notice board. Compulsory attendance was from nine to six sharp. So you weren't admitted if you didn't turn up by nine; I didn't accept any excuses. Afterwards, the tasks were assigned with sufficient breaks in between. In the afternoon it was always coffee and cake which one of them would buy or bring from home. All of this happened at regular intervals just like at a design studio. When I was at MetaDesign in the 1990s, for example, I always arrived around ten minutes late, mostly held up by some important phone call, to find seven members of staff sitting there waiting for me. Seven times ten minutes. If you multiply that idle time by the days of a week, a whole working day goes missing. And we really needed that day when things got tight towards the end of a project.

That is also why I established punctuality and discipline as an important principle both at work and at university – although that's not my nature really, as an easygoing person.

When you build groups, especially with people from different degree courses and even from different semesters, you have to be careful not to group together three older students who already know how things work. In that case, it's best to juggle them around a bit, because there are always some who may be silent but certainly not stupid.

Did teaching have any effect on your professional practice, on your design studios?

Sure! After about four years of course work, I knew most of the students very well, and therefore, who would be suitable for recruitment. Many people working at MetaDesign in the 1980s and 1990s had been my students.

So would you recommend that teaching staff continue their practical work at all costs?

Yes, I would. That's even a prerequisite in many cases. But there's sufficient theoretical stuff like brainstorming or team building you can teach without having much practical experience.

When it comes to team building, how do I get to know students in a short time so as to be able to intervene specifically, if necessary?

By forcing them to talk. I used to assign tasks on Friday and discuss them on Monday morning. After another day of experimenting, everybody had to present their results on Tuesday morning. Then you would already be in the picture and maybe discover a shy girl sitting at the back of class who hadn't spoken a word and whose name you didn't even remember. And she would present her work and come up with things, and wow, you'd just be stunned.

My students surprised me time and again. A Chinese student, tall and thin, for example, who hadn't spoken a word for two years but who'd always looked interested. After university, he had taken on some kind of job; then he suddenly turned up at my studio and showed me his work – I was absolutely amazed. He had learnt quite a lot, after all, but just didn't communicate it.

To what extent can an educator influence a development process that evolves inwardly rather than in dialogue?

It may sound rather banal, but praise is a method that does work after all. Sometimes you have to coach students who are obviously no design talents, praise their relatively uninspired drafts now and then and take about an hour's time to go through everything with them, showing them alternatives – just as you would with your own children. They are allowed to make mistakes and should not be left on their own. I often took that trouble, although I already knew that some of them would end up as taxi drivers.

What did you like most about teaching?

The feedback I received broadened my horizon terrifically because my students came up with ideas that I would never have thought of. And asked questions that I would never have asked. To see their hard work and amazing final results – that was a real moment of bliss.

How would you describe your teaching style?

I never really did any teaching. I did projects. I would always announce that we'd be operating under production-like circumstances despite the lack of commercial pressure to make the job work. You can't simulate that.

But you can simulate the pressure of practice and you can create deadlines. And I always did a time-out once or twice a day to deal with questions, for instance, on copyright issues, layout proportions, the golden ratio and its relationship to the Fibonacci sequence … or when everybody used Helvetica. You know, we often use terms that we cannot honestly explain … so I have taken to looking things up I don't know immediately, that goes for my professional work as well. At university, we would always discuss things like that straight away. Or the next day, I'd hold an additional 15-minute lecture or seminar on the topic. Just like it used to be at school: the room was darkened and we would watch a film. And while the film projector whirred, we would just relax. The pedagogical purpose was just to change the direction.

How did you provide feedback? Did you ask questions? Did you suggest 'trying something out' or something completely different?
Partially. In the morning, I would give a briefing. While all 16 of them were working, I would walk around peeping over their shoulders. In that respect, we always attached importance to doing real drawings and sketches, finding things out and gluing things together and not working on screens. Because if all of them were sitting in front of a computer they wouldn't be working in groups. Computer work could be done at home. In class, we would always put up everything on the wall or on whiteboards so that the others could see it as well! In that way, things got extremely lively, creating a spirit of togetherness. And rivalry, too. They would talk and sketch a lot. And some would say, 'I can't draw', and I would reply, 'Oh yes you can! Do a rough drawing', and would show them how. That is how they would overcome their fear of drawing. Two lines, two circles, that's it. A cigarette.

Besides that, I would always ask a lot of questions.

My method with students was also to say, 'I can't do that, so please explain it to me.' As far as working with Photoshop is concerned, for example, I am an absolute loser. And I didn't say that because I wanted to gain sympathy but because I really have no idea how it works. And that's okay, because I am not a jack-of-all-trades. People who know everything are a pain in the neck anyhow! [laughs] However, I always expected general knowledge. Politics. History!

What's so fascinating about teaching and did you learn anything you otherwise wouldn't have?
I never studied graphic design. I did a bit of art history, some English and quit my apprenticeship as a typesetter. But I somehow learnt that trade all the same. I had never seen a curriculum setting out what students are supposed to do. I secretly looked that up when I started my first job in Bielefeld. So, you learn from your students' questions and from your colleagues.

And quite generally in life that in order to answer questions you have to figure them out for yourself first.

One other aspect was the group work; I improved my delegating in that regard. Delegating also means not being too keen on working. [laughs]

And I learnt that you benefit from doing projects with people who all have different backgrounds and viewpoints … that's what I find so very rewarding. But also to put questions to students.

As a teacher, you constantly learn new things. Does that help to deepen your own insights?
Yes, it certainly does!

How would you describe your job? Is 'teaching' the right word for it?
I would actually describe it as solving problems collaboratively. You can only deal with my topic of complex design systems by doing a concrete project.

Have you ever repeated a project?
No, never! I always came up with one or two new projects every semester.

Here in your letterpress workshop it's all about 'grasping' things. Why is that still so important in today's digital world?
We all know that children touch everything because only then do they grasp the nature of things. When I see a round shape on the screen, for instance, how do I know it's a ball? Well, because I've experienced it before in a spatial context. Reading a text, for example, can be a slower process when leafing through a book than scrolling a digital text. But since we grow up in a spatial dimension and learn to do things by touching them, it is an advantage to turn pages if you have to repeat what you have read, because it's useful to know where the relevant content was – towards the beginning or the end of a book. That's an additional dimension. Earmarks, too. And I'm not arguing in favour of reading books, but simply pro human perception.

Another example: in metal typesetting, I have to touch everything before the actual printing, above all, what is not printed; for you cannot see black. That is why we read white, the contrast between the two. And when I need to get hold of the gaps between the lines and the spaces around them, then I have understood them. It's a physical experience. Not just the return button, but all of them are parts of the whole. I always like to compare that idea with a brick building: windows and doors of a building made of bricks always represent a multiple quantity of bricks. Architecture students who have built a wall themselves have a different, hands-on approach to architecture. Working on the computer, however, makes anything seem possible.

Analogously speaking, does that mean the digital world is like poured concrete?
Yes, you could put it that way. We have lost our sense of scale. It's all the same if a concrete wall is three by three or four by four metres. It must have a human scale, though. The Italian book, for example, still responds best to our needs. Since we still have only two hands with which we hold a book about 30 to 50 cm away from our eyes, because we still have two eyes side by side. That is why we have double pages instead of single ones.

Here, in the typography workshop, doing and grasping evolves playfully – a magic moment that makes you wish you could go on metal typesetting forever. Redundancy, for instance, is a problem in this trade because it costs extra effort. Setting more than one letter is more than double the work of setting just one. It's not a matter of quickly copying and pasting.

Did you have any particular trick to encourage students to read books?
First of all: we are reading more than ever! Nevertheless, you can still foster reading habits by bringing along interesting books. And what I do additionally is to try and encourage people to write. After the presentation, I asked everyone to hand in a written statement justifying their work. It's hugely important. In simple writing.

Did you go through those justifications with them?
Sure. How to write properly, use of syntax, omitting unnecessary things and adjectives and so on.

How did you foster creativity?
Oh my God. So you mean that c-word...

So people refer to creativity for want of anything better.
Correct!

All the same, what's your opinion on it?
Well it's totally irrelevant as far as I'm concerned. Because it's when I tell people to focus on ideas and then visualise them. Being creative means to express an idea you hadn't expressed before... it's a new idea. I don't need a cliché for that.

My job as a teacher is to communicate content based on certain rules. Grammar is a rule; writing from left to right is a rule, the same as being polite and punctual. Rules simply make life easier. Mobile phones are not allowed in class, for example.

And what if your students said that their concentration is better if they draw while listening to you?
Well, let them draw then! But not on the screen. It wouldn't do to get messages at the same time.

What was the biggest mistake you made in teaching?
Hard to put my finger on … maybe I didn't always think things through thoroughly. Sometimes I wasn't well-prepared, assuming that certain things are common knowledge.

And sometimes I got het up, I simply talked too much.

How important do you think grades are?
Complete nonsense. Because they are often meaningless, devoid of any value. Grades, if any, should take the form of honest assessments, not marks.

Absentees received no assessment, in which event grades were helpful. But despite all that, we still just dragged some of them along.

How did you encourage curiosity in your students?
I asked them questions that are hard to answer. That could be something like, 'What's the difference between an Olympiad and the Olympic Games?' Nobody knows that. As soon as they got home, though, they found out.

That way, they got used to the idea that questions always need to be answered.

Thanks a lot, Erik, for all your insights.

Takeshi Sunaga
teaches Interaction Design

Professor
Faculty of Fine Arts, Design
Tokyo University of the Arts (TUA)
Japan

In a very functionally furnished room, amicably smiling
Takeshi Sunaga explains why ideas should belong to no one
person and what that has to do with the eyes of a dragonfly.
He also emphasises the necessity of experiencing our social
life by asking questions. After the three-hour interview,
which he finalises by declaring to have said everything,
the sun has set. — December 2019

Thies: What motivated you to start teaching?
Sunaga: The reason I started teaching design was because I wanted to pass
on my experience of finding out 'what design actually is' to design students.
While I was studying design, I wanted to know what design really is, not just
how to do it. I used to ask my teacher that question. The teacher replied that
if you started designing as a career, you would know the answer. A few years
into my design career, I found the answer.

So may I ask you what design is?
Most importantly for me, the essence of design is not to shape things, but
to harmonise the relationships between things and people. In his book
The Sciences of the Artificial, political scientist and Nobel laureate Herbert
A. Simon uses the term 'interaction'. This would come close to the word I use:
harmonising – the fitness between the 'inner and outer environment' in
Simon's words.

A different meaning of design would be to create something which people
believe should exist, and to which they then give a form. However, the form
is not limited to an object as a thing; it could also be an event or a process
of becoming. Expression, imagination and creation are intrinsic to design
in that regard.

Could you explain that in detail based on an example project?
Of course. We did a long-term design project in a hospital once where the nursing staff wanted to improve their work processes. It all began with us having to redesign the user interface of an existing medical recording system (MRS). However, at the beginning of the project, we realised that it was first necessary to transform nursing practice before redesigning the MRS.

The nursing staff would measure the vital functions of their patients several times a day, for instance, their blood pressure and body temperature. Then they'd write those values on a sheet of paper, not on the terminal (PDA) of the MRS. Later on, they left the patient's room and input the information into the PDA. The staff explained that they used paper because they valued the dialogue with the patients – entering the data directly into the PDA would get in the way of this. We shifted the topic of this project from redesigning the user interface to transforming the way the nurses worked.

The new task was to build a collaboration with nurses. We aimed to develop a place where nurses would be allowed to 'express' their work at the hospital. It was to be an informative and insightful experience different from their usual work. To that end, we asked them to participate in an hour-long work-shop and write an essay about their most memorable experience at work. That way, we realised that healthcare involved two different activities: nursing – consisting of emotional work as an implicit job – and cognitive work as an explicit job. The existing MRS, however, only supported the cognitive work. We then attempted to draw a model that represented both activities. Our goal was to let nursing staff draw pictures of objects used daily in hospitals and to write essays about their own memorable job experiences. For the very first time at their workplace, they experienced the act of expressing their own minds and sharing these thoughts with each other.

Through this activity called 'Expression Workshop', together with the nurses, we all realised that 'expressing and sharing' nursing has the power to high-light the importance of nursing. As a result, the project team and nurses organised a programme which rotated the 'Expression Workshop' at ten wards of the hospital. The deliverables of the workshop, which consisted of essays and sketches by the nursing staff from the ward, clearly demonstrated the 'mind of nursing' within the hospital.

That's a great example. Do all your students participate in projects like that?
Graduate students participate in such projects. They contribute to the develop-ment of design for a year or two in different stages of the project.

Do you pursue a specific teaching method in projects like that?
I discuss that in detail in my contribution to the book titled *Gendai Dezain wo Manabu Hito no Tame ni* [For those who study contemporary design].

But first of all, I'd like to say that I hardly do any 'teaching' at all. I'm not much good at that. [laughs] In my design class, there are no answers. My design education is not based on a teacher who already knows the answer. It's more about finding solutions with students in the process and developing an attitude towards designing. Just because someone tells you how to do something doesn't automatically mean that you'll be capable of actually doing it yourself.

And why is that?
Only those who've done their own designs know how to do it. Only then does experience of the actual design process translate into knowledge of how to design. Students need to experience that first hand, otherwise they will only emulate others. They should do that with their whole body, with their hands, their feet or even in dancing with partners.

Do you have an example of that as well?
Yes, the 'Food Camp' project. This is a project to design 'eating'. It consists of gathering ingredients, cooking them and enjoying a meal together. It was organised as a social design study of the Toride Campus and the region. The students visited farmers, butchers and markets and asked a lot of questions about the essence of each job and then listened to what they had to say.

I accompanied a team on a visit to a farmer and listened to his stories about farming and business. When we parted, the farmer gave us a lot of vegetables as a gift. The key to this project was to visit the actual place and engage in a dialogue with the actors.

If we'd bought all the ingredients from the supermarket, it would have been a completely different experience of eating.

What were the students supposed to learn from that?
They learnt about the 'reality' of society, where outcomes of their design would have an effect. The reality is in their narratives. The story that is told becomes an additional ingredient added to the food that makes it a new dish. I wanted them to use the firewood they collected locally to cook the meal, to design activities in the process of cooking and eating, to create something that would lead them to the roots, to the origins. For that is design. Design doesn't mean arranging food on a beautiful plate and taking a photo of it.

How did the students respond to that kind of 'experiencing and asking questions'?
Many of them only understood in hindsight that speaking to people was a core component of the project. At the time, they complained, 'What do we have to do that for?'

Is it possible to generate an experience like that in other areas, too?
Sure. If you produce something, you can always go back to the roots. If you
make a poster, you can visit the factory that manufactures the paper. If it's
washi, that hand-processed Japanese paper, you can pay a visit to those people
who manufacture it by hand.

What did you say to those people who complained?
'If you try it out, you will understand.' Although discussions are interesting,
at that particular moment it was about being present in the world.

Are discussions nevertheless part of a project like that?
Yes of course. First, we discuss what the students will do with the project.
Then when the project is almost finished, after 'eating and cleaning up',
we discuss what the design of the project is.

What happens if two people have the same idea?
Concerning ideation, the general rule is that ideas and models generated
in my class are the common property of all course participants. Students
are allowed to adopt and develop any ideas from their fellow students.

Do your students always agree to that?
All participants in a project have to agree to that before we start.
　　On that basis, the class grows into a close-knit creative community,
where incredible things can happen. Figuratively speaking: a brain consists
of individual neurons. Those neurons all join to form a network. And many
of those brains unite to build an even greater network. Just like the compound
eyes of a dragonfly which can see in many different directions at the same
time. We practise open source because information should not be anyone's
property. The 'multiple brains' idea constitutes one of the most crucial parts
of my teachings.

Where did you get your approach to teaching from?
I was inspired by Kenji Ekuan from GK Design in Tokyo where I worked prior
to my teaching assignment and where team design was practised. I always say
to my students, 'You don't have to struggle on alone, let's do it together!'

How do you motivate your students to produce lots of ideas?
When my students have ideas or design something, I encourage them to
think and act by showing my own ideations and sketches. Besides that, I also
encourage them to draw more sketches than they ever thought possible:
not just 20 or 30 sketches, they have to do 70 sketches.

What are you particularly good at as a teacher?
Students have told me that I always listen carefully to what they have to say.

Do you put a special focus on listening?
Genuine interest and wholehearted attention are the sole keys to capture their hearts and minds. I have always done things that way, that's why it seems so natural to me.

What do you seek to teach your students?
Well, my aim is to educate people who will achieve great innovations, people who will change something in society or design completely new things.

   I taught Interaction Design at Tama Art University, and currently teach Societal Design at Tokyo University of the Arts. In that context, it's not designers who do the designing. It's society. And that is going to become increasingly important to be sure. For example, it's not enough just to make a smartphone easy to use. In addition to that, we also need to shape the possibilities and limits of access using the smartphone as a tool to shape our society. In order to do that, designers have to meet people involved in the practice and truly collaborate with them. It will not be design in a design studio but design in society. It is 'societal design'.

Will your students become specialists or generalists?
They will be generalists in design. They don't reduce a problem to a specific field but rather grasp it holistically. The most important task for designers as generalists is to create an environment in which practitioners are convinced that it is possible to design something with which they can solve their problem.

Do we need to change university structures in order to offer generalists an even better education?
Yes. I would like to remove all the borders between university departments, including those of all administrative offices, and redesign the structures in cooperation with professors from other disciplines.

Would it be possible to do that across other, entirely different, specialist areas?
I think that would even be crucial. Together with specialist areas outside art universities. Young teachers should be trained to reflect that. As they encounter different fields and get to know each other's ways of thinking and vocabulary, they will appreciate interdisciplinary communication.

Tokyo University of the Arts is currently involved in a student exchange with Tokyo Institute of Technology (TIT). Students from TIT come over to us and our design students take part in a design programme at TIT.

One thing I noticed is that mutual learning between disciplines is asymmetrical. For example, TIT students had less difficulty learning design at the design school, while design school students had more difficulty learning design engineering at the technical school.

What other advice would you give to young teachers?
It's necessary to talk a lot more about what one learns in the process of designing. Not only about the outcome of designing. You should have a dialogue and discussion on knowing about designing and the wisdom of design. When you start communicating with teachers from different disciplines, it is essential to put into words what you have noticed and understood. And by putting it into words, you should be able to recognise characteristics of your discipline and your speciality.

Many thanks, Takeshi.

Toshio Yamagata
teaches Graphic Design and Design Management

Professor
Department of Graphic Design
Tama Art University, Tokyo
Japan

*Kind, attentive eyes, 35 years of design for Shiseido at locations
in Paris and Tokyo, eleven years as university professor,
Toshio Yamagata talks about impulsive passion and about
the driving force that goes beyond, and that he is glad to see
his students make any amount of progress. He sometimes
stimulates that process by being silent.* — December 2019

**Thies: Let's get straight to the point: do you often have group discussions
with your students?**
Yamagata: Yes, but I think it's vital to speak to every single one of them personally. It even has to be face to face because they all have different problems,
especially when it comes to creativity. Mostly, I consider and discuss with my
students why they are not making any progress and offer them the opportunity
to reflect on that jointly.

**And how does that joint reflection happen, for example, when designing
a poster?**
Essentially, design begins with planning and conceptualisation.

In the past, I used to give my students tasks, but nowadays, I request them
to devise their own tasks, for example, I suggest topics such as Tokyo, family,
travelling or something like that. After that, they discover problems they would
like to solve, decide on how they want to express that in the poster and then
flesh out their ideas by means of a concept sheet. They need to decide what
they want to do and then visualise that idea. Then I teach them how a poster
finally evolves from the idea.

How does that process work in detail?
I'd like to give you an example: a student who was interested in sculpture was
experimenting with forms and cutting them out for her final project. People,
a hat, a mountain and many other things. When I saw that conglomeration of
hers, I couldn't quite figure out what she had in mind. However, while talking

to her, I noticed she was interested in human faces, so I suggested she should focus on faces only. From that idea, she developed the technique of positioning people on a certain spot, taking pictures of them from different angles and then creating a threedimensional work from all those perspectives that reminded you of neo-surrealism and cubism. In the end, she had 24 versions for which she also designed a box.

In that process, do you make suggestions, or do you find solutions collaboratively by asking questions and listening?
Conversations are the key here because it's not possible to elicit the students' deeper vision from the approaches they have tried out.

Do all the students listen to these one-to-one conversations?
Yes, the others are present as well. Normally, we gather around a few larger tables so that everyone can listen to what is being said. That particular student spoke about her – rather profound – ideas and I added my thoughts to them.

Do group discussions develop in that setting?
Sometimes I address specific students from the audience, but I have to admit that the students are not very good at group discussions.

Why is that?
Well, I think many students go to art university because they want to paint or draw pictures, which they are good at. However, my job is to turn them into designers and I therefore seek to educate them in fields like idea generation and communication.

How do you go about that?
Before asking 'how', we should first ask 'what'. When they choose a subject, they ought to have an opinion on it. So, to find out what they actually want to do, they jot down their thoughts in a notebook. I read the notes and help them with their style of expression, then I ask them to consider everything from other perspectives in order to find different approaches. In that way, we develop their ideas together.

And what happens then?
The students develop a concrete idea, their concept, from the basic idea. In order to do that, I let them produce anything they like first, which I then ask them to present to us all. Then we discuss the concept again and, depending on which technique the student is good at or wants to try out, I explain what photography or illustration, for example, is all about and how those techniques can be deployed. Afterwards, they continue to refine that.

How do you give a critical assessment of your students' work?
Some teachers just concentrate on all the bad things and criticise the students.
I try to do the opposite, telling them what they are good at, praising them a lot
and, in that way, I let them grow.

Is there any specific reason why you do it that way?
Yes, certainly. The reason is that in my time at the advertising department
of Shiseido, there was this very strict atmosphere. There were quite a lot of
older colleagues who were very intimidating. From them I learnt two methods,
one of them being reprehension. I was scolded for delivering something bad,
and I had to rework tasks over and over again. That happened frequently.
The other method involves non-verbal implicit communication, for instance,
by telling someone 'That won't do!' just by looking at them in a certain way.
With both methods, you are the subordinate. I was faced with that over decades
and used those methods myself when I was at Shiseido's.

However, when it comes to students, I am aware that they can't be professionals at this stage and, of course, they still make lots of mistakes. Both
methods would prevent them from making any further progress. That is why
I altered my approach; I am only strict with them in direct conversations if
they have been negligent. I never criticise them for their work. Sometimes I
resort to the old Japanese method of deliberately giving no answer. Eventually
my counterpart will say, 'I understand', and retreat. I use that method because
most people who work creatively have a natural sense of self-assessment and
actually know what they haven't done well. It is all about reaching the point
where you realise what you haven't done and what you still need to do.

**Does the person who retreats really understand what you intended to
criticise?**
I don't think that person will always understand what I mean, but they
automatically begin to notice the mistakes in their work. In Japan, this has
always been the way of doing things among craftspeople, between master
and apprentice.

Have you learnt something new through this method yourself?
Yes, I think so. Because if you want to work as a designer in the long term,
besides the impulsive passion you may feel initially, you also need motivation:
a driving force that goes beyond that. You need something enduring that
motivates you. If you are not sufficiently motivated to formulate and implement
your visions, you will probably quit the job after two or three years.

Besides that, you have to deliver something really good. It is simple
to satisfy customers. But if you want to create something that surpasses
their requirements, you have to consciously strive for that goal.

Have you ever learnt anything through your students?
Yes. For example, one of my students wanted to design a poster on philosopher Georges Bataille inspired by Japanese graphic designer Tadanori Yokoo who, in the age of modern design, had maintained his style of brush strokes, thus creating his own world. Since I had never read anything about the philosopher, I caught up on that as fast as I could and encouraged the student to stick to her ideas.

Is there a way to boost motivation?
I think motivation is the pleasure of discovering things – to stick with the previous example: I showed a book on graphic designer Tadanori Yokoo to the students, analysed it in my particular way and asked them to find out in a discussion whether there was something about that person that nobody had noticed.

Do you think that curiosity motivates people?
Yes, that is exactly what I wanted to say.

Is this the power, then, that fuels creativity?
Creativity is about discovering things. But to do that, you have to organise your thoughts, which also means you have to redefine your values. When, for example, you look at an artwork, you are confronted with new values and so you have no other alternative but to change your thoughts. You have to get rid of preconceived ideas in order to create something new. Although, strictly speaking, there is nothing new under the sun. In terms of design that means not just solving problems but encouraging people to discover something new.

You've just said that there is nothing new under the sun but also that design is about discovering something new. Isn't that a contradiction? What would you describe as new?
Nothing is new because everything has already existed, maybe 100 years ago. It's just that many people have already forgotten that.

That means that everything has already existed and is only rediscovered every now and then?
Yes – I often say, 'We are humans.' Most of us have two eyes, a nose and a mouth. Our eyes are not attached to our backs. Therefore, we have the same comfort or discomfort that Leonardo da Vinci had. People living 200 or 300 years ago had similar problems and the same physiognomy as we do today. And there are records of all those things that people have passed down to us, for example, in literature. The same applies to art: it is an expression of erstwhile human contemplation. But today, we just don't keep that in mind.

Sometimes it is also a feeling. For example, I don't know what it feels like to be in a war because I have never experienced one. So there must be many things under the sun we know nothing of.

Whatever I discover in the past needs to be translated into a new language in order to pass it on, for instance, to younger people, to the next generation. I think that is what designers do: we invent a new language.

That means putting something into a time-related context?
Yes, that is exactly what students should be able to do.

What else should they be able to do by the end of their time at university?
We want our students to have the grit to propose new values to society and hope that each of them will work as a designer throughout their lives without ever losing interest. Pablo Picasso's lifelong interest, for instance, was the question of what painting is. I think he created so many works because of this profound interest. He could have gone on and on forever and he would never have finished.

Besides that, I want them to become self-confident and learn to trust their own abilities and ideas.

Will the students be specialists or generalists by the end of their time at university? Wouldn't it be better to be an expert?
In my view, a designer is better off as a generalist, without being vague, as an all-rounder can quickly become. At the same time, you should also be a kind of specialist. Not in the sense of being manually skilled, but in that you have your own speciality, a kind of tree root that keeps you grounded; something you can always hold on to and that doesn't let you go.

What should they be able to achieve as qualified designers?
I am not quite sure, but my guess would be that the object of design is man. I think it's high time to reflect on human beings again.

Should we do good *for* the people?
Yes, exactly, that's how you could define design. As a human being, you have a multitude of feelings. If you reflect on how people think and what they are interested in, I think you could come up with plenty of good design ideas. Even if the media change and design trends come and go – what remains is man.

I encourage my students to observe people closely, in order to be able to design things for them. That applies to both product design and graphic design.

Ultimately, the ability to express oneself means being able to visualise one's design. It's about making ideas visible.

I think that is something we should definitely work on.

How important are grades in all these learning processes?

I don't think assessments are really necessary but they are mandatory. However, instead of assessing the final results of my students, I prefer to assess whether a student has grown as a person and worked harder than before. Besides, it's not about being the best in class, but about inspiring others.

What advice would you give to young professors? What should they be able to do well?

I think it's good to be in close touch with one's students. At the same time, it is okay to just accompany them for a while and then let them go. You have to invest a lot of time because every student is at a different level and they all need individual coaching.

As far as technical matters are concerned, you should give them direct instructions.

In Europe, we had the Bauhaus. Was there any school or movement like that in Japan or Asia that influenced you?

No. Although many Japanese designers were influenced by the Bauhaus, for me, it was not a benchmark. I think I was rather shaped by the philosophy of Shiseido.

Why and when did you become a teacher?

I was invited to shortly before I retired from Shiseido. At the time, I was talking to a photographer friend about my retirement and he asked me if I would like to start teaching. I replied, 'Well, not really, I'm planning to work as a freelance designer.' Nevertheless, he asked me to come to Tama Art University the next day. When I arrived, I was escorted straight to the President's room, and he said, 'Thank you very much!'

It was never my aim to become a teacher, but I was appointed. So suddenly, I had to reflect on the question of what students are. Ever since, I speak to my students all the time.

Thank you so much, Mr Yamagata.

Questions
never end

SAMPLE ASSIGNMENTS

SAMPLE ASSIGNMENTS

How do other teachers plan their lessons and which tasks do they use?
The sample assignments provided by the interviewees on the following
pages offer some insight. The selected tasks vary in terms of subject areas,
topics and scope, and show how diverse project work can be.

Katrin Androschin, Strategic Design
SRH Berlin University of Applied Sciences, Germany

Initial question for project work

Assignment:
In the master's degree in Strategic Design, we develop questions together with project partners: companies, start-ups, NGOs. At the beginning of the semester, there is a 'How Might We' question, which the students first need to research and edit openly. After several process steps, human or life-centred solutions are strategically thought out. They take into account social megatrends and show future prospects. All solutions are manufactured as prototypes to make them tangible and emotionally understandable for the target groups. The students are required to test, iterate and map out implementation scenarios as well as scaling potential.

Two sample questions that were posed at the beginning of the semester, and were repeatedly formulated and specified in the course of the semester, were:

1. How might smart clothing applications for the mobile society meet the needs of a sustainable future?
2. How can Strategic Design support our project partner (in the field of climate philanthropy) in inspiring their clients to fund progressive climate projects?

Paulus M. Dreibholz, Typography
University of Applied Arts Vienna, Austria

The new art of making books

Assignment:
Over the period of this project you are asked to engage with Ulises Carrión's article. You will develop a printed publication around this text that not only contains every part of it, but must follow and demonstrate your abilities to understand formal and conceptual structures of content and format and their respective implications.

Outline:
'A writer … does not write books. A writer writes texts.' This is how Ulises Carrión refers to the 'old art of bookmaking'. A designer designs a container, a structure for the text to sit in and gives shape to the words the author has given him to translate into a visual message.

Process:
Search, engage with and question the text.

Spend some time generating, developing and producing several ideas and approaches as to how your text can be interpreted using the format of a printed publication. Think about the content's meaning and how it could be visualised in an interpretive manner, using all possible variations and combinations of printed formats and typographic tools you can imagine.

For the second session, come back with at least three documented approaches represented by double page spreads for each idea and possibly a dummy publication.

Outcome:
The format of the project outcome is open, but needs to be print-based and strongly typographic in nature. You are welcome to generate and include images if your concept requires it. The purpose of this brief is to interpret and master the printed word, to show an expert understanding of the handling of text, language, typography, materials and production methods.

Tip:
It is important to test your ideas, to try and fail, rethink, try and succeed.
In short: it is important to produce! Don't rely on other people's experiments,
but conduct your own! Don't wait for 'permission' to conduct experiments, but
exercise full control over your project.

Time frame:
4 sessions

Reading:
- *The Detail in Typography*, Jost Hochuli
- *Elements of Typographic Style*, Robert Bringhurst
- *Die Kunst der Typographie*, Paul Renner
- *Notes on Book Design*, Derek Birdsall
- *Typography: My Way to Typography*, Wolfgang Weingart
- *Experimental Formats*, Roger Fawcett-Tang
- *Design is Attitude*, Helmut Schmid
- *Look at This: Contemporary Brochures, Catalogues and Documents*,
  Adrian Shaughnessy
- *Materials, Process, Print: Creative Solutions for Graphic Design*, Daniel Mason
- *New Typographic Design*, Roger Fawcett-Tang with David Jury
- *Sizes May Vary: A Workbook for Graphic Design*, Mark Boyce
- *Reading Form – A Call for Conscious Design*, Paulus M. Dreibholz

Nikolaus Hafermaas with Rob Ball, Transmedia Design
ArtCenter College of Design, Pasadena, USA

Travelism, the future of tourism

Assignment:
Travelling is a collection of choices, behaviours and actions. Travel starts
the moment you've identified the need or desire to 'go' and begun the process
of inspiration and selection of a destination. Transactionally, travel ends
the moment you return. But the impact of travel – from the emotional and
experiential afterglow to the environmental, social and economic effects –
can persist far into the future.

This project will explore:
- behaviours that drive both locals and visitors towards mutually and independently rewarding relationships, before, during and after the actual journey
- a notion of 'exploration' that includes locals and drives their own curiosity
  about where they live
- solutions to obstacles of access and authenticity such as climate change,
  gentrification, wealth inequality, available time, risk/reward tolerance
- new business and partnership opportunities
- new tools and methods such as media, products, services and campaigns
  that help destinations manage the flow of visitors and that foster a sense
  of authentic discovery
- new language around Travelism tailored specifically to the destinations
  NYC and Berlin
- new perspectives on the purpose and role of the NYC and Berlin DMOs
  (Destination Management Organisations)

Course learning outcomes:

CLO 1: develop a greater and deeper understanding of the business of hospitality and tourism

CLO 2: broaden research and documentation skills through qualitative and quantitative analysis in macro and micro environs

CLO 3: deepen investigative skills as a designer to understand and communicate a 'sense of place' through exploration

CLO 4: utilise design thinking and strategy to uncover new solutions for the tourism sector

CLO 5: improve collaborative skills with multi-disciplinary teams arriving at transdisciplinary solutions

CLO 6: help deepen a student's personal design voice

Creative deliverables within interdisciplinary teams of three to four students:
- conduct and document qualitative interviews with stakeholders in NYC and in Berlin: visitors, locals, hosts
- vividly document visited locations through imagery and artefacts
- identify pain points and design opportunities
- develop and visualise visitor and host personas and create various user scenarios and journeys
- create design solutions to enhance the travel experience and mitigate pain points
- collectively create and visualise a Travelism manifesto
- produce an immersive multimedia experience that brings to life the individual Travelism scenarios

Michael Hohl and Mathilde Scholz, Design Theory
Anhalt University of Applied Sciences, Dessau, Germany

Observing and drawing from description

Assignment:
An exercise in pairs. One person does the describing while the other person draws what is being described. Students are required to describe in words a small designed object (nothing natural) that is hidden from view. However, they are not allowed to mention the object's function or name.

This means you have to study the object closely and you soon notice how hard it is to find the words to describe what you see and feel clearly. We do not possess a precise language with which to describe things; we have to learn it first.

The exercise lasts about five to ten minutes after which roles are switched.

In the course of the exercise, constructivism and the limitations of language become tangible – simply amazing. Walking by, you see students drawing objects that you can identify immediately: small earplugs, for instance. In the process, the person drawing is often fully unaware of what they are currently drawing – because they already have something else in mind.

Learning effect:
- We all perceive the world differently;
- we need to study things closely;
- language has its limits. We cannot find the right words; and
- we have to learn to describe things precisely.

Experimenting with your mind and hands

Rathna Ramanathan and Sheena Calvert, Visual Communication
Royal College of Art (RCA), London, Great Britain

Proof

Assignment:
This eight-week project is founded on the belief that, as Rudnick noted, there is a crisis of graphic practices, providing us with distinct challenges for the future.

Proof is for those for whom the 'word' or text offers a starting point for creative inquiry and expression. It is an opportunity to use the research you've conducted in your dissertation, or if you have an interest in writing or in experimenting with codes and visual language.

Each week, over an eight-week period, is built around a combination of readings and focused workshop exercises (each with a particular provocation intended to motivate and inspire your thinking). We will investigate how you can produce communication material in an individual, personal yet impactful way that goes beyond the purely speculative.

We will start with the conclusion of a text that was transformative for you. It could be a paragraph you read that made you reconsider something or the conclusion of your dissertation. We will take a non-conformist, visually speculative approach to your work, asking *what if?* We will use this method of query to consider the concept of Stuart Candy's probable, preferable, plausible and possible futures in relation to your practice.

The project is grounded and structured to reflect the role of an independent practitioner-publisher. You will be working with your own content through phases of editing, drafting and designing to produce, publish and disseminate.

Our purpose is to move beyond designing communication for the way things are right now, to imagine communication for how things could be. We will seek audiences outside of the academic context to understand how to translate and create impactful communication and do this by speculating, imagining and dreaming to create work and graphic practices for the kind of world that we wish to live in.

Structure by week:
1. *Be curious* – Let Us Conclude | 2. *See more* – Metaphors of a Plausible Future | 3. *Think big* – Prototypes of a Probable Future | 4. *Make connect* – Images of a Preferable Future | 5. *Embrace paradox* – Provocations for a Possible Future | 6. *Take action* – Spec | 7. *Produce* – Look and Feel | 8. *Publish* – Let Us Begin

Stefan Sagmeister, Graphic Design,
School of Visual Arts in New York (SVA), USA

A person you want to touch

Assignment:
1. Select a person you want to touch. This should not be someone you know well, no partners, family members or friends.
2. Create a piece of design that touches this person within a certain time span.
3. Deliver that thing to that person and check if she/he was touched.

Kashiwa Sato, Design Thinking
Keio University SFC, Tokyo, Japan

Strategic Design on uncharted horizons

Assignment:

Objectives:

Generalising design methods to explore unexplored areas.

   Design is no longer simply a method of making products and buildings more attractive, but is now seen as a broad technology that positions the direction of science and technology itself, plans its relationship with society as an industry and designs the interaction between people and technology. In this class, we will investigate from scratch a field in which many designers are not involved, in which there are no examples of practice and where the students will learn design methods that enable social innovation in a project format.

Class outline:

In this class, using several 'unexplored areas' as examples, students will examine actual design strategies for these areas, and through a practical class format, propose a visual identity for the area. The class will also welcome guests who are experts in the field to discuss the design strategy. What vision do you have of how communication design can help?

Example theme:

One example of a major unexplored area is 'disaster prevention' in Japan. In addition to earthquakes, landslides and floods caused by typhoons and torrential rain, which have occurred in Japan in recent years, secondary disasters such as cut-off villages and water outages have become major problems. Although the Japan Meteorological Agency has compiled disaster prevention weather information and made it available on the web, it is difficult to know what to do in an emergency. There are no firm guidelines on what to do or how to prepare for such a situation.

Class process (eight sessions in total):
1. Students will be divided into groups of about seven people, and each group will consider what kind of solution should be presented on the issue. Once the groups have reached a consensus, they will consider what specific media to use, what companies and organisations to collaborate with, and what specific means, products and services to create as outputs.

2. In the above process, a progress report will be presented in class. The students will be asked questions not only by me, but also by other students in the group about any doubts or difficulties in understanding the construction of their idea, with the aim of improving the process.

3. The final session is a debriefing to report on the results. Other faculty members in charge of the course and I, as well as the participating students, vote to determine the ranking of the students.

Learning outcomes:
- knowing necessary steps/design methods for the real world
- assembling a team that meets for the first time
- building smooth communication skills
- focusing in a team on a single output
- clarifying the process in your thinking

Yasuhiro Sawada, Graphic Design
Tama Art University, Tokyo, Japan

Creation 1

Assignment:
Syllabus:
It's about a way of thinking that challenges common sense and finished
objects. And about a practice that explores in depth the unique expressive
power of one's own person. Only when the two are fused together does
a new creativity emerge that fascinates people. Graphic design is not
an act of competition on a fixed playing field, but an opportunity for
endless possibilities.

Task:
Create your own design.

- Duration: 6 months
- Topic: free
- Media: free

Free choice of topics and media means that these are discussed and
agreed upon with the teacher.

Mathilde Scholz, Integrated Design
Anhalt University of Applied Sciences, Dessau, Germany

Self-organised work in the seminar

Assignment:

Establishing an organisation system (or procedure):
The first session comprises an overview and the establishment of a structure that organises teamwork clearly. The teacher moderates the procedure with the aid of a visible agenda and defines the frame in order to establish a common understanding as to the direction the collaboration will take. In my seminar on how to work scientifically, students are required to create a guide that will help them in their future work.

The last item on the agenda is always to reflect on the session. This enables the teacher to react quickly to tensions.

Role hierarchy:
As an alternative to the personal hierarchy (due to their teaching role, teaching staff are at a hierarchically higher level than students), responsibilities are organised using roles, such as moderator or minutes taker, etc.

The moderator prepares the agenda for the session and considers *how* the tasks should be done. In the first session, the teacher does the moderating. Afterwards, the students take turns moderating. The person teaching then takes on the role of an expert for the content and coaches the moderator, raising awareness for teamwork and proposing methods to make quick joint decisions, for instance. The teacher needs to see the big picture: the atmosphere, the quality of the content and the project's direction.

Handing over:
This self-organised approach can only be successful if the students make the project their own. In order to do that, responsibility must be handed over to the students; this is done by the teacher after implementing the structure for self-organised work. After that, just let go and have faith.

Matthias Spaetgens, Conception
University of Applied Arts Vienna, Austria

Fatal distraction

Assignment:
Developing a campaign against the use of smartphones while driving

Background:
At least every tenth victim of a road accident dies due to driver distraction.
Distracted driving is even the number one cause of fatal accidents on motor-
ways, outpacing alcohol consumption and speeding by far. Checking your
smartphone is especially dangerous, as the risk of having an accident while
doing so is fivefold, and even tenfold while reading and texting messages.

Alarming conclusion: using your smartphone while driving has become
normal. Smartphones are reversing the years of decreasing trend in the
number of road accidents.

Bottom line:
It can happen to you sooner than you think.

Insights:
- Being inattentive for just one second at a speed of 100 km/h means you're
  driving blind for 28 metres – checking your smartphone for seven seconds
  means you're driving blind for about 200 metres.
- Multitasking is a myth. In reality, you can only concentrate on one thing
  at a time.

Media:
Social media, PR, moving image, event, poster

Implementation:
Please formulate the problem before presenting your overall concept, ideally
summarised in one or two sentences. You can then flesh out the information
campaign using scribbles, moodboards or other visualisation tools.

Takeshi Sunaga, Interaction Design
Tokyo University of the Arts (TUA), Japan

Verbalise your work

Assignment:
When a design project is completed, I usually provide design students with additional work. This is to verbalise their exploration and the fun experience they have created. The documentation should be based on the following framework:
- what you have designed;
- why you designed it;
- how you developed the designing; and finally
- what you have learnt through the designing.

Toshio Yamagata, Graphic Design and Design Management
Tama Art University, Tokyo, Japan

My topic

Assignment:
1. Choose one of the following thematic areas that interests you most: clothing, food, living and culture.
2. Identify a topic within the chosen area which you would like to develop and translate into a design.
3. Briefly describe what your message on the topic is and how you want to visualise it.
4. Choose a visual medium (poster, brochure or package) and develop ideas on how to use it and how it could help you to implement your design.

ACKNOWLEDGEMENTS

ACKNOWLEDGEMENTS

Acknowledgements are often hidden at the back of a book. However, I think it is important to place them more prominently here, because this project would not have been possible without the support of so many people.
At the heart of it was the endeavour to listen to other people in order to learn from them. The same is true for books you read or for printed and digital articles you discover, but also for conversations with numerous designers and non-designers. In the case of this book, I not only learnt from teachers who kindly shared their experience and knowledge with me – 24 of them in interviews – but also from my students. I would like to thank all those people very warmly.

I also wish to express my gratitude to Jan Svenungsson and Fritz Frenkler who encouraged me to launch this book project, as well as to Toshio Yamagata, Matthias Spaetgens, Katrin Androschin, Roswitha Janowski-Fritsch and Barbara Wimmer, Sabrina Horak, Ayako Otsu, Sunao Maruyama, Michael Schneider, Bernhard Poppe, Anton von Hinüber, Julia Hofmann, Marina Brandtner, Viktoria Horn, Susannah Leopold, Kate Howlett-Jones, Daniel Hendrickson, Katja Hasenöhrl, Doris Lang, Ludwig Übele, Lisa Schulz, Manuela Hausmann, Astrid Seme, Katja Richter, Martina Kupiak and Anja Hearing for their support. And special thanks to Paulus M. Dreibholz, who was a *big* help to me from the beginning of the project.

I am glad to be part of a great team in Matthias Spaetgens's Class of Ideas. My thanks go to that class as well as to the University of Applied Arts Vienna, Tama Art University Tokyo, iF Design Foundation and Superbude Wien, especially for their financial and moral support.

I learnt a lot – and *I listened*.

NOTES AND REFERENCES

NOTES AND REFERENCES

You will also find the links to all online sources mentioned here on teachinggraphicdesign.com and thiesdesign.com.

1 Williams, Raymond (1976): *Keywords: A Vocabulary of Culture and Society* (Reprint 2011), Routledge

2 Aynsley, Jeremy (2014): Graphic Design. In: De Bondt, Sara; de Smet, Catherine (eds.), *Graphic Design: History in the Writing*, Occasional Papers, p. 22

3 Simon, Herbert A. (1969, 1996): *The Sciences of the Artificial*, MIT Press, p. 111

4 iF Design Foundation (2021): *Designing Design Education*, av edition, p. 21

5 Baumgartner, Ekkehart (2021): The Thinking Hand. In: iF Design Foundation (ed.): *Designing Design Education*, av edition, p. 137

6 Lawson, Bryan (1980): *How Designers Think*, Architectural Press, p. 43

7 Papanek, Victor (2019): *Design for the Real World: Human Ecology and Social Change* (3rd edition), Thames & Hudson, p. 4

8 Bast, Gerald (2018): Die Kultivierung von Ungewissheit. In: Universität für angewandte Kunst Wien (ed.): *Digitale Transformationen*, Brandstätter Verlag, pp. 14ff

9 Projector Institute (2018, 24 April): *Interview with Michael Wolff*, https://prjctr-institute.medium.com/interview-with-michael-wolff-4626d901af22

10 The Cooper Union (2021, 6 December): *Intercultural and decolonial: exploring frameworks for typographic practice with Rathna Ramanathan* (video document), Herb Lubalin Lecture Series, www.youtube.com/watch?v=oLU6L3fDMAE

11 World Economic Forum (2020): *The Future of Jobs Report 2020: Infographics*, www.weforum.org/reports/the-future-of-jobs-report-2020/in-full/infographics-e4e69e4de7

12 Garland, Ken (1962), cited in Shaughnessy, Adrian (2012): *Ken Garland Structure and Substance*, Unit Editions, p. 55

13 Cohen, David K. (2011): *Teaching and Its Predicaments*, Harvard University Press, p. 4

14 Postman, Neil; Weingartner, Charles (1969): *Teaching as a Subversive Activity*, Dell Publishing, p. 66

15 Ambady, Nalini; Rosenthal, Robert (1993): Half a Minute: Predicting Teacher Evaluations From Thin Slices of Nonverbal Behavior and Physical Attractiveness. In: *Journal of Personality and Social Psychology*, vol. 64, no. 3, pp. 431–441

16 Hattie, John; Yates, Gregory C.R. (2013): *Visible Learning and the Science of How We Learn*, Routledge, ch. 4

17 Hattie, John; Yates, Gregory C.R. (2013): *Visible Learning and the Science of How We Learn*, Routledge, ch. 4

18 form Design Podcast (4 April 2022): *Sammeln als Haltung – Alexander von Vegesack über seinen Lebensweg als Objektbesessener* (podcast), form Designmagazin, https://podcasts.apple.com/de/podcast/alexander-von-vegesack-ich-hab-mich-einfach-in-objekte/id1533806115?i=1000556195321

19 Amelang, Manfred; Bartussek, Dieter (2001): *Differentielle Psychologie und Persönlichkeitsforschung*, Kohlhammer

20 Hattie, John; Yates, Gregory C. R. (2013): *Visible Learning and the Science of How We Learn*, Routledge, pp. 93ff

21 Anderson, James (9 March 2016): *10 teachers' tips for wannabe fashion students*, i-D Magazine, https://i-d.co/article/10-teachers-tips-for-wannabe-fashion-students/

22 Weber, Matt (2016, 19 October): *Harvard EdCast: I Wish My Teacher Knew* (podcast, interview with Kyle Schwartz), Harvard EdCast, www.gse.harvard.edu/news/16/10/harvard-edcast-i-wish-my-teacher-knew

23 Shaughnessy, Adrian (2013): *Essays Scratching the Surface*, Unit Editions, pp. 263f

24 Groys, Boris (2009): Education by Infection. In: Madoff, Steven Henry (ed.): *Art School (Propositions for the 21st Century)*, MIT Press, p. 27

25 Kornfeld, Stella; Meisel, Celeste; Scheer, Melanie; Scholz, Mathilde; Wilke, Hannes (2021): *perMA – Prototyp einer neuen Lernkultur*, Anhalt University of Applied Sciences, www.perma-dessau.de, p. 80

26 Hollis, Richard (2015): Principles before Style: Questions in Design History. In: Heller, Steven (ed.): *The Education of a Graphic Designer* (ebook), Allworth Press, p. 171

27 Rogers, Carl R.; Farson, Richard Evans (1957): *Active Listening*, Industrial Relations Center, University of Chicago

28 Nichols, Michael P.; Straus, Martha B. (2021): *The Lost Art of Listening* (3rd edition), The Guilford Press, p. 10

29 Shaughnessy, Adrian (2012): *Ken Garland Structure and Substance*, Unit Editions, p. 56

30 Koudenburg, Namkje; Postmes, Tom; Gordijn, Ernestine H. (2011): Disrupting the flow: How brief silences in group conversations affect social needs. In: *Journal of Experimental Social Psychology*, vol. 47, issue 2, pp. 512–515

31 Westerkamp, Hildegard (2001, 1 January): *Soundwalking*, www.hildegardwesterkamp.ca/writings/writings-by/?post_id=13&title=soundwalking

32 International Council of Design (2020): *Professional Code of Conduct for Designers*, www.theicod.org/storage/app/media/resources/ICO_Professional_Code_of_Conduct.pdf

33 Rogers, Carl R. (1995): *On Becoming a Person*, Houghton Mifflin Company, p. 17

34 Strack, Fritz; Martin, Leonard L.; Stepper, Sabine (1988): Inhibiting and Facilitating Conditions of the Human Smile: A Nonobtrusive Test of the Facial Feedback Hypothesis. In: *Journal of Personality and Social Psychology*, vol. 54, no. 5, pp. 768–777

35 Maidel, Romina; Behrends, Jakob (2012): „Design muss sich als Disziplin positionieren". Volker Albus hebt die Bedeutung des Schreibens hervor (audio document). In: *Sprache für die Form*, no. 1, www.designrhetorik.de/design-muss-sich-als-disziplin-positionieren/

36 Hattie, John; Yates, Gregory C. R. (2013): *Visible Learning and the Science of How We Learn*, Routledge, pp. 187ff

37 Fried, Carrie B. (2007): In-class laptop use and its effects on student learning. In: *Computers & Education*, https://doi:10.1016/j.compedu.2006.09.006

38 Glaser, Milton (2001, 11 November): *Ten Things I Have Learned, Part of an AIGA Talk in London*, www.miltonglaser.com/files/Essays-10things-8400.pdf Amongst others, Milton Glaser also designed the 'I love NY' and DC Comics logos and was the first graphic designer to receive the National Medal of the Arts, which is the highest honour awarded to artists and patrons of the arts by the United States Congress.

39 **On cybernetics:**
Wiener, Norbert (1948): *Cybernetics: Or Control and Communication in the Animal and the Machine*, MIT Press
YouTube (2016): *Paul Pangaro: What Is Cybernetics?* (video document), www.youtube.com/watch?v=Oad8Ro8j_fE
On cybernetics and design:
Dubberly, Hugh; Pangaro, Paul (2019, 1 January): *Cybernetics and Design: Conversations for Action*, www.dubberly.com/articles/cybernetics-and-design-conversations-for-action-v2.html
Glanville, Ranulph (2014): How design and cybernetics reflect each other. In: *Proceedings of RSD3, Third Symposium of Relating Systems Thinking to Design*, 15–17 October 2014, Oslo, Norway, http://openresearch.ocadu.ca/id/eprint/2053/
On cybernetics and teaching:
Michael Hohl combined the processes of cybernetics and design with other perspectives and ideas and translated it to teaching. Together with Mathilde Scholz he developed the concept of transformative teaching. Kornfeld, Stella; Meisel, Celeste; Scheer, Melanie; Scholz, Mathilde; Wilke, Hannes (2021): *perMA – Prototyp einer neuen Lernkultur*, Anhalt University of Applied Sciences, www.perma-dessau.de

40 Polanyi, Michael (1966): *The Tacit Dimension*, Doubleday & Company

41 Schön, Donald A. (2016, 1983): *The Reflective Practitioner: How Professionals Think in Action*, Routledge

42 Design Council (2019, 17 May): *Framework for Innovation: Design Council's evolved Double Diamond*, www.designcouncil.org.uk/our-work/skills-learning/tools-frameworks/framework-for-innovation-design-councils-evolved-double-diamond

43 Norman, Don (2013): *The Design of Everyday Things*, Basic Books

44 Auping, Michael (2007): 30 Years: *Interviews and Outtakes*, Prestel, p. 16

45 Weibel, Peter (2018): Dinge und Daten. In: Universität für angewandte Kunst Wien (ed.): *Digitale Transformationen*, Brandstätter Verlag, pp. 262–264

46 Kornfeld, Stella; Meisel, Celeste; Scheer, Melanie; Scholz, Mathilde; Wilke, Hannes (2021): *perMA – Prototyp einer neuen Lernkultur*, Anhalt University of Applied Sciences, www.perma-dessau.de, pp. 105–110

47 Freire, Paulo (2005): *Pedagogy of the Oppressed* (30th anniversary edition), Continuum, p. 87

48 Dreibholz, Paulus M. (2016): *Reading Form – A Call for Conscious Design*, Vienna (Gaffa Editions)

49 Dreibholz, Paulus M. (2010): *MAtters Transcript*, London (Gaffa Limited), pp. 9–10

50 Ward, Henry (2012, 2 November): *Interview with John Baldessari.* www.henryhward.com/interview-with-john-baldessari

51 This interview was preceded by a lecture given by Sven Ingmar Thies on the subject of 'German Design History and Education' followed by a podium discussion with Yasuhiro Sawada and Toshio Yamagata at Tama Art University Tokyo on 5 December 2019.

52 Lloyd-Jones, Teleri (2020, 3 November): *Dr Rahna Ramanathan announced as our new Dean of Academic Strategy*, www.arts.ac.uk/colleges/central-saint-martins/stories/rathna-ramanathan-new-dean

53 Renninger, LeeAnn (2020, 10 February): *LeeAnn Renninger: The secret to giving great feedback* (video document), TED Talks, www.ted.com/talks/leeann_renninger_the_secret_to_giving_great_feedback

54 This interview was preceded by a lecture given by Sven Ingmar Thies on the subject of 'German Design History and Education' followed by a podium discussion with Yasuhiro Sawada and Toshio Yamagata at Tama Art University Tokyo on 5 December 2019.

55 Kornfeld, Stella; Meisel, Celeste; Scheer, Melanie; Scholz, Mathilde; Wilke, Hannes (2021): *perMA – Prototyp einer neuen Lernkultur*, Anhalt University of Applied Sciences, www.perma-dessau.de

56 In visual art, horror vacui (Latin for 'fear of empty space') refers to the desire to fill the entire surface of a space or an artwork with detail (cf. https://en.wikipedia.org/wiki/Horror_vacui_(art))

All of the above links were accessed on 18 January 2025.

Recommended reading

Besides the other sources cited in the publication, the printed and digital texts listed below have provided a wealth of inspiration not only for my teaching, but also for this book. This selection not only addresses teaching and graphic design, but also provides insights beyond the realm of design.

You will also find the links to all online sources mentioned here on teachinggraphicdesign.com and thiesdesign.com.

Books

Aicher, Otl (2015): *analogous and digital* (2nd edition), Ernst & Sohn

Bayne, Siân; Evans, Peter; Ewins, Rory; Knox, Jeremy; Lamb, James; Macleod, Hamish; O'Shea, Clara; Ross, Jen; Sheail, Philippa; Sinclair, Christine (2020): *The Manifesto for Teaching Online*, MIT Press

Berzbach, Frank (2013): *Die Kunst, ein kreatives Leben zu führen. Anregung zu Achtsamkeit*, Hermann Schmidt

Brookhart, Susan M. (2017): *How to Give Effective Feedback to Your Students* (2nd edition), ASCD

Buchholz, Kai; Theinert, Justus (2007): *Designlehren. Wege deutscher Gestaltungsausbildung*, Arnoldsche Art Publishers

Burkhardt, Christoph (2017): *Denkfehler Innovation. Warum Fehlentscheidungen oft der Grund für Fortschritt sind*, Springer Gabler

Carr, Nicholas (2010): *The Shallows: What the Internet Is Doing to Our Brains*, W. W. Norton & Company

Cross, Nigel (2007): *Designerly Ways of Knowing*, Birkhäuser

Davis, Meredith (2017): *Teaching Design: A guide to curriculum and pedagogy for college design faculty and teachers who use design in their classrooms*, Allworth Press

De Bono, Edward (2016): *Lateral Thinking*, Penguin Random House

Dewey, John (1916): *Democracy and Education: An introduction to the philosophy of education*, Macmillan

Dewey, John (1934, 2005): *Art as Experience*, Penguin Books

Dobelli, Rolf (2012): *Die Kunst des klugen Handelns*, Hanser

Dobelli, Rolf (2014): *The Art of Thinking Clearly*, Harper Collins

Dubberly, Hugh; Pangaro, Paul (2019): Cybernetics and Design: Conversations for Actions. In: Fischer, Thomas; Herr, Christine M. (eds.): *Design Cybernetics: Navigating the New*, Springer

Freitag, Andreas (2015): *Von Marken und Menschen. Arbeit, Führung und das gute Leben*, Verlag Hermann Schmidt

Frenkler, Fritz (ed.) (2020): *The Report. Industrial Design at the Technical University of Munich*, Technical University of Munich, Faculty of Architecture

Frutiger, Adrian (1981): *Der Mensch und seine Zeichen*, Fourier Verlag

Gladwell, Malcolm (2006): *Blink! The Power of Thinking Without Thinking*, Penguin Books

Grenny, Joseph; Patterson, Kerry; McMillan, Ron; Switzler, Al; Gregory, Emily (2022): *Crucial conversations: Tools for Talking When Stakes are High* (3rd edition), McGraw Hill

Hara, Kenya (2015): *Ex-formation*, Lars Müller Publishers

Heiz, André Vladimir (2012): *Grundlagen der Gestaltung*, Niggli Verlag

Hohl, Michael; Scholz, Mathilde (2020): Theorie designen: Ein neues, partizipatives Lehrformat für Designtheorie im ersten Semester. In: Park, June H. (ed.): *Designwissenschaft trifft Bildungswissenschaft*, kopaed, pp. 30–39

Hollis, Richard (2012, 2017): *Writings about Graphic Design*, Occasional Papers

Kahneman, Daniel (2012): *Thinking, Fast and Slow*, Penguin Books

Klaus, Katja; Bittner, Regina (eds.) (2019): *Gestaltungsproben. Gespräche zum Bauhausunterricht*, Spector Books

Kries, Mateo; Klein, Amelie; Clarke, Alison J. (eds.) (2018): *Victor Papanek: The Politics of Design* (exhibition catalogue), Vitra Design Museum, Victor J. Papanek Foundation, University of Applied Arts Vienna

Kroeger, Michael (2008): *Paul Rand: Conversations with Students*, Princeton Architectural Press

Laurillard, Diana (2012): *Teaching as a Design Science: Building Pedagogical Patterns for Learning and Technology*, Routledge

Lidwell, William; Holden, Kritina; Butler, Jill (2003): *Universal Principles of Design: A Cross-disciplinary Reference*, Rockport Publishers

Madoff, Steven Henry (ed.) (2009): *Art School (Propositions for the 21st Century)*, MIT Press

Maeda, John (2006): *The Laws of Simplicity*, MIT Press

Malsy, Victor; Teufel, Philipp; Gejko, Fjodor (eds.) (2007): *Helmut Schmid: Gestaltung ist Haltung / Design Is Attitude*, Birkhäuser

McNiff, Shaun (1998): *Trust the Process: An Artist's Guide to Letting Go*, Shambhala Publications

Moggridge, Bill (2007): *Designing Interactions*, MIT Press

Nonaka, Ikujiro; Takeuchi, Hirotaka (1995): *The Knowledge-Creating Company: How Japanese Companies Create the Dynamics of Innovation*, Oxford University Press

Olins, Wally (2014): *Brand New: The Shape of Brands to Come*, Thames & Hudson

Oswalt, Philipp (ed.) (2019): *Hannes Meyers neue Bauhauslehre: Von Dessau bis Mexiko*, Birkhäuser

Pfeffer, Florian (2014): *To Do: Die neue Rolle der Gestaltung in einer veränderten Welt: Strategien, Werkzeuge, Geschäftsmodelle*, Verlag Hermann Schmidt

Selwyn, Neil (2019): *Should Robots Replace Teachers? AI and the Future of Education*, Polity Press

Stanier, Michael Bungay (2016): *The Coaching Habit: Say Less, Ask More & Change the Way You Lead Forever*, Box of Crayons Press

Tenorth, Heinz-Elmar (ed.) (2012): *Klassiker der Pädagogik* (2nd edition), C.H. Beck

Watzlawick, Paul (1983, 1993): *The Situation Is Hopeless, But Not Serious: The Pursuit of Unhappiness*, W. W. Norton & Company

Weinbaum, Alexandra; Allen, David; Blythe, Tina; Simon, Katherine; Seidel, Steve; Rubin, Catherine (2004): *Teaching as Inquiry: Asking Hard Questions to Improve Practice and Student Achievement*, Teachers College Press

Weinschenk, Susan M. (2011): *100 Things Every Designer Needs to Know About People*, New Riders

Welzer, Harald (2013): *Selbst denken. Eine Anleitung zum Widerstand* (6th edition), S. Fischer

Westover, Tara (2022): *Educated: A Memoir*, Random House

Wick, Rainer K. (2009): *Bauhaus: Kunst und Pädagogik*, Athena Verlag

Wood, Luke; Haylock, Brad (eds.) (2020): *One and Many Mirrors: Perspectives on Graphic Design Education*, Occasional Papers

Wyss, Ruedi (ed.), Binder, Ulrich (2013): *Gestaltung der Grundlagen: Aus dem Gestalterischen Propädeutikum der Zürcher Hochschule der Künste*, Niggli Verlag

Online sources

AIGA (2017, 21 August): *AIGA Designer 2025: Why design education should pay attention to trends*, https://educators.aiga.org/wp-content/uploads/2017/08/DESIGNER-2025-SUMMARY.pdf

Bennett, Audrey G.; Vulpinari, Omar (eds.) (2011): *Icograda Design Education Manifesto 2011, Taipei/Montreal 2011*, www.theicod.org/storage/app/media/resources/Icograda%20Documents/IcogradaEducationManifesto_2011.pdf

Integrierte Qualitätsoffensive in Lehre und Studium (2016): *Methodensammlung: Für Dozierende der Heinrich-Heine-Universität*, Heinrich Heine University Düsseldorf, www.diversity.hhu.de/fileadmin/redaktion/Diversity_Portal/Dateien/Methodenbuch_Stand151216.pdf

Davis, Meredith (2016): 'Normal science' and the changing practices of design and design education. In: *Visible Language*, vol. 50, no. 1, https://journals.uc.edu/index.php/vl/article/view/5913

DERC (2020): *Charting the Future of Design Education: A Report by the Design Education Review Committee*, http://designsingapore.org/wp-content/uploads/2022/06/DERC_Report_v2_updatedJune2020.pdf

Dubberly, Hugh (2004): *How Do You Design?*, Dubberly Design Office, www.dubberly.com/wp-content/uploads/2008/06/ddo_designprocess.pdf

Facione, Peter A. (2020): *Critical Thinking: What It Is and Why It Counts* (updated edition), www.researchgate.net/publication/251303244_Critical_Thinking_What_It_Is_and_Why_It_Counts

IDEO (2013): *Design Thinking for Educators: Toolkit*, available at: https://page. ideo.com/design-thinking-edu-toolkit

Iguchi, Toshino; Suga, Yasuko (eds.) (2017): *Design Education beyond Boundaries: The Second Asian Conference of Design History and Theory*, Saitama University, https://acdht.com/download/2017/all_corol.pdf

IIT Institute of Design (ID) (2020): *Lead with Purpose: Design's central role in realizing executive vision*, https://id.iit.edu/wp-content/uploads/2020/01/IIT-ID-Pathways-Report-2020.pdf

Queen's University (n.d.): *Teaching and Learning in Higher Education* (online course), www.queensu.ca/ctl/resources/online-modules

Singh, Sapna; Sanders, Liz; Irwin, Terry; Stappers, Pieter Jan; Lotz, Nicole; Bohemia, Erik (2016): The Future of Design Education. In: Lloyd, P.; Bohemia, E. (eds.), *Future Focused Thinking – DRS International Conference 2016*, 27–30 June, Brighton, United Kingdom, https://dl.designresearch society.org/drs-conference-papers/drs2016/conversations/12

All of the above links were accessed on 18 January 2025.

Photo credits

Page 1:   Class of Ideas © Katja Hasenöhrl
Page 2:   Thies © Katja Hasenöhrl
Page 4:   Androschin, Ave © Thies Design
Page 5:   Dreibholz © Katja Hasenöhrl
Page 6:   Frenkler © Thies Design
          Hafermaas © Graft Brandlab
Page 7:   Hartwig © Thies Design
          He © Jianping He & hesign
Page 8:   Hohl, Kato © Thies Design
          Joost © Till Vill
Page 9:   Mateus-Berr © Katja Hasenöhrl
Page 10: Matsushita © Thies Design
          Pirker © TU Graz
Page 11: Ramanathan © Naomi James
Page 12: Renninger © LeeAnn Renninger
          Saga © Thies Design
          Sagmeister © David Johansson,
          Design Network
Page 13: Sato, Sawada © Thies Design
Page 14: Scholz © Thies Design
Page 15: Spaetgens © Katja Hasenöhrl
          Spiekermann © Thies Design
Page 16: Sunaga, Yamagata © Thies Design

About the author

Born and raised in Hamburg, Germany, Sven Ingmar Thies studied graphic design at Braunschweig University of Art and completed his final thesis in Tokyo and Yokohama.

Since his time at university, he has focused on a holistic design approach that seamlessly connects to other design disciplines, other specialist areas or even to handicrafts. This conviction was intensified further by two professional engagements at Henrion, Ludlow & Schmidt in London, where brands were holistically developed, and at Kitayama Institute in Tokyo, where he learnt about the interplay between architecture and design during a two-year postgraduate scholarship.

Besides being involved in project-related work for brand agencies Landor (today, Landor & Fitch) and Enterprise IG (today, Superunion), he founded Thies Design in 1998, which develops tailored brand experiences for enterprises and institutions.

In addition to his professional activities, Sven Ingmar Thies has taught graphic design at the University of Applied Arts Vienna's Class of Ideas since 2011.

Sven Ingmar Thies (ed.)

Concept, author and interviews:
Sven Ingmar Thies

Project Management 'Edition
Angewandte' on behalf of the
University of Applied Arts Vienna:
Barbara Wimmer, Vienna

Transcription: Anton von Hinüber,
Julia Hofmann, Sabrina Horak,
Ayako Otsu
Translation from German into
English: Marina Brandtner,
Susannah Leopold
Proofreading/Copyediting: Daniel
Hendrickson, Viktoria Horn, Kate
Howlett-Jones, Susannah Leopold
Book design: thiesdesign.com,
Mylène Martz, Sven Ingmar Thies
Image editing: pixelstorm.at
Printing: Beltz Grafische Betriebe,
Bad Langensalza

Library of Congress Control
Number: 2025930313

Bibliographic information published by the German National
Library
The German National Library lists
this publication in the Deutsche
Nationalbibliografie; detailed
bibliographic data are available on
the Internet at http://dnb.dnb.de.

ISSN 1866-248X
ISBN 978-3-0356-2964-4
e-ISBN (PDF) 978-3-0356-2966-8

German print version:
ISBN 978-3-0356-2965-1

© 2025
Birkhäuser Verlag GmbH, Basel
Im Westfeld 8, 4055 Basel,
Switzerland
Part of Walter de Gruyter GmbH,
Berlin/Boston

www.birkhauser.com
www.degruyter.com

Questions about General Product
Safety Regulation
productsafety@degruyterbrill.com